*Selected Chapters from*

# Investment Analysis and Portfolio Management

## Jerome B. Cohen
*Professor of Finance and Dean (Emeritus)*
*Bernard M. Baruch College*
*The City University of New York*

## Edward D. Zinbarg
*Senior Vice President*
*The Prudential Insurance Company of America*

## Arthur Zeikel
*President and Chief Investment Officer*
*Merrill Lynch Asset Management, Inc.*

**Special Edition for CFA Candidates**

**IRWIN**
*Professional Publishing*
Burr Ridge, Illinois
New York, New York

Richard D. Irwin, Inc., 1993

*Printed in the United States of America.*

ISBN 0-256-03624-1

1 2 3 4 5 6 7 8 9 0 VB 0 9 8 7 6 5 4 3

# CHAPTER

# 7

# *Business Cycles and Investment Strategy*

*Better is one forethought than two after.*
Erasmus

This chapter surveys the relationships between stock prices, interest rates, and the broad movements of economic activity which are referred to as the business cycle. The survey suggests that an ability to anticipate forthcoming changes in business conditions can be used to improve the timing of security purchases and sales. The final section of the chapter is a logical extension of this discussion. If economic forecasting can be helpful to the investor, how should the investor go about making or using such forecasts? Obviously, in a single section of a single chapter we cannot present all there is to know about the subject of economic forecasting. But we can encourage familiarity with some of the most useful tools employed by forecasters.

## ▪ *BUSINESS CYCLES AND STOCK PRICES*

Substantial evidence suggests that an ability to foresee business cycle turning points several months ahead improves the ability to foresee major turning points in the general level of stock prices. The evidence does not imply that every bear market must be accompanied by an economic recession or vice versa. However, the tendency for stock prices to decline prior to an economic downturn has been so pronounced

***TABLE 7–1***    ***Stock Market and Economic Peaks***

| Date of Peak in S&P 500 | Date of Peak in Industrial Production | No. of Months Market Peak Led Economic Peak |
|---|---|---|
| Dec. 1952 | Jul. 1953 | 7 |
| Jul. 1956 | Feb. 1957 | 7 |
| Jul. 1959 | Jan. 1960 | 6 |
| Jan. 1966 | Oct. 1966 | 9 |
| Nov. 1968 | Mar. 1969 | 4 |
| Dec. 1972 | Nov. 1973 | 11 |
| Nov. 1976 | Dec. 1977 | 13 |
| Nov. 1980 | Aug. 1981 | 9 |
| Average | | 8 |

SOURCE: Goldman Sachs Research, March 1986.

that if a recession or a slowdown of economic growth appears to lie ahead, the investor should consider that the odds are high it will be preceded by a significant stock market downturn some months in advance. For example, the data in Table 7–1 shows that, on average, the market tends to peak eight months before the economy, as a whole, turns down.

Table 7–2, on the other hand, shows in general, the market tends to bottom (and enter a new bull phase) several months prior to a trough in economic activity.

It is essential to stress the fact that stock price peaks and troughs typically have preceded turning points of general business activity. Many investors are invariably surprised when, in the midst of rather dreary business news, stock prices rise, and in the midst of prosperity, stock prices fall. But such is the nature of the stock market.

Several theories have been offered to explain the stock market's apparent forecasting ability. One is that investors collectively have good foresight and that they act on

***TABLE 7–2***    ***Stock Market and Economic Troughs***

| Date of Trough in S&P 500 | Date of Trough in Economic Activity* | No. of Months Market Trough Led Economic Trough |
|---|---|---|
| Dec. 1957 | Feb. 1958 | 2 |
| Oct. 1960 | Dec. 1960 | 2 |
| Oct. 1966 | Jun. 1967 | 8 |
| Jun. 1970 | Sept. 1970 | 3 |
| Oct. 1974 | Feb. 1975 | 4 |
| Mar. 1978 | Mar. 1978 | 0 |
| Jul. 1982 | Aug. 1982 | 1 |
| Average | | 3 |

*Year-over-year change in spread between growth in industrial production and growth in employment.
SOURCE: Goldman Sachs Research, June 1985.

the basis of what they think is going to happen to business activity rather than on the basis of what they currently see happening. Another argument is that investors act on the basis of current rather than anticipated future developments but that the chief current indicators they watch—corporate profits and profit margins—tend to turn in advance of general business activity. Therefore, profit-oriented investors coincidentally bid stock prices up and drive them down in advance of general business activity. Yet a third theory is that stock price reversals help cause subsequent economic reversals by affecting consumer and business confidence and spending decisions. Finally, various monetary explanations for the stock price lead have been offered, as will be noted in later sections. Perhaps the truth lies closest to a combination of all these hypotheses.

Let us look at the record more closely. Table 7–3, based on National Bureau of Economic Research data (described later in this chapter), shows the relationship between business cycle movements and the stock market over the entire period for which data are available. Henry L. Wojtyla, who prepared the analysis, divided recessionary periods of economic activity into three groupings: mild, average, and severe. In mild recessions, according to Wojtyla's analysis, the stock market tends to decline about 20 percent, with the market's peak preceding the economy's peak by an average of five months (see Panel A). At the trough, the market leads the economy by an average of three months.

Among average recessions (Panel B), the associated stock market corrections are slightly deeper, and the leads are a bit longer. Associated with severe recessions (Panel C) are stock market declines averaging 39 percent but with lead times somewhat similar to less severe recessions.

### TABLE 7–3  Recessions and the Stock Market

| Post-war Cycles | Cycle Number | Rank | Peak | | Trough | | Industrial Production | | Associated Market Declines | | | |
|---|---|---|---|---|---|---|---|---|---|---|---|---|
| | | | | | | | Duration (months) | Drop (percent) | Duration (months) | Drop (percent) | Lead at Peak (months) | Lead at Trough (months) |
| **A. Mild Recessions** | | | | | | | | | | | | |
| * | 42. | 1. | Aug. | 1966 | March | 1967 | 7 | 0 | 9 | −18 | 7 | 5 |
| | 13. | 2. | Dec. | 1845 | June | 1846 | 6 | −4 | 13 | −15 | 0 | −7 |
| * | 43. | 3. | Dec. | 1969 | Nov. | 1970 | 11 | −6 | 18 | −23 | 12 | 5 |
| | 9. | 4. | Jan. | 1828 | Dec. | 1829 | 23 | −3 | 15 | −15 | 3 | 11 |
| | 19. | 5. | June | 1869 | Dec. | 1870 | 18 | −8 | 17 | −16 | −2 | −1 |
| | 15. | 6. | March | 1854 | Dec. | 1854 | 9 | −10 | 25 | −39 | 15 | −1 |
| | 34. | 7. | Oct. | 1926 | Nov. | 1927 | 13 | −6 | | No market decline | | |
| * | 41. | 8. | April | 1960 | Feb. | 1961 | 10 | −9 | 15 | −11 | 9 | 4 |
| | 8. | 9. | May | 1825 | Nov. | 1826 | 18 | −8 | 27 | −16 | 6 | −3 |
| | 1. | 10. | Sept. | 1792 | May | 1793 | 8 | −9 | 8 | −20 | 8 | 8 |
| | 10. | 11. | Oct. | 1833 | July | 1834 | 9 | −9 | 8 | −15 | 4 | 5 |
| | 22. | 12. | March | 1887 | April | 1888 | 13 | −11 | 10 | −9 | −2 | 1 |
| | 18. | 13. | April | 1865 | Dec. | 1867 | 32 | −11 | 36 | −36 | 12 | 8 |
| | 29. | 14. | Jan. | 1910 | Jan. | 1912 | 24 | −9 | 22 | −25 | 1 | 3 |
| | 17. | 15. | Oct. | 1860 | June | 1861 | 8 | −14 | 9 | −25 | 1 | 0 |
| | | | Average | | | | 14 | −8 | 17 | −21 | 5 | 3 |

**TABLE 7–3** *(concluded)*

| Post-war Cycles | Cycle Number | Rank | Peak | | Trough | | Industrial Production | | Associated Market Declines | | | |
|---|---|---|---|---|---|---|---|---|---|---|---|---|
| | | | | | | | Duration (months) | Drop (percent) | Duration (months) | Drop (percent) | Lead at Peak (months) | Lead at Trough (months) |
| **B. Average Recessions** | | | | | | | | | | | | |
| * | 45. | 16. | Jan. | 1980 | Nov. | 1982 | 34 | −12 | 21 | −21 | −10 | 3 |
| | 26. | 17. | June | 1899 | Dec. | 1900 | 18 | −12 | 7 | −21 | −5 | 6 |
| | 27. | 18. | Sept. | 1902 | Aug. | 1904 | 23 | −14 | 29 | −44 | 15 | 9 |
| * | 39. | 19. | July | 1953 | May | 1954 | 10 | −9 | 8 | −12 | 6 | 8 |
| | 3. | 20. | April | 1801 | April | 1803 | 24 | −24 | 16 | −44 | 6 | 14 |
| | 14. | 21. | June | 1847 | Dec. | 1848 | 18 | −12 | 15 | −23 | −2 | 1 |
| | 23. | 22. | July | 1890 | May | 1891 | 10 | −17 | 18 | −27 | 13 | 5 |
| * | 38. | 23. | Nov. | 1948 | Oct. | 1949 | 11 | −10 | 12 | −18 | 5 | 4 |
| | 2. | 24. | May | 1796 | July | 1798 | 26 | −11 | 31 | −29 | 13 | 8 |
| | 4. | 25. | Dec. | 1806 | July | 1808 | 19 | −34 | 14 | −53 | 4 | 9 |
| | 6. | 26. | Nov. | 1815 | June | 1817 | 19 | −16 | 12 | −8 | 2 | 9 |
| | 16. | 27. | June | 1857 | Dec. | 1858 | 18 | −21 | 27 | −48 | 23 | 14 |
| | 33. | 28. | May | 1923 | July | 1924 | 14 | −18 | 7 | −19 | 2 | 9 |
| | 31. | 29. | Aug. | 1918 | March | 1919 | 7 | −17 | 12 | −34 | 21 | 16 |
| | 40. | 30. | Aug. | 1957 | April | 1958 | 8 | −13 | 5 | −18 | 1 | 4 |
| | | | Average | | | | 17 | −16 | 16 | −28 | 6 | 8 |
| **C. Severe Recessions** | | | | | | | | | | | | |
| | 30. | 31. | Jan. | 1913 | Dec. | 1914 | 23 | −19 | 28 | −17 | 3 | −2 |
| | 25. | 32. | Dec. | 1895 | June | 1897 | 18 | −15 | 14 | −30 | 6 | 10 |
| | 5. | 33. | March | 1810 | Dec. | 1812 | 33 | −18 | 41 | −36 | 5 | −3 |
| | 7. | 34. | Aug. | 1818 | Dec. | 1820 | 28 | −18 | 13 | −13 | −4 | 11 |
| * | 44. | 35. | Nov. | 1973 | March | 1975 | 16 | −15 | 23 | −44 | 10 | 3 |
| | 12. | 36. | March | 1839 | April | 1843 | 49 | −19 | 52 | −36 | 6 | 3 |
| | 20. | 37. | Oct. | 1873 | March | 1879 | 65 | −27 | 40 | −38 | −4 | 21 |
| | 21. | 38. | March | 1882 | May | 1885 | 38 | −28 | 36 | −25 | 9 | 11 |
| | 28. | 39. | May | 1907 | June | 1908 | 13 | −28 | 13 | −45 | 7 | 7 |
| | 11. | 40. | Dec. | 1836 | April | 1838 | 16 | −28 | 22 | −34 | 16 | 10 |
| | 24. | 41. | Jan. | 1893 | June | 1894 | 17 | −27 | 9 | −39 | 2 | 10 |
| | 32. | 42. | Jan. | 1920 | July | 1921 | 18 | −32 | 22 | −44 | 3 | −1 |
| | 37. | 43. | Feb. | 1945 | Oct. | 1945 | 8 | −35 | No market decline | | | |
| | 36. | 44. | May | 1937 | June | 1938 | 13 | −32 | 14 | −44 | 2 | 1 |
| | 35. | 45. | Aug. | 1929 | March | 1933 | 43 | −52 | 33 | −85 | −1 | 9 |
| | | | Average | | | | 27 | −26 | 26 | −39 | 5 | 6 |
| | | | Average for postwar cycles | | | | 13 | −9 | 14 | −20 | 5 | 4 |
| | | | Combined average | | | | 19 | −17 | 19 | −29 | 6 | 6 |

| Peak | | Trough | | Duration (months) | Drop (percent) |
|---|---|---|---|---|---|
| Other Market Declines | | | | | |
| Nov. | 1830 | Nov. | 1831 | 12 | −16 |
| Feb. | 1934 | March | 1935 | 13 | −19 |
| Oct. | 1938 | April | 1942 | 42 | −39 |
| May | 1946 | Feb. | 1948 | 21 | −23 |
| Dec. | 1961 | June | 1962 | 6 | −23 |
| Sept. | 1976 | March | 1978 | 18 | −17 |

SOURCE: Rosenkrantz, Ehrenkrantz, Lyon & Ross, Inc., June, 1983.

**FIGURE 7–1   Bear Markets and Economic Recessions**

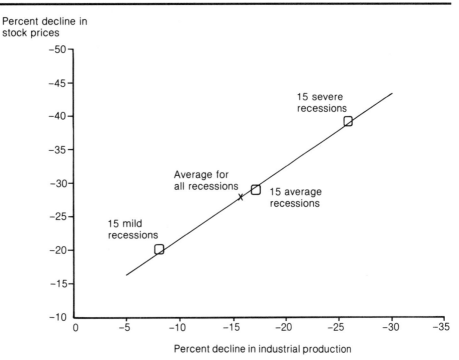

SOURCE: Rosenkrantz, Ehrenkrantz, Lyon & Ross, Inc., June 1983.

Figure 7–1 summarizes the entire business cycle history in a somewhat different fashion. Of course, the process of averaging different cycles masks a good deal of variation. Moreover, some observers have argued that changes in the regulation governing financial markets will tend to disrupt the historical relationship between business cycle movements and the stock market. We will have more to say about this later in the chapter.

## From the General to the Specific

Since an ability to foresee business cycle turning points normally would improve one's ability to foresee major turning points in the stock market as a whole, would it also improve one's ability to select the particular stocks to be most affected by the change in overall trend? The relative price changes of individual stocks over short periods of time reflect many factors. These factors include relative changes in company sales, earnings, and dividends, but they also include the degree to which different stocks had been overpriced or underpriced prior to the turning point of the general market. To the extent that accurate forecasts of the overall economy can improve forecasts of relative changes in the prosperity of different industries, forecasts of relative price changes of stocks in different industries should be improved.

Some industry groupings typically (but not always) achieve earnings gains in years when overall profits decline.[1] Historically, office and business equipment, electric utilities, soft drinks, and tobacco stocks are the S&P groups that have been best in this regard.

Because recession years and the beginning stages of an economic recovery tend to be good periods of stock market performance[2], substantial research efforts are directed towards identifying industry groups and individual stocks likely to outperform the broad market averages during the early stages of a new bull market. Merrill Lynch, for example, has studied relative stock group performance during the first six months of bull market cycles and the last four months of bear market cycles. Table 7–4 is a convenient reference listing of Merrill Lynch's major conclusions. Figure

**TABLE 7–4  Group Performance in the Business Cycle**

| Master Group | Dominant Investment Characteristics | Best Relative Performance | Worst Relative Performance |
|---|---|---|---|
| **Cyclical stocks:** | | | |
| Credit cyclicals . . . . . . . . . . . . | Sensitive to interest rates—performance best when interest rates low. Most groups building-related. | Early and middle bull markets. | Early and middle bear markets, with the exception of forest products. |
| Consumer cyclicals . . . . . . . . . | Consumer durables and non-durables. Profits vary with economic cycle. | Early and middle bull markets. | Early and middle bear markets. Exception is hotel/motel. |
| Capital goods . . . . . . . . . . . . . (cyclical only) | Many groups depend on capacity utilization. | Middle and late bull markets. | Late bear markets. |
| Energy . . . . . . . . . . . . . . . . . . (cyclical only) | Closely tied to economic cycle. | Early bull markets. | Early bear markets. |
| Basic industries . . . . . . . . . . . . | Profits depend on industrial capacity utilization. Prices may benefit from supply shortages near economic peaks. | Early and middle bear markets. Economic peaks. | Early or middle bull markets, depending on source of demand for products. |
| Financial . . . . . . . . . . . . . . . . | Banks, insurance, and gold mining. | Late bull and late bear markets. Economic troughs. | Early bull markets. |
| Transportation . . . . . . . . . . . . . | Surface transportation. | Early bull markets. | Early bear markets. |
| **Defensive stocks:** | | | |
| Defensive consumer . . . . . . . . Staples | Nonvolatile consumer goods. | Late bear markets. | Early bull markets. |
| Energy . . . . . . . . . . . . . . . . . (defensive only) | Major international and domestic oils. Volatility introduced by OPEC power. | Late bear markets. | Early bull markets. |
| Utilities . . . . . . . . . . . . . . . . . | Large liquidity and operating stabilty. | Late bear markets. | Early bull markets. |

---

[1]There have been, since 1950, 12 years in which earnings on the S&P 500 were lower than the previous year, the latest being 1982. For a year-by-year review of industry group earnings see p. 254 of the previous edition of this text.

[2]According to Goldman Sachs, for example, "The average level of the market in the 12 months subsequent to an economic trough has, since 1948, been higher than the average stock price level in the 12 months preceding an economic trough."

**TABLE 7–4 *(concluded)***

| Master Group | Dominant Investment Characteristics | Best Relative Performance | Worst Relative Performance |
|---|---|---|---|
| **Growth stocks:** | | | |
| Consumer growth . . . . . . . . . | Combination of growth and defensive characteristics. Several subgroups: offer high yields. | Cosmetics, soft drinks and drugs: late bear markets. Other subgroups: early bull markets. | Cosmetics, soft drinks, and drugs do not vary in any regular cyclical pattern for this group. Other subgroups: late bear markets. |
| Capital goods— . . . . . . . . . . technology Capital goods (growth only) | Linked to capital investment spending cycle, which tends to lag behind the economic cycle. | Early and middle bull markets. | Late bear markets. |
| Energy . . . . . . . . . . . . . . . (growth only) | Linked to economic cycle and to OPEC. | Early bull markets but varies. | Varies. |

SOURCE: Merrill Lynch.

7–2 shows the relationship of common stock group performance to the economic cycle.

The important findings of the Merrill Lynch study were:

1. Industries that outperform the market in the early phase of a bull market are those that are characterized by superior growth qualities or that are especially sensitive to the expected turning of the business cycle. Credit-sensitive stocks, excluding utilities,[3] stand out among those sensitive to the business cycle as beneficiaries of the anticipated decline in interest rates.

2. Industries that outperform other groups in the early phase of a bull market usually have high betas. Industries that outperform the average in the late phase of a bear market usually have low betas. The beta correlations are extremely high.

3. Basic industries are especially poor early bull-market performers because they usually do not meet the criteria noted above.

4. Industries with historical market patterns that suggest they should be underweighted in the early phase of a bull market are those that thrive in the economic environment of high capacity utilization usually created in the middle or late-middle stages of a recovery. In general, those industries are classified as intermediate goods and services, and they also tend to have minimal exposure to the capital spending cycle.

We are obliged to end this portion of our discussion with some serious words of warning. Too many investors believe that timing investment decisions with business cycle changes can be reduced to some form of a mechanical decision-making

---

[3]Utility issues, generally considered among the most interest-sensitive groups, were not found to be early bull-market performers. While these issues tend to do well *immediately* following turns in interest rates, utility stocks lose relative momentum fairly quickly because, according to Merrill Lynch analysts who conducted the study, of their low betas (which offset the momentum created by the sensitivity to lower interest rates).

*FIGURE 7–2    Business Cycle and Relative Stock Performance*

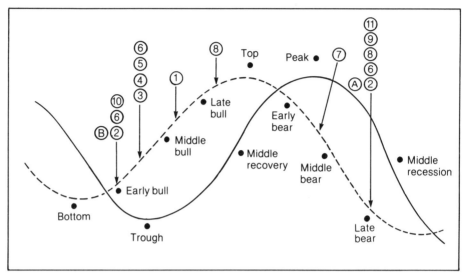

Key:
Solid line = economic cycle.
Broken line = stock market cycle.
 1 = Capital goods.
2a = Consumer growth—cosmetics, soft drinks, drugs.
2b = Consumer growth—other subgroups.
 3 = Consumer cyclicals
 4 = Credit cyclicals.

 5 = Capital goods—technology.
 6 = Energy.
 7 = Basic industries.
 8 = Financial.
 9 = Defensive consumer staples.
10 = Transportation.
11 = Utilities

SOURCE: Merrill Lynch.

process. That is, when something which has happened before happens again, it triggers a response that would have worked well the last time around. Not so.

The purpose of understanding past patterns is to establish a framework within which unfolding events must be placed. Then the goal of effective analysis is to determine whether or not past patterns should or should not be expected to hold. Such judgments require that investors seek to determine whether the operating characteristics of companies and industries have changed in their sensitivity to business cycle conditions. Then the assessment must be made as to whether or not expected events have already been discounted by the market pricing mechanism. This general concept is an important one for participants in the investment process to understand clearly. Exogenous factors frequently disturb expectations based on historical experience.

# ■ *BUSINESS CYCLES AND INTEREST RATES*

Interest rate cycles, as well as stock price cycles, have been closely related to the ebb and flow of general business activity. Essentially, interest rates have tended to rise as the business cycle matures.

Geoffrey H. Moore, of the National Bureau of Economic Research, a leading busi-

***TABLE 7–5    Changes in Real Interest Rates Around Business Cycle Turning Points***

| Recession | During Prerecession Period | During Recession |
|---|---|---|
| 1953-QII to 1954-QII | −0.55% | −0.99% |
| 1957-QIII to 1958-QII | +1.05 | −0.30 |
| 1960-QII to 1961-QI | +1.90 | −0.03 |
| 1969-QIV to 1970-QIV | +1.82 | −1.50 |
| 1973-QIV to 1975-QI | +0.64 | −6.16 |
| 1980-QI to 1980-QIII | +4.57 | −5.68 |
| 1981-QIII to 1982-QIV | +7.96 | −3.69 |

Note: Prerecession periods are the four quarters preceding the cyclical peak. Figures are changes in real interest rates over the designated intervals.
SOURCE: Morgan Stanley.

ness cycle research organization, recently summarized the causal factors for this pattern as follows: (1) the rising demand for business credit, both for operating purposes and for capital investment; (2) the rising demand for mortgage credit, both residential and nonresidential; (3) the rising demand for consumer credit; (4) the widening expectation of an increase in the rate of inflation, which makes lenders reluctant to lend at the same interest rate and borrowers more willing to pay a higher rate; and (5) the sluggish response of the supply of lendable funds to the pressures. During a business cycle contraction, according to Moore and others, all or most of these factors operate in reverse and (tend to) bring interest rates down.[4]

Taking a different perspective, Table 7–5 shows the relationship of *real* (i.e. net of inflation) interest rate changes and the business cycle. According to John D. Paulus of Morgan Stanley who prepared this study, "With a single exception, recession periods have all been preceded by increases in real interest rates. Similarly, every recovery has been kicked off by a decline in real rates during an economic contraction."[5]

Portfolio managers who predicate their investment maneuvers on interest rate developments believe, in general, that short-term interest rates turn before long rates. However, despite these convictions by some practitioners it is important to point out that other researchers have come to different conclusions, and the general subject of whether short-term interest rates turn before long-term rates remains very debatable.[6]

Whatever pattern the future may hold, market participants continue to watch interest rate movements, particularly in the short area, closely, in order to gain some insight into unfolding business cycle and stock market developments.[7]

---

[4]Geoffrey H. Moore, "Business Cycles, Inflation, and Forecasting," *National Bureau of Economic Research Studies in Business Cycles,* no. 24, (Cambridge, Mass.: Ballinger Publishing, 1983), p. 150.

[5]John D. Paulus, "Real Interest Rates and the Economic Recovery," *Economic Research,* May 11, 1983, p. 2. Real interest rates are defined as, "the 90-day commercial paper rate minus a four-quarter weighted average of current and past inflation as measured by the GNP deflator."

[6]See, David L. Lindsay, "Interest Rates and the Business Cycle," *The Babson Staff Letter,* May 11, 1984; and Ronald A. Glantz, "How to Forecast Interest Rate Peaks," *Paine Webber,* July 18, 1984.

[7]Capital market theorists have reported empirical research findings which indicate that inclusion of an interest rate factor adds substantial explanatory power to a simple single-market model. See, for example, Mark J. Flannery and Christopher M. James, "The Effect of Interest Rate Changes on the Common Stock Returns of Financial Institutions," *The Journal of Finance,* September 1984.

Merrill Lynch has identified four economic time series that have been somewhat reliable in identifying turning points in short-term interest rates. To be useful in this regard, according to Merrill Lynch, a series must be available on a timely basis, must shift direction decisively at or near a peak or trough in rates, and should not give off frequent false signals. Few, if any, of the series lead interest rate turns on a consistent basis. The four series are: Index of Spot Prices of Industrial Raw Materials, Business Demand for Short Term Credit, Index of Industrial Production, Growth in Money Supply.

However reliable these or other indicators may appear to be statistically, the actual record of interest rate forecasters is not too impressive. For example, a consensus of forecasts failed to project either the big rate rise in the first half of 1984 or the large drop in the second.[8] (See Figure 7–3.)

**FIGURE 7–3** **Proportion of Forecasters Expecting Rates to Rise and Proportion Expecting a Decline, Month by Month, 1984**

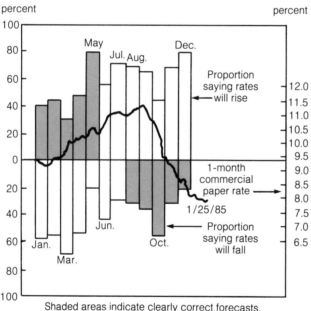

Shaded areas indicate clearly correct forecasts.

SOURCE: Citicorp, *Economic Week*.

# ▪ *INVESTMENT TIMING IMPLICATIONS*

*Stocks.* Elaine M. Garzarelli, Director of Quantitative Analysis for Shearson Lehman Brothers, has observed that, "every time since 1967 that the S&P 500 dropped by double digits, it was preceded by a 20 percent rise in the three month Treasury bill rate.

Moreover, a decline in interest rates has preceded five of the last six bull markets.

---

[8]Peter Crawford, Citicorp *Economic Week* 13, no. 7 (February 19, 1985).

**FIGURE 7–4    Stocks Have Way to Go in 1986 Based on the Current Bond Rally . . .**

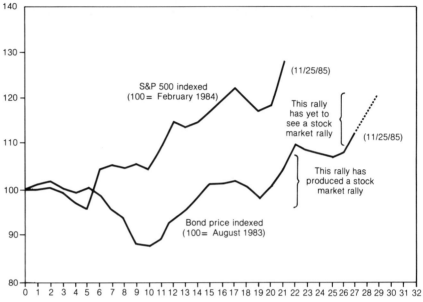

Months from respective start dates

SOURCE: Prudential-Bache Securities

Thus, investors have come to recognize that the stock market tends to move inversely to interest rates, with a lag that varies from three to nine months. Figure 7–4 shows how one analyst forecasted the stock market outlook for 1986 based on this relationship.[9]

***Bonds.*** Typically, since interest-rate turns have more or less coincided with business cycle peaks, the best time to buy bonds is when the crest of economic activity has been reached, not before. Bond prices under this scenario are at their lowest point, interest rates are at their highest. The best time to sell bonds is when a new economic advance begins following a recession. At such times, bond prices are usually high (interest rates low).

Which specific bond maturities are most or least attractive depends importantly on the dynamics of the business cycle as it produces changes in the yield curve, a term used to describe the relationship, at a given point in time, between bonds of very similar quality but of different maturities. Also known as the term structure of interest rates, this concept will be described more fully in Chapter 14. Briefly, the cyclical characteristics of the yield curve are as follows:

**1.**   Up to maturities of about three years—the "short end" of yield curve—longer term securities tend to have higher yields than shorter term securities, whether the *level* of interest rates is high or low.

[9]Fred Fraenkel and Linda M. Baker, "Rates Still Lead the Market," *Investment Weekly,* Prudential Bache Securities, November 27, 1985.

***FIGURE 7–5    Yield Spreads and the Stock Market***

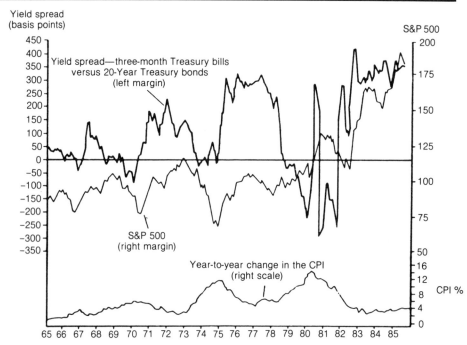

SOURCE: Morgan Stanley Economic Research; Data Resources, Inc.

2. From three years to about 15 years, that is, between the boundaries of relatively short-term and relatively long-term securities, the yield curve gradually changes shape as the level of rates rises. The curve moves from upward sloping, to flat, to downward sloping. Downward sloping means that longer term securities tend to have lower yields than shorter term securities.
3. Beyond maturities of about 15 years, yield usually does not change significantly as maturity is extended. That is, the long end of the yield curve typically is rather flat regardless of level.

Changes in the yield curve are also of interest to common stock investors. Figure 7–5 shows the spread between 20-year Treasury bonds and 3-month Treasury bills, matched against the S&P 500, going back to 1965. According to Byron R. Wien, Portfolio Strategist for Morgan Stanley:

> An inverted yield curve [i.e., bill rates higher than bond yields] results from Federal Reserve restraint, and tight money is bad for stock prices. A dip below the zero line tipped off investors about a decline in 1966 but proved to be a false signal in 1967. When the yield curve turned negative again in 1968, it was clearly the top of the market for many stocks, although the averages themselves moved forward for a while.
>
> The yield curve continued to serve watchful investors when it turned deeply negative prior to the 1970 bear market. In 1973, however, the market had already registered a decline, so it didn't totally anticipate the shift in trend.
>
> The S&P 500 underwent a fairly important correction from 1976 to the first

quarter of 1978 and was recovering before the yield curve turned negative in 1979. The factor that seems to have confused the indicator was inflation, which troughed in 1976 and rose for the remainder of the decade, accelerating in 1979 and 1980.

In the early eighties, however, the yield curve seemed to regain its old predictive powers. It plummeted into negative territory in mid-1980, giving those who hadn't lost faith adequate time to sell their positions before the November peak. Then, it turned positive in late 1981, providing adequate (perhaps too much) time to acquire stocks before the August 1982 bottom. The curve has been strongly positive ever since, so you would have been fully invested during the 1983–1984 correction, but that's a hazy memory overshadowed by the strong market environment we have had this year. All in all, over the last 20 years, the negative yield curve indicator has been helpful in five of its eight opportunities.[10]

Looking out, Wien concludes that "On the basis of the yield curve's present configuration, it looks as if it makes sense to remain bullish."[11]

Bond investors are also concerned about the business cycle influence on "quality" spreads, i.e., the difference in available yield between securities with similar maturities, but different investment quality. Figure 7–6 shows that the timing of peaks and troughs in quality spreads are closely related to business conditions. According to Tracy G. Herrick:

> The troughs in the quality cycle have occurred just as a business expansion ends, or a recession begins. This is a period when bankruptcies fall to a relatively low level. A period of rising prosperity tends to dull the edge of credit reviews. Investors begin to believe that they have little to fear from lending to virtually any borrower.
>
> However, within less than a year of business recession, this sanguine view of lending has abruptly reversed. Quality spreads then have regularly doubled. Often, this doubling has occurred within the final three months of a recession. The announcement of a major corporate bankruptcy has signaled the abrupt change, as occurred with the bankruptcy of Penn-Central in 1970. In addition, the experience during the spring of 1980 showed that unexpected corporate losses can serve as a shock to push quality spreads sharply higher, almost as if they were a coiled spring that had been released.[12]

These relationships are more than a statistical coincidence. The spread between expected stock returns in short-term interest rates narrows as the economic advance progresses—stock yields falling and bond yields rising. This gradually begins to draw income-minded investors away from stocks and into bonds. In addition, capital-gains-minded investors begin selling stocks as corporate profit margins narrow and economic recession begins to threaten. The proceeds of these sales either are put into the bank or into fixed-income securities. The shifting of funds out of the stock market weakens stock prices prior to the peak of business activity, but dividends are still high or rising. Therefore, stock yields begin to reverse their downward movement prior to the business peak.

Eventually the economy reaches a peak and turns down. Interest rates ultimately move down as well. Dividends reach a plateau or decline, but stock prices decline faster, and stock yields therefore rise. The yield spread thus becomes gradually less favorable to bond investment. Income seekers begin switching back into stocks, and

[10]Byron R. Wien, "Taking A Spin Around the Yield Curve," *Investment Strategy*, Morgan Stanley, November 25, 1985, p. 2.

[11]Wien, "Taking A Spin Around the Yield Curve," p. 2.

[12]Tracy G. Herrick, "The Money Analyst," *Jefferies and Company*, December 1984, p. 1.

**FIGURE 7–6    Quality Spreads and the Business Cycle**

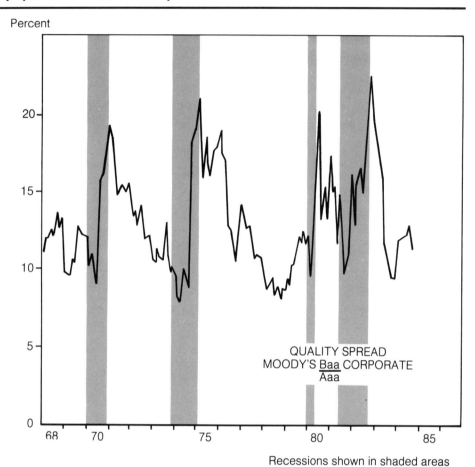

SOURCE: Jefferies and Company.

bargain hunters do likewise in anticipation of eventual recovery. The expansion process begins anew shortly thereafter.

There is another dimension to the impact of changing interest rates on stock prices. As will be shown in Chapter 10, the discount rate, or interest factor, is an important ingredient in most common stock valuation techniques. All other things being equal, rising interest rates reduce and falling interest rates enhance the present value of common stock holdings, particularly for long-term investors.

However, declines in economic activity may no longer, in the minds of many observers, presuppose a drop in short-term interest rates, and vice versa. These expectations are predicated upon changes brought about by the deregulation of financial markets. In essence, in the new "deregulated environment" lending institutions are no longer constrained by rising interest rates. For example, financial market deregulation has fostered the development of a wide variety of floating rate financial instruments, which not only exacerbates the cyclical swings in interest rates, but allows financial intermediaries to quickly pass on the cost of funds to the final borrower. Federal Reserve Board interest rate policy, in this new environment, is likely to be a less effective regulator of the economy than heretofore. Here's how Henry Kaufman summarized this important new development:

> Financial deregulation does not lower interest rates generally; rather, it has the following implications. First it brings uniformity to different interest rates. Local and regional sources of funds are now subject to the bidding of the U.S. and international money markets. Second financial deregulation raises the cost of funds to financial intermediaries, as they attempt to enlarge the scope of their activities. Third, *the advent of floating rates and the elimination of interest rate ceilings permit financial intermediaries to escape the direct discipline of rising interest rates. The result is that when restraint is necessary, the central bank is required to exert even greater market pressure than before.* Fourth, the combination of deregulation and a monetarist policy will result in *substantial interest rate volatility.*[13]

Another aspect to deregulation is the suspicion that the time between peaks in the level of economic activity will lengthen and the relationship between market peaks and economic peaks will become obsolete. In other words, bull markets are likely to end very early in the economic expansion. According to Steven G. Einhorn of Goldman Sachs, "The level of real interest rates needed to bring about recession is likely higher than has been required in the past because there is no supply of credit constraints to weaken the economy." According to Einhorn the most recent market cycle is consistent with this expectation. For example, the S&P 500 peaked in November 1983 (as of that writing). The historical relationship as indicated in Table 7–6 suggested the onset of a recession in mid-1984. As of this writing, early 1986, the economic outlook does not yet *resemble* the start of a new recession. Thus, an unprecedented amount of time has elapsed between peak in share prices, albeit, an interim and a peak in the economy.[14]

All of these portfolio management considerations are intertwined with the nation's inflation experience. Most of the time, recessions have been associated with a diminution of inflationary pressures and economic recovery with an acceleration of price advances. Interest rates, as we have discussed, followed a similar pattern. From 1965 to the mid-1980s, however, inflation did not diminish with the onset of recessions, in fact or in the expectations of the marketplace. If anything, the inflationary expectations generated in the late stages of prosperity continued to spiral upward after the economy peaked, thus explaining the soaring level of bond yields in the face of declining industrial production in 1981-82. Only in the very late stages have investors been confident enough to expect diminishing inflationary pressures, an attitude which has tended to persist beyond the economic trough and carried bond yields down to the point where investors realized that they had become duped once again into thinking that the inflation cancer had been cured.

More recently, the pattern of inflation, investor expectations, and the business cycle shifted once again. Throughout the 1983–85 expansionary period most economists and investors anticipated that continued economic strength would be accompanied by an increase in inflationary pressures, not only in the United States but

---

[13]Henry Kaufman, "Fallen Financial Dogmas and Beliefs," Salomon Brothers, Inc., June 13, 1985.
[14]Steven G. Einhorn, "Risk, Return, and Equity Valuation," *Portfolio Strategy,"* Goldman Sachs, July 10, 1984.

**TABLE 7–6    Market and Economic Peaks**

| Date of Peak in S&P 500 | Date of Peak in Industrial Production | Number of Months Market Peak Led Economic Peak |
|---|---|---|
| Dec. 1952 | Jul. 1953 | 7 |
| Jul. 1956 | Feb. 1957 | 7 |
| Jul. 1959 | Jan. 1960 | 6 |
| Jan. 1966 | Oct. 1966 | 9 |
| Nov. 1968 | Mar. 1969 | 4 |
| Dec. 1972 | Nov. 1973 | 11 |
| Nov. 1976 | Dec. 1977 | 13 |
| Nov. 1980 | Aug. 1981 | 9 |
| Average | | 8 |
| Nov. 1983 | Dec. 1985 or later | 25 + |

SOURCE: Goldman Sachs, March 1986.

around the world as well. Quite the reverse took place. That is, despite continued economic strength, the level of inflation remained surprisingly low. Here's how Morgan Guaranty Trust summarized the paradox:

> Five years ago, "price disinflation," let alone outright "deflation," had virtually vanished from the lexicon of economists and policymakers. Today, following the remarkable and still-continuing decline of inflation in industrial countries, those seemingly archaic terms are taking on new life. Lenders and borrowers—farmers, commodity producers, manufacturers, and sovereign governments—are seeking to fathom whether present experience is a mere interlude preceding the return of 1970s style inflation or the beginning of a new era of low inflation.[15]

# ■ BUSINESS CYCLE FORECASTING

## A Business Cycle Chronology

For more than 50 years, the National Bureau of Economic Research, a private nonprofit organization, has sponsored the research efforts of America's leading students of the business cycle. Their data show that 10 complete cycles have taken place since 1933, or about one every five years. By comparison, in the preceding century and a half, there were 34 cycles observed or about one every four years. In other words, the frequency of cycles has somewhat diminished. However, the biggest business cycle change, according to Moore and Zarnowitz:

> is the shift in the length of contractions compared to expansions. In the period for which only annual dates are available, 1790 to 1855, contractions averaged about 24

---

[15]World Financial Markets, "Countering World Deflation," Morgan Guaranty Trust Company of New York, December 1985. See also "Waking Up to the Glut Economy," *New York Times*, December 8, 1985.

months, expansions 31 months. Then from 1854 to 1933, when monthly dates are available, the average durations are 22 and 25 months respectively. But since 1933 the average contraction has lasted only 11 months while expansions have averaged 49 months (27 months when the wartime expansions are included).

Thus, since the depression of the early 1930s, the contraction phase of the business cycle has been reduced by about a year, while the expansion phase has been extended by two years. Before 1933, recessions lasted almost as long as expansions. Since then, expansions have been more than four times as long as recessions: the economy has been in recession less than 20 percent of the time.

Recessions have not only become shorter but also much more uniform in length. Using the standard deviation as a measure, the variability among contractions in 1790–1855 was 18 months; in 1854–1933, 14 months; while in 1933–1982 it was only three months. In this sense, recessions have become more predictable. On the other hand, expansions have become less uniform in length. Between 1790–1855 the standard deviation of durations of expansions was 18 months, the same as for the contractions. From 1854 to 1933, the standard deviation of expansions was nine months. But from 1933 to 1983, it was 27 months. Expansions have become nine times as variable as contractions.[16]

Thus, no two business cycles are exactly alike, and the timing of business cycles has not been consistent enough to warrant purely calendar-oriented judgments as to the probability of a peak or trough occurring at any given time. Furthermore, even the National Bureau readings frequently do not describe trends in the business picture in a fully satisfactory manner.

For example, the NBER announced in mid-1983 that the trough of the last recession occurred in November 1982—seven months after the turn. This declaration differed from both the consensus of leading economists and government officials who believed the cyclical bottom was reached seven months earlier.[17]

## Business Cycle Physiology

Most modern business economists have become increasingly impressed with the almost endless variety of the cyclical fluctuations they are trying to forecast. Nevertheless, the unique aspects of each individual cycle usually fit into a common framework which has been referred to as "the cumulative process" or "the self-generating cycle." The essential characteristics of this framework can be described briefly.

If we break into a cycle as revival is beginning, we find business sales and inventories at a depressed level and considerable excess plant capacity. As sales begin to rise and profit expectations improve, business leaders start planning for production increases. They expand working hours and gradually rehire previously laid-off workers. This increases employee incomes and stimulates personal consumption expenditures. With sales and profits rising, the managers begin to expand and modernize production facilities. These purchases from the capital goods industries create still

---

[16]Geoffrey H. Moore and Victor Zarnowitz, "The Development and Role of the National Bureau's Business Cycle Chronologies," National Bureau of Economic Research, Inc, Cambridge, Mass., Working Paper No. 1394, July 1984, p. 24. See also, Nicholas D. Kristoff, "Are the Economy's Up's and Down's Intensifying?" *New York Times*, April 21, 1985.

[17]Eric N. Berg, "Ending Recession, Officially," *New York Times*, July 9, 1983, p. 34.

more jobs and incomes and more consumption by workers in those industries. And so the expansion *cumulates*.

Workers, machines, and materials eventually are being utilized at capacity, and demand exerts upward pressure on prices and wages. Business leaders go increasingly into debt to finance expanding inventories, receivables, and fixed assets. Interest rates rise. Soon costs are rising faster than prices, and profit margins deteriorate. This coincides with the gradual realization that productive capacity has outstripped potential sales. Business executives become uneasy and pull in their reins. They reduce their orders for heavy equipment, cut back on the rate of inventory accumulation, repay loans, lay off marginal personnel, and even sell some of their personal common stock holdings. Caution spreads as incomes are reduced. Consumers postpone purchases of durable goods, business executives slash inventories sharply, and the cumulative process is at work in a downward direction.

As the downturn continues, credit terms ease and interest rates fall. The monetary authorities usually reinforce the ease. Housing construction often picks up as reduced mortgage rates, lowered downpayments, and extended maturities bring monthly carrying charges to a level which buyers are willing to undertake despite the recessionary atmosphere. Government spending acts as a strong prop to the economy. The stock market, after a sizable shake-out, stabilizes and begins to move up. Soon consumers realize that the worst is over and begin to unloosen their purse strings. A new revival is in the making.

In recent years, observers have identified another dimension to business cycle movements known as growth cyclical slowdowns.[18] Essentially, growth cycles represent fluctuations around the long-term growth trend of a nation's economy, i.e. a trend-adjusted business cycle. Actually, Solomon Fabricant coined the term "growth cycle" to describe a period in which the economy slows dramatically, but keeps sputtering forward.[19]

## Leading Economic Indicators

It should be clear from the brief physiology of a business cycle above that fluctuations of the whole of economic activity reflect fluctuations of the economy's many parts. Moreover, while the parts tend to move in unison, there is also a sequence observable. When one part changes direction, it pushes another part, which pushes still another. It is logical, therefore, that if we wish to predict turning points of the whole economy, we should try to isolate and study those parts which usually turn *before* the whole.

The search for leading, coincident and lagging indicators of general economic activity has been one of the major continuing projects of the National Bureau of Economic Research (NBER). *Business Conditions Digest* classifies indicators by their participation in the stage of the economic process and their relationship to business cycle movements, as shown in Table 7–10. Panels A and B of Table 7–7 are a cross-

---

[18]See Nicholas D. Kristof, "Handling Growth Recessions," *"New York Times,"* December 13, 1984, p. D-1.

[19]For a good current analysis of growth cycles, both domestic and for international economies, see Moore, et al., "The Development and Role of the National Bureau's Business Cycle Chronologies," p. 27.

**TABLE 7-7  Cross-classification of Cyclical Indicators by Economic Process and Cyclical Timing**

## A. Timing at Business cycle Peaks

| Economic Process / Cyclical Timing | I. Employment and Unemployment (18 series) | II. Production and Income (10 series) | III. Consumption, Trade, Orders, and Deliveries (13 series) | IV. Fixed Capital Investment (18 series) | V. Inventories and Inventory Investment (9 series) | VI. Prices, Costs, and Profits (17 series) | VII. Money and Credit (26 series) |
|---|---|---|---|---|---|---|---|
| Leading (L) Indicators (62 series) | Marginal employment adjustments (6 series) Job vacancies (2 series) Comprehensive employment (1 series) Comprehensive unemployment (3 series) | Capacity utilization (2 series) | New and unfilled orders and deliveries (6 series) Consumption (2 series) | Formation of business enterprises (2 series) Business Investment commitments (5 series) Residential construction (3 series) | Inventory investment (4 series) Inventories on hand and on order (1 series) | Stock prices (1 series) Commodity prices (1 series) Profits and profit margins (7 series) Cash flows (2 series) | Money flows (3 series) Real money supply (2 series) Credit flows (4 series) Credit difficulties (2 series) Bank reserves (2 series) Interest rates (1 series) |
| Roughly Coincidental (C) Indicators (23 series) | Comprehensive employment (1 series) | Comprehensive output and real income (4 series) Industrial production (4 series) | Consumption and trade (4 series) | Backlog of investment commitments (1 series) Business investment expenditures (5 series) | | | Velocity of money (2 series) Interest rates (2 series) |
| Lagging (Lg) Indicators (18 series) | Duration of unemployment (2 series) | | | Business investment expenditures (1 series) | Inventories on hand and on order (4 series) | Unit labor costs and labor share (4 series) | Interest rates (4 series) Outstanding debt (3 series) |
| Timing Unclassified (U) (8 series) | Comprehensive employment (3 series) | | Trade (1 series) | Business investment commitments (1 series) | | Commodity prices (1 series) Profit share (1 series) | Interest rates (1 series) |

TABLE 7-7 (Concluded)

## B. Timing at Business Cycle Troughs

| Economic Process / Cyclical Timing | I. Employment and Unemployment (18 series) | II. Production and Income (10 series) | III. Consumption, Trade, Orders, and Deliveries (13 series) | IV. Fixed Capital Investment (18 series) | V. Inventories and Inventory Investment (9 series) | VI. Prices, Costs, and Profits (17 series) | VII. Money and Credit (26 series) |
|---|---|---|---|---|---|---|---|
| Leading (L) Indicators (47 series) | Marginal employment adjustments (3 series) | Industrial production (1 series) | New and unfilled orders and deliveries (5 series) Consumption and trade (4 series) | Formation of business enterprises (2 series) Business investment commitments (4 series) Residential construction (3 series) | Inventory investment (4 series) | Stock prices (1 series) Commodity prices (2 series) Profits and profit margins (6 series) Cash flows (2 series) | Money flows (2 series) Real money supply (2 series) Credit flows (4 series) Credit difficulties (2 series) |
| Roughly Coincidental (C) Indicators (23 series) | Marginal employment adjustments (2 series) Comprehensive employment (4 series) | Comprehensive output and real income (4 series) Industrial production (3 series) Capacity utilization (2 series) | Consumption and trade (3 series) | Business investment commitments (1 series) | | Profits (2 series) | Money flow (1 series) Velocity of money (1 series) |
| Lagging (Lg) Indicators (40 series) | Marginal employment adjustments (1 series) Job vacancies (12 series) Comprehensive employment (1 series) Comprehensive and duration of unemployment (5 series) | | Unfilled orders (1 series) | Business investment commitments (2 series) Business investment expenditures (6 series) | Inventories on hand and on order (5 series) | Unit labor costs and labor share (4 series) | Velocity of money (1 series) Bank reserves (1 series) Interest rates (8 series) Outstanding debt (3 series) |
| Timing Unclassified (U) (1 series) | | | | | | | Bank reserves (1 series) |

**FIGURE 7–7** *How to Read* Business Conditions Digest *Charts*

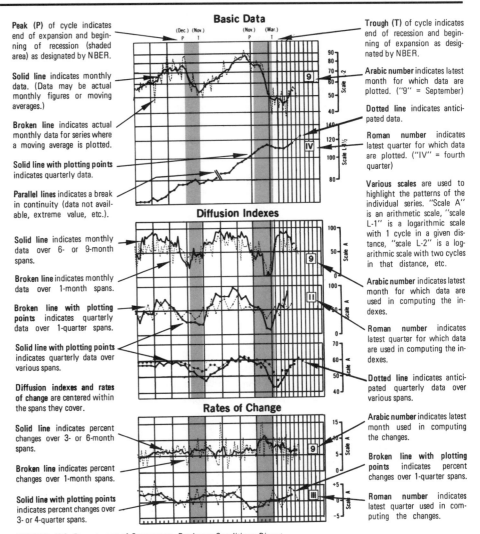

Peak (P) of cycle indicates end of expansion and beginning of recession (shaded area) as designated by NBER.

Solid line indicates monthly data. (Data may be actual monthly figures or moving averages.)

Broken line indicates actual monthly data for series where a moving average is plotted.

Solid line with plotting points indicates quarterly data.

Parallel lines indicates a break in continuity (data not available, extreme value, etc.).

Solid line indicates monthly data over 6- or 9-month spans.

Broken line indicates monthly data over 1-month spans.

Broken line with plotting points indicates quarterly data over 1-quarter spans.

Solid line with plotting points indicates quarterly data over various spans.

Diffusion indexes and rates of change are centered within the spans they cover.

Solid line indicates percent changes over 3- or 6-month spans.

Broken line indicates percent changes over 1-month spans.

Solid line with plotting points indicates percent changes over 3- or 4-quarter spans.

**Basic Data**

**Diffusion Indexes**

**Rates of Change**

Trough (T) of cycle indicates end of recession and beginning of expansion as designated by NBER.

Arabic number indicates latest month for which data are plotted. ("9" = September)

Dotted line indicates anticipated data.

Roman number indicates latest quarter for which data are plotted. ("IV" = fourth quarter)

Various scales are used to highlight the patterns of the individual series. "Scale A" is an arithmetic scale, "scale L-1" is a logarithmic scale with 1 cycle in a given distance, "scale L-2" is a logarithmic scale with two cycles in that distance, etc.

Arabic number indicates latest month for which data are used in computing the indexes.

Roman number indicates latest quarter for which data are used in computing the indexes.

Dotted line indicates anticipated quarterly data over various spans.

Arabic number indicates latest month used in computing the changes.

Broken line with plotting points indicates percent changes over 1-quarter spans.

Roman number indicates latest quarter used in computing the changes.

SOURCE: U.S. Department of Commerce, *Business Conditions Digest.*

classification of cyclical indicators based on an analysis of respective series involved at five business cycle peaks and troughs. Each tabulation distinguishes seven major economic processes and four types of cyclical timing. The titles in the cells identify subgroups of the given economic process with the given timing characteristic. The number of series in each such group is given in parentheses following the title.[20] Figure 7–7 contains a key designed to help read the various charts contained in *Business Conditions Digest.*

---

[20]Complete information on how individual indicators are classified by timing at peaks, troughs, and on turns, along with selected measures, is provided in *The 1984 Handbook of Cyclical Indicators*, U.S. Department of Commerce, Bureau of Economic Analysis.

**TABLE 7–8   Leading Indicators of Economic Activity**

Average weekly hours of production of nonsupervisory workers, manufacturing.

Average weekly initial claims for unemployment insurance, state programs.

Manufacturers' new orders in 1972 dollars, consumer goods and materials industries.

Vendor performance, percent of companies receiving slower deliveries (percent).

Net business formation.

Contracts and orders for plant and equipment in 1972 dollars.

New building permits, private housing units.

Change in manufacturing and trade inventories on hand and on order in 1972 dollars.

Change in sensitive materials prices.

Stock prices, 500 common stocks.

Money supply; M-2 adjusted for inflation.

Change in business and consumer credit outstanding.

SOURCE: *Business Conditions Digest,* U. S. Department of Commerce.

The NBER has selected 12 leaders which come closest to meeting ideal characteristics, such as smoothness of movement from month to month, and consistency and logic of relationship to the general business cycle. These 12 are identified in Table 7–8.

As a valuable supplement to the individual indicators, there is a composite index which combines the leading indicators into a single statistical series. Table 7–9 summarizes the performance record of the composite indexes of leading indicators. In six of eight recessions, the Composite Index of Leading Indicators (CLI) provided a useful signal: a prediction zero to 12 months before the downturn. In two cases, however, the CLI failed to provide a useful signal. First, it gave no prior warning of the 1981 recession. Second, before the 1957 recession, it gave a premature signal, a warning 14 months in advance. On balance, however, Palash and Radecki, who reviewed the data carefully, concluded: "The much-maligned CLI, we find, can predict turning points substantially better than is generally recognized."[21]

The leading indicators are, for the most part, measures of anticipations or new commitments. As such, they have a "look ahead" quality and are highly sensitive to changes in the economic climate as perceived in the marketplace.[22] Consequently, as Figure 7–8 indicates, the index of leading indicators tends to move closely with the stock market (which is one of the 12 leading indicators). One noticeable exception took place in 1974. This divergence according to Goldman Sachs is attributed to the psychological influence of the OPEC oil price increase, Watergate, and so on, which accentuated the decline in domestic economic developments.[23] The coincident indi-

---

[21]Carl J. Palash and Lawrence J. Radecki, "Using Monetary and Financial Variables to Predict Cyclical Downturns," *Quarterly Review,* Federal Reserve Bank of New York, Summer 1985, p. 39. See also Douglas M. Woodham, "Are Leading Indicators Signaling a Recession?" *Quarterly Review,* Federal Reserve Bank of New York, Autumn 1984. Both studies contain detailed analysis of the composite indices' past "false" signals.

[22]Philip A. Klein and Geoffrey H. Moore, "The Leading Indicator Approach to Economic Forecasting—Retrospect and Prospect," *Journal of Forecasting,* 2 (December 1982), p. 119.

[23]Leon G. Cooperman, "Portfolio Strategy," Goldman Sachs, January 1986, p. 5.

**TABLE 7–9** *Performance of the Composite Index of Leading Indicators (1950–83)*

| Peak in Business Cycle | Amount of Lead Time Provided (in months) |
|---|---|
| 7/53 | 1 |
| 8/57 | Premature (14) |
| 4/60 | 5 |
| 12/66 | 6 |
| 12/69 | 1 |
| 11/73 | 3 |
| 1/80 | 6 |
| 7/81 | No Signal |

SOURCE: Federal Reserve Bank of New York.

cators are comprehensive measures of economic performance, pertaining to output, employment, income, and trade. They are the measures to which everyone looks to determine whether the nation is prosperous or depressed. The lagging indicators are more sluggish in their reactions to the economic climate, but they serve two useful functions. First, since they are usually very smooth, they help to confirm changes in trend that are first reflected in the more erratic leading and coincident indicators. Second, their very sluggishness can be an asset in cyclical analysis. As imbalances in the economy are developing or subsiding, the lagging indicators frequently provide the earliest warnings of all, as when rapid increases in costs of production outstrip price increases and threaten profit margins, thus inhibiting new commitments to invest, which are among the leading indicators.[24]

There also are composites of the coincident and lagging indicators. The latter are used as checks on the validity of turns in the leading index. That is, if the leading indicator index seems to have turned down, that fact should be confirmed by subsequent downturns of, first, the coincident index and, next, the lagging index.

Here's how a leading Wall Street economist surveyed the future based on his reading of economic indicators at the end of 1985:

> The leading indicators' signal of a recovering economy became firmer in October. The composite index rose 0.3 percent, its sixth consecutive rise, and September's increase was revised up from 0.1 percent to 0.4 percent. A healthy 60 percent of the components contributed to the expansion, well in the range characterizing normal expansion stages of past business cycles. The most sluggish measure on this chart is the ratio of coincident to lagging indicators, which was unchanged in October. This ratio tends to have longer lead times at business cycle peaks than the other indicators. However, its record is more uneven at business cycle troughs. On two prior occasions—1949 and 1970—it turned up after the economy recovered. Therefore, its failure to respond to date is not necessarily inconsistent with a general economic upturn being in place.[25]

Of course, the investor cannot wait until all the confirming signals have been given before taking action to sell or buy stocks and bonds. It will be too late. But if quick

[24]Klein et al., "The Leading Indicator Approach to Economic Forecasting—Retrospect and Prospect."
[25]Gary Wenglowski, "The Pocket Chartroom," Goldman Sachs, December 1985, p. 23.

FIGURE 7-8  *Comparison of 12 Leading Indicators, Ratio for Coincident to Lagging Indicators, and the S&P 400*

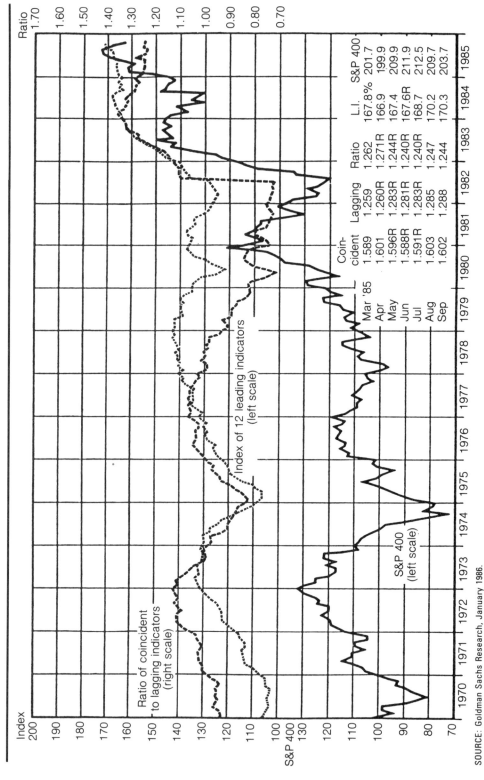

SOURCE: Goldman Sachs Research, January 1986.

action is taken, say, by selling stocks when the composite leading index looks like it is turning down, but the composite coincident index subsequently fails to turn down, the investor would be well advised to conclude that a mistake has been made and should buy back into stocks.

We do not mean to imply, of course, that stocks should be sold just because a single economic indicator turns down. Indeed, a whole variety of factors should be reviewed, and action should be taken when a consensus emerges. Nevertheless, it must be emphasized that if you wait until all the evidence is in hand, the market's move will have passed you by.

*Monetary Indicators.* Among the NBER's selected list of leading indicators is a measure of money supply (M-2), as defined by the Federal Reserve Board. In light of many financial developments over the past few years, the monetary authorities determined a few years ago that the signficance of widely used measures of money and credit had been reduced. Some of these developments have been associated with the emergence in recent years of new monetary assets—for example, negotiable order of withdrawal (NOW) accounts and money market mutual fund shares; others have altered the basic character of standard monetary assets, for example, the growing similarity of and the growing substitution between the deposits of thrift institutions and those of commercial banks.[26] Consequently, in late 1979 the Federal Reserve Board of Governors introduced a new set of definitions to be used by observers in order to track changes in money supply conditions more closely. In presenting this new data base, the Fed noted:

> Given the changes in financial practices in recent years, the new measures should aid both the Federal Reserve and the public in interpreting monetary developments. However, many of the changes in the payments mechanism and in the character of financial assets that necessitated such a redefinition—some of which are ongoing— have also added significantly to the complexity of the monetary system. As a consequence, it is recognized that no one set of monetary aggregates can satisfy every purpose or every user. For this reason, the principal components of the new measures, along with several related series, will be published regularly with the new aggregates. In this way, users will be able to analyze separately the components and to construct alternative measures.

The new monetary definitions were subsequently accompanied by a significant shift in the focus of Federal Reserve Board policy decisions, from concern over the so-called federal funds rate (the interbank borrowing/lending rate) to emphasis on controlling the supply of bank reserves as the primary means of reducing inflation.[27] Here is how Prudential's *Economic Review* summarized other changes in Federal Reserve operating procedures in recent years.

> In the 30 years prior to October 1982, the Fed followed a monetary strategy which was basically easy until such time as the rising inflation rate became a major public concern. At that point, policy would be reversed to reduce the inflation rate, until

---

[26]A good discussion of many of these developments can be found in Benjamin M. Friedman, "Money, Credit, and Interest Rates in the Business Cycle," forthcoming in Robert J. Gordon (ed.) *The American Business Cycle: Continuity and Change* (Chicago: University of Chicago Press, 1986). See also Stephen H. Axelrod, "U.S. Monetary Policy in Recent Years," *Federal Reserve Bulletin*, Washington, D.C., January 1985.

[27]See, for example, Carl J. Palash and Lawrence J. Radecki, "Using Monetary and Financial Variables to Predict Cyclical Downturns," *Quarterly Review*," Federal Reserve Bank of New York, Summer 1985, p. 36.

such time as the unemployment rate increased to politically unacceptable levels. During the 1950s and 1960s the trigger point on inflation was between 3 percent and 4 percent. In the 1970s it took an inflation rate of nearly 10 percent to trigger monetary policy. The greater tolerance for inflation in the 1970s is probably related to the fact that it was widely believed that much of the inflation in that period was due to oil shocks and other factors external to Federal Reserve control.

As there is a relatively long lag between easy monetary policy and inflation, the old monetary strategy implied relatively long periods of easy money. Because there is a relatively short lag between tight money and unemployment, there were relatively short periods of tight monetary policy. Thus, the typical business cycle pattern of 8 to 16 quarters of steady growth in real GNP followed by 2 to 5 quarters of contraction in real GNP.

A good case can be made that since about October 1982 the Fed has followed a new monetary strategy designed to prevent a reacceleration of inflation with the business cycle expansion. Instead of allowing monetary policy to remain easy until the inflation rate actually rose to politically unacceptable levels, monetary policy now becomes restrictive whenever the growth of nominal GNP exceeded some target level which if continued would increase the inflation rate. Because GNP responds within three to six months of a monetary stimulus, the information needed to change policy comes much quicker.[28]

This attitudinal change in Fed policy was accompanied by a shift in focus as to the importance of monetary aggregates in implementing policy goals.[29] As Benjamin Friedman of Harvard University points out:

> From 1970 onward, quantity targets for the growth of various aggregate measures of money and credit, including especially the narrowly defined money stock (M1), played a generally increasing albeit sporadic role in the formulation and implementation of monetary policy. In 1979 the Federal Reserve announced a renewed emphasis on these quantity growth targets and adopted new operating procedures, based on the growth rate of nonborrowed bank reserves, for achieving them. In 1982 the M1 target was publicly suspended, however, and the weight placed on even the broader money and credit targets in 1982 and 1983 was uncertain.[30]

It should be noted that the influence of money on economic activity is at the center of a good deal of dispute among economists. Some view money as a prime mover of the economy, as a causal factor of business cycles. Others see money as a sort of lubricating oil—a good supply is necessary to keep the economic engine running, but it doesn't cause movement by itself.

In addition to their theoretical disputes, economists also argue about the empirical evidence. For example, Benjamin M. Friedman, in a very thoughtful and thorough analysis conducted for the National Bureau of Economic Research, points out: "As of the time of writing, the role of quantity growth targets in U.S. monetary policy may be central, irrelevant or, more likely, somewhere in between."[31]

Whatever the true case may be, monetary aggregates are relied upon by many investment practitioners as good (if not reliable) indicators of the potential impact

---

[28]The Prudential, *Economic Review,* March 1985.

[29]Some observers believe that the new Federal Reserve policy of targeting monetary aggregates instead of interest rates was the most probable reason for increased volatility in all types of economic behavior. See, for example, Palash et al., "Using Monetary and Financial Variables to Predict Cyclical Downturns."

[30]Friedman, "Money, Credit, and Interest Rates in the Business Cycle," 1986.

[31]Friedman, "Money, Credit, and Interest Rates in the Business Cycle," 1986.

FIGURE 7-9  Comparison of Two Money Supply Measures and the S&P 400

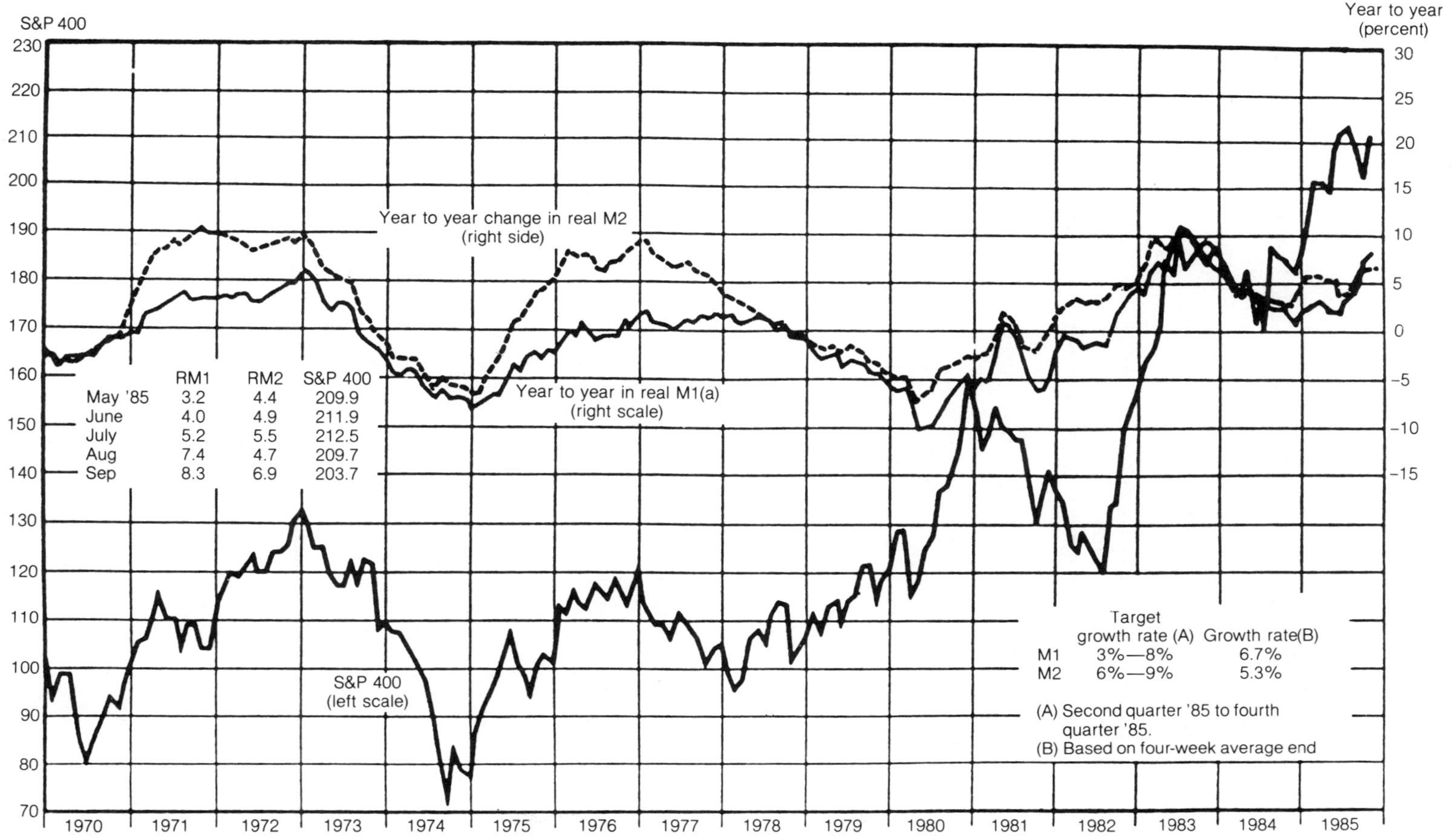

SOURCE: Goldman Sachs Research.

241

that monetary policy decisions will have on aggregate economic activity, and consequently, on portfolio decisions. There seem to be two factors at work. One, investment market participants are constantly buffeted with "evidence" supporting, even proving, the contention that money supply growth and stock price movements are positively and highly correlated. See Figure 7–9.

Secondly, evidence exists that of all the business financial and economic news emanating out of Washington, announcements regarding money supply have a particularly significant (negative) impact on stock prices. That is, announced increases in money supply that are surprisingly large tend to drive stock prices down, at least for a while. This contrasts sharply with the view that "only limited evidence supports the view that either inflation or real economic activity surprises affect stock prices."[32]

Finally, on the matter of monetary aggregates, practicing investors have come to recognize that no one series can be expected to act as the "best indicator" or as a harbinger of economic trends. In fact, each of the aggregates has some measurement claim as a leading indicator of business cycle peaks. Each usually warned of a coming recession, but all five produced instances of premature signals, failures to provide a signal, or both.[33] As can be seen in Table 7–10, each of the monetary variables has some legitimate claim as a leading indicator of business cycle peaks.

Therefore, the best advice that can be given to analysts and investors is to examine several monetary series rather than any single one. Such an approach would also be in keeping with the observation that the "Fed picks that measure of the money supply that has the most stable relationship to GNP."[34]

**Anticipation Surveys.**     The economic and monetary indicators discussed thus far are all measures of what might be called accomplished facts—orders *placed,* hours *worked,* prices of *transactions,* changes in *existing* money supply, and so forth. In addition to these accomplished facts, economists have available for analysis a group of surveys of spending *intentions* of business leaders and consumers. These surveys are conducted by various governmental and private organizations, and the investor should be familiar with at least some of them.

Probably the most widely used group of surveys are those relating to business spending for plant and equipment. In October each year, the economists of McGraw-Hill, Inc., conduct a survey of business capital expenditure plans for the year ahead. The results are published in *Business Week* during the month of November. In December, the Department of Commerce publishes (in the *Survey of Current Business*) an estimate of capital spending in the first quarter of the coming year based on a survey conducted through government auspices. By March, the Department of Commerce has run another survey, this time covering expectations for the first and second quarters and for the full year. In April, McGraw-Hill publishes the results of a follow-up to their October survey, and in June and September, Commerce provides estimates for the current and succeeding quarters based on still more surveys. In addition to this abundance of data, the Conference Board compiles a quarterly record

---

[32]Douglas K. Pearce and V. Vance Roley, "Stock Prices and Economic News," National Bureau of Economic Research, Working Paper No. 1296, March 1984.

[33]Palash et al., "Using Monetary and Financial Variables to Predict Cyclical Downturns," p. 41.

[34]The Prudential, *Economic Review,* March 1985.

**TABLE 7–10    Monetary Variables in Business Cycle Turning Points**

| Peak in Business Cycle | Amount of Lead Time Provided | | | | | |
|---|---|---|---|---|---|---|
| | **M1** | **M2** | **M3** | **Total Debt** | **CP Rate** | **Leading Indicators** |
| 7/53 . . . . . . . . . . . . | 2 | No signal | No signal | * | No signal | 1 |
| 8/57 . . . . . . . . . . . . | Premature (14) | Premature (19) | Premature (19) | * | Premature (24) | Premature (14) |
| 4/60 . . . . . . . . . . . . | 2 | 5 | 5 | No signal | 12 | 5 |
| 12/66 . . . . . . . . . . . . | 2 | 5 | 5 | 2 | 6 | 6 |
| 12/69 . . . . . . . . . . . . | 3 | 7 | 8 | 3 | 6 | 1 |
| 11/73 . . . . . . . . . . . . | No signal | 6 | 0 | No signal | 7 | 3 |
| 1/80 . . . . . . . . . . . . | No signal | Premature (27) | 10 | 6 | Premature (24) | 6 |
| 1/81 . . . . . . . . . . . . | No signal | No signal | No signal | 8 | 12 | No signal |
| False signals . . . . . . . | None | 6/64–9/64 | None | None | 2/51–5/52 5/64–6/64 | 4/51–5/52 |

*Data for total debt are not available.
SOURCE: Federal Reserve Bank of New York.

of budgetary appropriations for future capital spending by the boards of directors of America's largest corporations. These findings are discussed and interpreted in the monthly Board's publication, *Manufacturing Industrial Statistics* (available through private subscription).

Since capital spending plays such an important role in our economy (many economists believe it is the single most important generating factor in the business cycle), a successful forecast of such spending obviously is desirable. While the surveys do not have a perfect record, use of the data usually results in a correct forecast of the direction of capital spending, although not necessarily in a correct forecast of magnitude.

During recent years, consumers have joined business executives as objects of economic surveyors' attentions. While no one claims that consumers plan their future spending in the same sense as business leaders do, it seems reasonable to hypothesize that families talk things over some time prior to purchasing major items, such as automobiles, houses, home furnishings, and appliances, and perhaps even some nondurables, such as clothing. Surely impulse buying cannot be the only driving force behind consumer spending, particularly on expensive durable goods. Although consumer spending intentions are subject to swift revisions due to unexpected changes in employment conditions, fluctuations in purchases of consumer durables are such a key element in the business cycle that all available evidence should be brought to the fore in an attempt to forecast these fluctuations.

Since 1946, the Institute for Social Research of the University of Michigan has conducted several nationwide surveys each year in an attempt to determine changes in consumer attitudes and in their intentions to purchase durable goods. Richard Curtin, Director of Surveys on Consumer Attitudes defines the purpose of the survey as follows:

> The survey measures are not intended to establish the absolute level of consumer sentiment at any given time. They are intended to measure change. Comparisons with previous measurements indicate the direction of change in consumer attitudes

and expectations, and to some extent, the degree of that change. Moreover, the analytic focus is not only on the direction of change but also on understanding why these changes in consumer attitudes and expectations occur, and how these changes relate to subsequent shifts in consumer behavior.[35]

The findings are made public via books, publications of the Department of Commerce, and press conferences. Other organizations, notably the Bureau of the Census and the Conference Board, have built upon the work of the Institute for Social Research, but have taken issue with the Center's emphasis on attitudes as distinguished from intentions.[36] A much debated question among economists is whether attitude data really add significantly to the forecasting potential of intentions data.[37]

It may seem as if there is no efficient way to organize this mass of survey data, monetary data, and other leading indicators in such a way as to derive an overview of what is developing in the nation's economy and a forecast of what is to come. But there is. Economists approach the problem by utilizing what is known as a GNP model.

## *The GNP Model*

The word *model* in the context of economic forecasting often refers to a complex set of mathematical equations. But it also may be used simply to convey an impression of *structure*. The gross national product (GNP) is a framework within which economic information may be arranged in an orderly fashion. Analysts can bring to bear whatever amount of mathematics they desire in their attempt to gain insight from this information.

Gross national product, simply defined, is the market value of the nation's output of goods and services. Its measurement can be approached from either of two directions: *(a)* By adding up the incomes generated by the economy—wages, salaries, profits, interest, and rent; or *(b)* by adding up the expenditures of consumers, businesses, and governments (plus net exports). For short-term forecasting purposes, the expenditure approach is more useful than the income approach. What one does is to forecast each major expenditure component of GNP, add up the component forecasts, and thus forecast the movement of aggregate economic activity as measured by GNP. This is why GNP model building is often referred to as sector analysis.

GNP data are compiled by the Department of Commerce every quarter (on a seasonally adjusted annual rate basis), and are published in most complete detail in the *Survey of Current Business*. The data are revised frequently as new information becomes available, and the analyst must be careful to work with the most up-to-date statistics. Extensive revisions usually are published in each July issue of the *Survey,* and historical data are presented in a special biennial (even years) supplement entitled *Business Statistics*. Detailed descriptive material on the conceptual underpin-

[35]Richard T. Curtin, "Indicators of Consumer Behavior: The University of Michigan Surveys of Consumers," *Public Opinion Quarterly* 46, p. 340, by the Trustees of Columbia University, 1982.

[36]Consumer surveys patterned after the Institute's work are now conducted in a dozen other countries, including Western Europe, Australia, Japan, and Canada.

[37]The most recent book by the pioneer in this field is George Katona, *Psychological Economics,* (New York: Elsevier, 1975). See also, Richard T. Curtin, "Curtin on Katona," in *Political Economy and Public Policy: Contemporary Economists in Perspective,* Vol. 1, ed. William Breit and Kenneth G. Elzinva, (New York: Jai Press, 1983).

**TABLE 7–11    *Major Components of Gross National Product, 1985 ($ billions)***

| | |
|---|---:|
| Personal consumption expenditures: | |
| Durable goods | $355 |
| Nondurable goods and services | 896 |
| Services | 1,285 |
| Total | $2,536 |
| Gross private domestic investment: | |
| Residential construction (including farm) | 180 |
| Business capital spending | 451 |
| Business inventory accumulation | −8 |
| Total | 623 |
| Government purchases of goods and services: | |
| Federal | 347 |
| State and local | 499 |
| Total | 846 |
| Net exports of goods and services | −89 |
| Gross national product | $3,916 |

SOURCE: *Survey of Current Business,* October 1985.

nings of national income accounting have been published in supplementary volumes entitled *The Input-Output Structure of the U.S. Economy.* An analytically convenient statement of the U.S. GNP accounts is shown in Table 7–11.

As noted previously, the economic forecasters' tasks are to enter the numbers they believe are most realistic for each calendar quarter of the period they are forecasting. To do this, they make use of any and every piece of evidence they think is pertinent. The latter point should be stressed. Sector analysis permits a maximum degree of analytical flexibility and ingenuity. As one analyst has put it, a GNP model has "a ravenous appetite for any data, evidence or insight concerning the current situation and outlook."

## Achieving Internal Consistency in a Forecast

Since investment timing depends more on a proper forecast of the *direction* than of the *magnitude* of economic change, it may seem unnecessary to attempt quantitative forecasts of the GNP sectors. Quantification is desirable, however. In the first place, without quantification the significance of each component of the economic outlook cannot be assessed properly. For example, a decline in defense spending may be foreseen, and a rise in residential construction may be foreseen. But without an estimate of the magnitude of the change in each sector, the analyst cannot determine direction of change of the two sectors *combined.*

Furthermore, the various GNP sectors are interrelated. For example, consumer spending for durable goods, such as furniture and appliances, is related to purchases of homes; these expenditures affect saving; saving affects business investment; business investment affects consumer incomes, thereby affecting consumer spending. The circles go on and on. Since the major economic sectors are so fundamentally interrelated, an overall forecast based on a summation of individual sector forecasts must be internally consistent. The sectors must be in reasonable proportion to the whole and to each other—reasonable in the sense of conforming to the analyst's theory of business cycles and reasonable in the light of past empirical relationships. The only way to achieve internal consistency is to quantify.

With regard to internal consistency, it also must be recognized that the entire discussion thus far has been in terms of the expenditure, or demand, components of gross national product. Forecasters cannot rest easy, however, until they compare estimates of national spending with some measures of *supply* potential—that is, with some measures of national productive capacity. They must try to determine what their projections of gross national product imply for the rate of employment, for example. Can the projected demand for goods and services in fact be supplied by the available labor force? Or will the need for labor become so intense that product bottlenecks will result? On the other hand, does the projected demand fall far short of the productive capacity of the economy, leaving a high degree of slack in labor utilization? Similarly, what are the implications for plant and equipment adequacy?

If the forecast's implied rate of utilization of physical and human resources is very high, the forecasters may consider either scaling down their projections or maintaining their projections but adding a substantial price increase factor. On the other hand, if a preliminary forecast indicates that gross national product will be far below the economy's productive capacity, the forecasters must consider the possibility of federal government measures designed to take up the slack. Such considerations, however, must be predicated on whether the prevailing political environment will be conducive to the prospect of increasing federal budget deficits in order to stimulate the economy. The current popularity of supply-side economics raises substantial doubts that enlarged federal spending will be the primary means of correcting a business cycle downturn.

The latest 1985 *Economic Report of the President* adds this perspective:

> Activist fiscal policy—whether on the spending or the tax side—can be upsetting to private decisionmaking. Changes in jobs, place of residence, and business investment in plant and equipment are based on long-term expectations and plans; frequent changes in government tax and spending policy make efficient decisions more difficult. Fiscal policy adjustments are often unpredictable, and this uncertainty complicates both business and consumer planning. Indeed, because business cycle fluctuations themselves have proven so difficult to forecast, government responses to business fluctuations are necessarily difficult to forecast.[38]

## Sources and Uses of Funds Model

Closely allied to the GNP model is an analytical structure which is widely used in interest rate forecasting. It is known as sources and uses of funds analysis. The object of sources and uses of funds analysis is to quantify the individual supply and demand forces at work in the money and capital markets and thereby to determine whether the balance of forces lies in the direction of higher or lower interest rates. For example, Table 7–12 shows the major components of sources and uses of investment

[38]*Economic Report of the President,* Council of Economic Advisors (Washington, D.C.: U.S. Government Printing Office, February 1985), p. 58. It is ironic that this statement preceded, by a year, the massive tax revision proposals of 1986.

*TABLE 7–12    Net Demand and Supply for Funds ($ Billions)*

### 1. Summary of supply and Demand for Credit
(Annual Net Increases in Amounts Outstanding, Dollars in Billions)

|  | 1979 | 1980 | 1981 | 1982 | 1983 | 1984E | 1985P | Amt. Out. 31 Dec 84E | Table Reference |
|---|---|---|---|---|---|---|---|---|---|
| **Net demand** | | | | | | | | | |
| Privately held mortgages | $113.1 | $84.2 | $73.7 | $15.9 | $83.7 | $148.5 | $136.4 | $1,485.5 | 2 |
| Corporate and foreign bonds | 35.7 | 40.2 | 34.9 | 39.1 | 37.9 | 50.5 | 45.3 | 656.9 | 3 |
| Total long-term private | 148.8 | 124.3 | 108.6 | 54.9 | 121.7 | 199.0 | 181.7 | 2,142.4 | |
| Short-term business borrowing | 98.0 | 67.1 | 117.3 | 47.5 | 60.1 | 141.6 | 153.2 | 1,006.7 | 8 |
| Short-term other borrowing | 49.3 | 11.2 | 37.7 | 27.7 | 60.5 | 97.9 | 120.7 | 695.5 | 8 |
| Total short-term private | 147.2 | 78.3 | 155.0 | 75.2 | 120.6 | 239.5 | 273.9 | 1,702.2 | |
| Privately held federal debt | 76.2 | 118.7 | 123.0 | 214.1 | 241.0 | 257.3 | 277.9 | 1,728.1 | 6 |
| Tax-exempt notes and bonds | 27.8 | 31.9 | 29.5 | 63.9 | 54.3 | 66.5 | 63.2 | 542.8 | 4 |
| Total government debt | 104.0 | 150.6 | 152.4 | 278.0 | 295.3 | 323.8 | 341.1 | 2,270.9 | |
| **Total net demand for credit** | **$400.0** | **353.3** | **$416.0** | **$408.1** | **$537.6** | **$762.4** | **$796.7** | **$6,115.6** | ▼ |
| **Net supply*** | | | | | | | | | |
| Thrift institutions | $56.5 | $54.5 | $27.8 | $31.3 | $136.8 | $155.8 | $171.7 | $1,117.1 | 9 |
| Insurance, pensions, endowments | 77.9 | 88.2 | 89.2 | 107.1 | 96.1 | 105.3 | 105.4 | 1,190.2 | 9 |
| Investment companies | 29.3 | 15.9 | 72.4 | 52.4 | 6.0 | 49.9 | 58.0 | 261.3 | 9 |
| Other nonbank finance | 27.8 | 13.1 | 28.8 | 4.9 | 12.0 | 50.6 | 41.3 | 307.8 | 9 |
| Total nonbank finance | 191.4 | 171.7 | 218.1 | 195.6 | 250.9 | 361.5 | 376.5 | 2,876.3 | |
| Commercial banks | 122.2 | 101.4 | 107.6 | 107.2 | 140.2 | 169.0 | 164.8 | 1,761.6 | 10 |
| Nonfinancial corporations | 7.0 | 1.8 | 18.4 | 13.6 | 22.8 | 12.6 | 23.1 | 160.6 | 11 |
| State and local governments | 7.1 | 0.6 | 2.0 | 10.3 | 17.2 | 11.0 | 9.7 | 93.6 | 11 |
| Foreign investors | −4.6 | 23.2 | 16.3 | 18.1 | 28.5 | 30.7 | 30.8 | 283.2 | 11 |
| Subtotal | 323.1 | 298.7 | 362.4 | 344.8 | 459.5 | 584.8 | 604.8 | 5,175.3 | |
| Residual: households direct | 76.9 | 54.6 | 53.7 | 63.3 | 78.1 | 177.6 | 191.9 | 940.4 | 12 |
| **Total net supply of credit** | **$400.0** | **$353.3** | **$416.0** | **$408.1** | **$537.6** | **$762.4** | **$796.7** | **$6,115.6** | ▲ |
| **Memo** | | | | | | | | | |
| Net issuance corporate stock | $−1.9 | $18.2 | $11.9 | $19.5 | $27.8 | $−89.1 | $−26.8 | $2,030.0 | |
| Total credit and stock | 398.1 | 371.5 | 427.9 | 427.6 | 565.3 | 673.3 | 769.9 | 8,145.6 | |
| **Percentage of total absorbed by** | | | | | | | | | |
| Households | 56.2% | 42.9% | 40.1% | 28.8% | 40.6% | 45.8% | 44.3% | | |
| Nonfinancial business | 24.3 | 25.3 | 25.1 | 18.5 | 15.0 | 9.6 | 15.2 | | |
| Financial institutions | 7.3 | 10.1 | 11.8 | 4.4 | 8.4 | −2.7 | 5.1 | | |
| Government | 7.9 | 15.6 | 17.6 | 45.7 | 33.5 | 46.4 | 34.2 | | |
| Foreigners | 4.3 | 6.1 | 5.4 | 2.6 | 2.5 | 0.9 | 1.2 | | |

*Excludes funds for equities and other demands not tablulated above.

SOURCE: Salomon Brothers, 1986.

funds, based on data contained in Federal Reserve flow-of-funds tabulations. These tabulations are updated quarterly in the *Federal Reserve Bulletin*.

Since, by definition, sources and uses of funds must always balance, it may be wondered how such tabulations can be useful in forecasting interest rates. After all, changes in interest rates, like changes in any prices, come about because of *imbalances* in supply and demand. Unsatisfied demands for funds pull interest rates upward, and pressures of excess supplies push them down.

Admittedly, it would be very helpful to have statistics on ex ante sources and uses of funds which would reveal such imbalances. But even a balanced ex post framework can be useful. In the first place, as analysts attempt to forecast the various components of the sources and uses statement—as they strike a balance between the forecast supplies and demands—they develop a feel for the ex ante gap between supply and demand. Another clue to the probable direction of interest rate changes is the magnitude of noninstitutional sources of funds which the forecaster envisions in estimating forthcoming sources and uses of investment funds.

Institutional investors are under considerable pressure to commit their funds whether interest rates are high or low. Therefore, when demands for funds are expected to be low relative to the available institutional supply, interest rates usually can be expected to decline. But when demands are forecast to rise rapidly relative to institutional supply, they cannot be met unless higher interest rates cause funds to be forthcoming from other sources, such as individuals. Here is how Henry Kaufman describes the ever changing nature of the overall process:

> There is a kind of dynamic balance between the financial needs of households and business corporations that tends to follow a natural shifting pattern over the course of the business cycle. In the early stages of expansion, households increase their borrowing needs in order to satisfy pent-up demands, and this benefits the business sector's internal cash generation. At this stage, business capital formation is typically limited by large excess capacity. Later in the cycle, household demands are closer to satiation, which naturally slows the growth of business internal cash flows—just as businesses are accelerating their own spending to alleviate their stretched-out production capacity.[39]

***A Final Word on Forecasting.***     It may be surprising to readers of this book to realize that detailed economic forecasts have been fairly inaccurate. A number of important studies call attention to the limited predictive value of detailed economic forecasts reaching out further than a few quarters.[40] For example, Leonard Silk of the *New York Times* has reported on a study which found that "no single forecaster has been observed to earn a long record of superior overall accuracy, and indeed nothing in the study would encourage us to expect any individual to reach this elusive goal."[41] Errors in turning point forecasts, that is, the prediction that an important economic variable, or some aggregate of series, is about to change direction, are even less reliable. Part of the problem, according to a classic explanation by Victor Zarnowitz, is that "forecasters draw, to a large extent, upon the same raw materials," that is, on information that is widely accessible, and they variously influence one another. Few if any of them can be regarded as independent producers, though some meet this description more than others.[42] A comparable problem is that forecasters often place undue weight on recent conditions when predicting future events and fail to consider the impact of countervailing trends. Peter L. Bernstein recently pointed out that "In November 1980, the consensus of the Blue Chip survey of economic

[39]See Henry Kaufman, James McKeon, and Nancy Kimelman, "1985 Prospects for Financial Markets," Salomon Brothers, Inc., December 11, 1984.

[40]*Business Week* recently reviewed a variety of predictions for 1984 and in retrospect concluded "that the economics profession by and large had another disastrous year predicting the future." See, "What Good are Economists?" February 4, 1985, p. 60. See, also, Stephen K. McNees, "Which Forecast Should You Use?" *New England Economic Review*, July-August 1985.

[41]Leonard Silk, "How to Win at Forecasting," Economic Scene, *New York Times*, July 27, 1983.

[42]Victor Zarnowitz, *An Appraisal of Short-Term Economic Forecasts* (New York: National Bureau of Economic Research, 1967), p. 7.

forecasters predicted an average rate of inflation of 8.9 percent for the first half of the 1980s and 7.6 percent for the latter half." The actual inflation rate for 1985 was less than 3.5 percent. Bernstein notes, "As usual, the economists were extrapolating the recent past into the more distant future."[43]

Furthermore, poor forecasting is not limited to economists in the United States. *The Economist* magazine of London recently examined the forecasting record of the British Treasury along with three important independent economic forecasters and concluded "all forecasts should carry a government health warning, but some are less dangerous than others."[44]

Thus, investors who incorporate business cycle forecasting into their portfolio management decision-making procedures are well advised to remember that the way people actually behave is captured by few—if any—forecasting models.[45] History abounds with examples of this fundamental principle which the well-known observer of Wall Street, Ray De Voe (an appreciator of such happenings), calls the "forecasters' trap." One of the more humorous but appropriate examples is related by Shepherd Mead in "How to Get to the Future Before It Gets to You."[46] Its relevance to popular forecasts over pending oil shortages a few years ago should also not be lost. Stepping back in time to 1850, Mead engages several model builders to study the developing problems of pollution in New York City. The main causes of concern are chewing tobacco and horses—more precisely, spit and horse manure. In 1850 the spit level in the gutter was half an inch high, and the manure level in the middle of the road was half an inch too.

By 1860 each had reached a level of one inch, and using prevailing rates of growth as a basis of a forecast, levels of two inches were expected by 1870 and four inches by 1880. Looking further ahead, by 1970 it was expected that there would be 2,048 inches of spit and horse manure in the streets. That comes to 170 feet, 8 inches of each.

Clearly, investors were well advised to buy plug tobacco and horse oat company common stocks. Could growth ever be more assured?

Unfortunately, forecasts of that kind fail to recognize: (1) that people, when the spit and manure level reached the second and third story, would begin to do something about it; (2) that oat and tobacco supplies could not be available to meet demand; and (3) most importantly, that cigarette smoking would replace chewing tobacco and automobiles would replace horses.

The point is that investors must supplement traditional forecasting methods with common sense judgments about the future.

---

[43]Peter L. Bernstein, "What's Happened to Inflation Expectations?" Peter L. Bernstein, Inc., December 1, 1985.

[44]"Better than a Blindfold and a Pin," *The Economist,* November 9, 1985, p. 71.

[45]This important point was reinforced by Karen Arenson of the *New York Times* when she noted that "models work best when the future resembles the past. They work least well when major shifts in economic behavior are taking place." See Karen W. Arenson, "Useful, Yes; Infallible, Hardly," *New York Times,* April 26, 1981.

[46]Shepherd Mead, "How to Get to the Future Before It Gets to You," (New York: Hawthorn Books, 1974) p. 15. For those interested in going further on this point, the best compendium of inaccurate forecasts is M. Hirsh Goldberg, *The Blunder Book* (New York: William Morrow and Company, Inc. 1984). See also, Christopher Cerf and Victor Navaskey, *The Experts Speak* (New York: Random House, 1984).

# ■ *SUMMARY*

Historical precedent, as outlined in the first part of this chapter, suggests various investment strategies which may be employed profitably if investors develop an ability to forecast major economic turning points about four to six months in advance—or if they rely on the counsel of others who have such an ability. (Of course, many investors will adopt a buy-and-hold strategy which ignores cyclical swings.) The precise implementation of these strategies depends on how aggressive, self-confident, and flexible an investor is. For example, large institutional investors are much less flexible than individual investors. Nevertheless, the general nature of the strategies is as follows:

1.  If investors suspect that the prosperity phase of the business cycle is coming to an end but are not yet firmly convinced of the fact, they might continue buying common stocks but confine purchases to companies whose sales are likely to be least vulnerable to recession and whose stocks price-earnings ratios still seem relatively attractive.

2.  When investors become convinced that a recession lies shortly ahead, even though the stock market is still strong, they should have the courage to stop making new common stock commitments. Investable funds should be kept liquid at this stage—that is, in bank time deposits or in short-term securities. Long-term bond investments probably are not yet appropriate, since interest rates are likely still to be rising. But the typical flat or downward-sloping shape of the yield curve at such times suggests that a good rate of return will be secured even on liquid investments.

3.  When the recession gets underway and stock prices are falling rapidly, interest rates are likely to be at a peak, and liquid funds should be shifted into high-quality bonds of long maturity. These are likely to appreciate most in value when the cyclical decline in interest rates takes place.

4.  In the midst of the recession, yield spreads between high-quality and lower-quality bonds, and between bonds and mortgages, may become relatively wide. Income oriented investors often find it worthwhile to shift funds from high-quality bonds to these higher-yielding investments at such time.

5.  When investors perceive the forthcoming end of the recession, a renewed stock buying program is in order—particularly the stocks of cyclical and glamour-growth companies which probably were severely depressed during the bear market. Profits on long-maturity bonds can be realized through sales, although some further rise in bond prices can be anticipated, with the proceeds of the sales to be invested in common stocks.[47]

It must be recognized, of course, that the business-cycle approach to investment timing has faults as well as virtues. First, since many full-time professional economists have only mediocre forecasting records, investors who are not economists cannot be expected to do very well in forecasting on their own—or in evaluating the forecasts of professionals. Second, even a consistent record of perfect forecasts is

---

[47]All of these investment operations, of course, should take place within an overall policy framework regarding the appropriate percentages of total assets to be allocated to stocks versus fixed-income investments, as described in Chapters 17 and 18 of this book.

unlikely to result in consistently correct investment timing. For although the timing relationships among stock price, interest rate, and business cycle turning points have been reasonably stable, they have not been, and doubtless will not in the future be, unchanging. Consequently, many investors supplement business cycle analysis with the tools of technical analysis described in the next chapter.

---

# SUGGESTED READINGS

Arnott, Robert D., and William A. Copeland. "The Business Cycle and Security Selection." *Financial Analysts Journal,* March-April 1985.

Bernstein, Peter L., and Theodore N. Silbert. "Are Economic Forecasters Worth Listening To?" *Harvard Business Review,* September-October 1984.

Black, Fischer. "The Trouble with Economic Models." *Financial Analysts Journal,* March-April 1982.

*Business Conditions Digest.* U.S. Department of Commerce, Bureau of Economic Analysis, monthly.

Canto, Victor A. et al. *The Financial Analyst's Guide to Monetary Policy.* New York: Praeger Publishers, 1986.

*Economic Report of the President.* Council of Economic Advisers. Washington, D.C.: U.S. Government Printing Office, annually.

Friedman, Benjamin M. "Money, Credit, and Interest Rates in the Business Cycle." National Bureau of Economic Research, Working Paper No. 1982, October 1984.

Jeffrey, Robert H. "The Folly of Stock Market Timing." *Harvard Business Review* July-August, 1984.

McNees, Stephen K. "Which Forecast Should You Use?" *New England Economic Review,* July-August 1985.

Moore, Geoffrey H. *Business Cycles, Inflation, and Forecasting.* 2nd ed. Cambridge, Mass.: Ballinger Publishing Company, 1983.

Moore, Geoffrey H., and Victor Zarnowitz. "The Development and Role of the Nation Bureau's Business Cycle Chronologies." National Bureau of Economic Research, Inc., Working Paper No. 1394, July 1984.

Piccini, Raymond. "Stock Market Behavior Around Business Cycle Peaks." *Financial Analysts Journal,* July-August 1980.

Stoken, Dick A. *Cycles.* New York: McGraw-Hill, 1978.

# CHAPTER

## 10

# *Common Stock Valuation*

*The greatest of all gifts is the power to estimate things at their true worth.*

LaRochefoucauld

Some companies are worth more dead than alive. Their breakup value—the amount that would remain after selling their assets and paying off their debts—is greater than the price at which their shares trade in the open market. Corporate raiders are always on the lookout for such companies and are willing to pay a premium over market price to buy up their shares, as long as the liquidating value is high enough to make the effort worthwhile. Thus, one might say that, at a minimum, a share of stock is worth its estimated breakup value (net liquidating value of the company divided by the number of shares outstanding). Of course, as discussed in the previous chapter, the liquidating value of a company's net assets often is not apparent from a simple perusal of its published balance sheets. Even when it can be determined, however, in most cases companies are worth more as going concerns, and their stocks sell at higher prices than liquidating value. Therefore, while the estimation of breakup values occupies a significant portion of the time of many Wall Street analysts,[1] most stock valuation methods are aimed at determining going-concern values.

## ■ PRESENT VALUE THEORY

Theorists argue that the best measure of going-concern value is the present value of expected future cash flows from an investment. Therefore, common stock investors should follow three steps: (1) estimate the future earnings per share of a company,

---

[1]Stuart Weiss, "Breakup Value Is Wall Street's New Buzzword," *Business Week,* July 8, 1985.

(2) make a judgment about the proportion of earnings likely to be paid as dividends, and (3) calculate the present value of the projected dividend stream by discounting the dividends at a required rate of return that reflects the degree of uncertainty about the accuracy of the estimates.

Valuation by discounting estimated dividend flows frequently is attacked as unrealistic.[2] First, it is not possible to forecast dividends many years into the future with a high degree of accuracy. Second, the dominant objective of millions of investors in common stocks is to sell the stocks at a profit rather than to sit around collecting dividends.

The logic of the second argument is probably more easily rebutted than the first. Consider the hypothetical example of a corporation which has written into its bylaws a perpetual prohibition of dividend payments or of return of capital to stockholders via sale of assets or by any other means. With these bylaws, no rational investor would be willing to purchase the corporation's stock, no matter how high its earnings or how low the asking price. (We exclude from consideration purchasing stock in order to become an operating officer and thus receive a salary, or purchasing the stock in the hope of changing the bylaws.) Of course, people sometimes become irrational or follow the greater fool theory, whereby each buyer assumes that he or she will be able to sell at a higher price to a greater fool. For example, in the tulip mania in Europe a few centuries ago, people bought and sold tulip bulbs at fantastic prices without the vaguest intention of actually planting the bulbs to get flowers.[3] But such bubbles must inevitably burst. Our hypothetical corporation's stock might trade for a while, but people must eventually recognize that they are buying and selling a mere piece of paper, without any value in the absence of an ability to pay dividends or liquidate. Thus, while much of a stock's value to an investor undoubtedly lies in the prospect of price appreciation, prices cannot be divorced from dividend prospects.[4]

Arguments regarding the difficulty of forecasting dividends into the distant future are more difficult to rebut. Indeed, we shall not try to rebut. Rather, our belief is that several different valuation methods should be applied. Investors should try to find stocks whose market prices appear low or high based on alternative estimates of value. Therefore, we will review in this chapter not only the classical discounted dividend approach to valuation but also more pragmatic approaches relying on:

**a.** price/earnings ratios,

**b.** price/sales ratios, and

**c.** price/book value ratios.

---

[2]See, for example, Robert J. Shiller, "Do Stock Prices Move Too Much To Be Justified by Subsequent Changes in Dividends?" *American Economic Review*, June 1981.

[3]For a fine account of this and other speculative manias, see Charles Mackay, *Extraordinary Popular Delusions and The Madness of Crowds*. Originally published in 1841; reprinted by Investors Library, Inc., Palisades Park, N.J.

[4]For some empirical studies in support of this argument, see John A. Cole, "Are Dividend Surprises Independently Important?" *The Journal of Portfolio Management*, Summer 1984; and Paul Asquith and David W. Mullins, Jr., "The Impact of Initiating Dividend Payments on Shareholders' Wealth," *The Journal of Business*, January 1983. Nevertheless, skepticism persists, as suggested by the Shiller article. Also see Suzanne Wittebort, "Do Investors Really Care About Dividends?," *Institutional Investor*, March 1981.

# ■ *PRESENT VALUE MATHEMATICS*

## *The Basic Concept*

The concept of present value is really quite simple and can be prosaically illustrated. Assume that Mr. A wants to borrow money from Ms. B, repayable at a future date. Ms. B is willing to grant the loan but feels that, considering the risks involved, she is entitled to a 10 percent annual rate of return. This being the case, how much money will B advance to A on A's IOU for $1,000 payable one year hence? The answer is $909.09. If B lends $909.09 and gets back $1,000.00 one year later, she has earned $90.91 interest during the year ($1,000 − $909.09), which is 10 percent of the amount loaned. Thus, $909.09 is the present value of $1,000 payable one year hence at a discount rate of 10 percent (in present value calculations, the interest rate is known as the discount rate). Algebraically, the relationships in this example can be described in two ways:

$$
\begin{aligned}
1.\ \text{Future value} &= \text{Present value} \times (1 + \text{Interest rate}) \\
\$1,000.00 &= \$909.09 \quad\quad \times\ 1.10 \\
2.\ \text{Present value} &= \text{Future value}/(1 + \text{Interest rate}) \\
\$909.09 &= \$1,000.00\ /\ 1.10
\end{aligned}
$$

Suppose, now, that the $1,000 IOU was to be payable two years hence instead of one year hence. If B still wants a 10 percent per annum rate of return, she would be willing to lend $826.45. This can be seen as follows:

$$
\begin{aligned}
\text{Year 1: } \$826.45 \times 1.10 &= \$909.09\ (\$826.45 + \$82.64) \\
\text{Year 2: } \$909.09 \times 1.10 &= \$1,000.00\ (\$909.09 + \$90.91)
\end{aligned}
$$

As a generalization, we can state that:

$$
\begin{aligned}
\text{Future value} &= \text{Present value} \times (1 + i)^n \\
\text{Present value} &= \text{Future value}/(1 + i)^n
\end{aligned}
$$

where:

$i$ = Annual compound interest rate or discount rate (compounding means that interest is to be earned not only on the initial principal amount but also on each interest payment).

$n$ = Number of years between the present and the future value.

We can further generalize for cases where interest is to be compounded more frequently than once a year. For example, bonds usually pay interest twice a year, stocks usually pay dividends quarterly, and many savings banks compound interest daily. The more generalized formulas would be:

$$
\begin{aligned}
\text{Future value} &= \text{Present value} \times [1 + (i/m)]^{mn} \\
\text{Present value} &= \text{Future value}/[1 + (i/m)]^{mn}
\end{aligned}
$$

where:

$i$ = Stated, or nominal annual interest or discount rate.

$m$ = Number of compounding periods each year.

$n$ = Number of years between present and future value.

# Present and Future Value Tables

In order to simplify such calculations, tables have been developed for the future value of \$1 and the present value of \$1.[5] Tables 10–1 and 10–2 are typical. Note that each column represents a different interest rate, and each row represents a different number of compounding periods. To illustrate the use of these tables, consider the following questions:

1. If you borrow \$5,000 and promise to repay the loan after five years, with interest at 10 percent, compounded annually, how much will you have to repay?
2. If you promise to pay me \$5,000 after 10 years, how much should I be willing to lend you today if I demand 12 percent interest, compounded annually?
3. Suppose, in question 2, that I demand 12 percent compounded quarterly?

To answer question 1, go to Table 10–1. Run your finger down to the row for period 5 and across to the 10 percent column. You will find the number 1.6105. This means that the future value of \$1 after five years, at 10 percent compounded annually, is \$1.6105. Since the loan is \$5,000, multiply \$5,000 by 1.6105, and the answer is that you will have to repay \$8,052.50.

To answer question 2, go to Table 10–2. Run your finger down to the row for period 10 and across to the 12 percent column. You will find the number .3220. This means that the present value of \$1 payable 10 years from now is only 32 cents, at a 12 percent annual discount rate. Since you promise to pay me \$5,000 in 10 years, I will lend you \$1,610 (\$5,000 × 0.3220).

To answer question 3, stay at Table 10–2 but go to the 40-period row (10 years,

**TABLE 10–1   Future Value of \$1 Payable at End of N Periods**

| N | 1% | 2% | 3% | 4% | 5% | 6% | 7% | 8% | 9% | 10% | 12% | 14% | 15% | 16% | 18% | 20% |
|---|---|---|---|---|---|---|---|---|---|---|---|---|---|---|---|---|
| 1 | 1.0100 | 1.0200 | 1.0300 | 1.0400 | 1.0500 | 1.0600 | 1.0700 | 1.0800 | 1.0900 | 1.1000 | 1.1200 | 1.1400 | 1.1500 | 1.1600 | 1.1800 | 1.2000 |
| 2 | 1.0201 | 1.0404 | 1.0609 | 1.0816 | 1.1025 | 1.1236 | 1.1449 | 1.1664 | 1.1881 | 1.2100 | 1.2544 | 1.2996 | 1.3225 | 1.3456 | 1.3924 | 1.4400 |
| 3 | 1.0303 | 1.0612 | 1.0927 | 1.1249 | 1.1576 | 1.1910 | 1.2250 | 1.2597 | 1.2950 | 1.3310 | 1.4049 | 1.4815 | 1.5209 | 1.5609 | 1.6430 | 1.7280 |
| 4 | 1.0406 | 1.0824 | 1.1255 | 1.1699 | 1.2155 | 1.2625 | 1.3108 | 1.3605 | 1.4116 | 1.4641 | 1.5735 | 1.6890 | 1.7490 | 1.8106 | 1.9388 | 2.0736 |
| 5 | 1.0510 | 1.1041 | 1.1593 | 1.2167 | 1.2763 | 1.3382 | 1.4026 | 1.4693 | 1.5386 | 1.6105 | 1.7623 | 1.9254 | 2.0114 | 2.1003 | 2.2878 | 2.4883 |
| 6 | 1.0615 | 1.1262 | 1.1941 | 1.2653 | 1.3401 | 1.4185 | 1.5007 | 1.5869 | 1.6771 | 1.7716 | 1.9738 | 2.1950 | 2.3131 | 2.4364 | 2.6996 | 2.9860 |
| 7 | 1.0721 | 1.1487 | 1.2299 | 1.3159 | 1.4071 | 1.5036 | 1.6058 | 1.7138 | 1.8280 | 1.9487 | 2.2107 | 2.5023 | 2.6600 | 2.8262 | 3.1855 | 3.5832 |
| 8 | 1.0829 | 1.1717 | 1.2668 | 1.3686 | 1.4775 | 1.5938 | 1.7182 | 1.8509 | 1.9926 | 2.1436 | 2.4760 | 2.8526 | 3.0590 | 3.2784 | 3.7589 | 4.2998 |
| 9 | 1.0937 | 1.1951 | 1.3048 | 1.4233 | 1.5513 | 1.6895 | 1.8385 | 1.9990 | 2.1719 | 2.3579 | 2.7731 | 3.2519 | 3.5179 | 3.8030 | 4.4355 | 5.1598 |
| 10 | 1.1046 | 1.2190 | 1.3439 | 1.4802 | 1.6289 | 1.7908 | 1.9672 | 2.1589 | 2.3674 | 2.5937 | 3.1058 | 3.7072 | 4.0456 | 4.4114 | 5.2338 | 6.1917 |
| 11 | 1.1157 | 1.2434 | 1.3842 | 1.5395 | 1.7103 | 1.8983 | 2.1049 | 2.3316 | 2.5804 | 2.8531 | 3.4785 | 4.2262 | 4.6524 | 5.1173 | 6.1759 | 7.4301 |
| 12 | 1.1268 | 1.2682 | 1.4258 | 1.6010 | 1.7959 | 2.0122 | 2.2522 | 2.5182 | 2.8127 | 3.1384 | 3.8960 | 4.8179 | 5.3502 | 5.9360 | 7.2876 | 8.9161 |
| 13 | 1.1381 | 1.2936 | 1.4685 | 1.6651 | 1.8856 | 2.1329 | 2.4098 | 2.7196 | 3.0658 | 3.4523 | 4.3635 | 5.4924 | 6.1528 | 6.8858 | 8.5994 | 10.699 |
| 14 | 1.1495 | 1.3195 | 1.5126 | 1.7317 | 1.9799 | 2.2609 | 2.5785 | 2.9372 | 3.3417 | 3.7975 | 4.8871 | 6.2613 | 7.0757 | 7.9875 | 10.147 | 12.839 |
| 15 | 1.1610 | 1.3459 | 1.5580 | 1.8009 | 2.0789 | 2.3966 | 2.7590 | 3.1722 | 3.6425 | 4.1772 | 5.4736 | 7.1379 | 8.1371 | 9.2655 | 11.973 | 15.407 |
| 16 | 1.1726 | 1.3728 | 1.6047 | 1.8730 | 2.1829 | 2.5404 | 2.9522 | 3.4259 | 3.9703 | 4.5950 | 6.1304 | 8.1372 | 9.3576 | 10.748 | 14.129 | 18.488 |
| 17 | 1.1843 | 1.4002 | 1.6528 | 1.9479 | 2.2920 | 2.6928 | 3.1588 | 3.7000 | 4.3276 | 5.0545 | 6.8660 | 9.2765 | 10.761 | 12.467 | 16.672 | 22.186 |
| 18 | 1.1961 | 1.4282 | 1.7024 | 2.0258 | 2.4066 | 2.8543 | 3.3799 | 3.9960 | 4.7171 | 5.5599 | 7.6900 | 10.575 | 12.375 | 14.462 | 19.673 | 26.623 |
| 19 | 1.2081 | 1.4568 | 1.7535 | 2.1068 | 2.5270 | 3.0256 | 3.6165 | 4.3157 | 5.1417 | 6.1159 | 8.6128 | 12.055 | 14.231 | 16.776 | 23.214 | 31.948 |
| 20 | 1.2202 | 1.4859 | 1.8061 | 2.1911 | 2.6533 | 3.2071 | 3.8697 | 4.6610 | 5.6044 | 6.7275 | 9.6463 | 13.743 | 16.366 | 19.460 | 27.393 | 38.337 |
| 25 | 1.2824 | 1.6406 | 2.0938 | 2.6658 | 3.3864 | 4.2919 | 5.4274 | 6.8485 | 8.6231 | 10.834 | 17.000 | 26.461 | 32.918 | 40.874 | 62.668 | 95.396 |
| 30 | 1.3478 | 1.8114 | 2.4273 | 3.2434 | 4.3219 | 5.7435 | 7.6123 | 10.062 | 13.267 | 17.449 | 29.959 | 50.950 | 66.211 | 85.849 | 143.37 | 237.37 |
| 40 | 1.4889 | 2.2080 | 3.2620 | 4.8010 | 7.0400 | 10.285 | 14.974 | 21.724 | 31.409 | 45.259 | 93.050 | 188.88 | 267.86 | 378.72 | 750.37 | 1469.7 |
| 50 | 1.6446 | 2.6916 | 4.3839 | 7.1067 | 11.467 | 18.420 | 29.457 | 46.901 | 74.357 | 117.39 | 289.00 | 700.23 | 1083.6 | 1670.7 | 3927.3 | 9100.4 |
| 60 | 1.8167 | 3.2810 | 5.8916 | 10.519 | 18.679 | 32.987 | 57.946 | 101.25 | 176.03 | 304.48 | 897.59 | 2595.9 | 4383.9 | 7370.1 | 20555. | 56347. |

---

[5]Most good handheld calculators will also do the job conveniently.

**TABLE 10–2  Present Value of $1 Payable at End of N Periods**

| N | 1% | 2% | 3% | 4% | 5% | 6% | 7% | 8% | 9% | 10% | 12% | 14% | 15% | 16% | 18% | 20% |
|---|----|----|----|----|----|----|----|----|----|-----|-----|-----|-----|-----|-----|-----|
| 1 | .9901 | .9804 | .9709 | .9615 | .9524 | .9434 | .9346 | .9259 | .9174 | .9091 | .8929 | .8772 | .8696 | .8621 | .8475 | .8333 |
| 2 | .9803 | .9612 | .9426 | .9246 | .9070 | .8900 | .8734 | .8573 | .8417 | .8264 | .7972 | .7695 | .7561 | .7432 | .7182 | .6944 |
| 3 | .9706 | .9423 | .9151 | .8890 | .8638 | .8396 | .8163 | .7938 | .7722 | .7513 | .7118 | .6750 | .6575 | .6407 | .6086 | .5787 |
| 4 | .9610 | .9238 | .8885 | .8548 | .8227 | .7921 | .7629 | .7350 | .7084 | .6830 | .6355 | .5921 | .5718 | .5523 | .5158 | .4823 |
| 5 | .9515 | .9057 | .8626 | .8219 | .7835 | .7473 | .7130 | .6806 | .6499 | .6209 | .5674 | .5194 | .4972 | .4761 | .4371 | .4019 |
| 6 | .9420 | .8880 | .8375 | .7903 | .7462 | .7050 | .6663 | .6302 | .5963 | .5645 | .5066 | .4556 | .4323 | .4104 | .3704 | .3349 |
| 7 | .9327 | .8706 | .8131 | .7599 | .7107 | .6651 | .6227 | .5835 | .5470 | .5132 | .4523 | .3996 | .3759 | .3538 | .3139 | .2791 |
| 8 | .9235 | .8535 | .7894 | .7307 | .6768 | .6274 | .5820 | .5403 | .5019 | .4665 | .4039 | .3506 | .3269 | .3050 | .2660 | .2326 |
| 9 | .9143 | .8368 | .7664 | .7026 | .6446 | .5919 | .5439 | .5002 | .4604 | .4241 | .3606 | .3075 | .2843 | .2630 | .2255 | .1938 |
| 10 | .9053 | .8203 | .7441 | .6756 | .6139 | .5584 | .5083 | .4632 | .4224 | .3855 | .3220 | .2697 | .2472 | .2267 | .1911 | .1615 |
| 11 | .8963 | .8043 | .7224 | .6496 | .5847 | .5268 | .4751 | .4289 | .3875 | .3505 | .2875 | .2366 | .2149 | .1954 | .1619 | .1346 |
| 12 | .8874 | .7885 | .7014 | .6246 | .5568 | .4970 | .4440 | .3971 | .3555 | .3186 | .2567 | .2076 | .1869 | .1685 | .1372 | .1122 |
| 13 | .8787 | .7730 | .6810 | .6006 | .5303 | .4688 | .4150 | .3677 | .3262 | .2897 | .2292 | .1821 | .1625 | .1452 | .1163 | .0935 |
| 14 | .8700 | .7579 | .6611 | .5775 | .5051 | .4423 | .3878 | .3405 | .2992 | .2633 | .2046 | .1597 | .1413 | .1252 | .0985 | .0779 |
| 15 | .8613 | .7430 | .6419 | .5553 | .4810 | .4173 | .3624 | .3152 | .2745 | .2394 | .1827 | .1401 | .1229 | .1079 | .0835 | .0649 |
| 16 | .8528 | .7284 | .6232 | .5339 | .4581 | .3936 | .3387 | .2919 | .2519 | .2176 | .1631 | .1229 | .1069 | .0930 | .0708 | .0541 |
| 17 | .8444 | .7142 | .6050 | .5134 | .4363 | .3714 | .3166 | .2703 | .2311 | .1978 | .1456 | .1078 | .0929 | .0802 | .0600 | .0451 |
| 18 | .8360 | .7002 | .5874 | .4936 | .4155 | .3503 | .2959 | .2502 | .2120 | .1799 | .1300 | .0946 | .0808 | .0691 | .0508 | .0376 |
| 19 | .8277 | .6864 | .5703 | .4746 | .3957 | .3305 | .2765 | .2317 | .1945 | .1635 | .1161 | .0829 | .0703 | .0596 | .0431 | .0313 |
| 20 | .8195 | .6730 | .5537 | .4564 | .3769 | .3118 | .2584 | .2145 | .1784 | .1486 | .1037 | .0728 | .0611 | .0514 | .0365 | .0261 |
| 25 | .7798 | .6095 | .4776 | .3751 | .2953 | .2330 | .1842 | .1460 | .1160 | .0923 | .0588 | .0378 | .0304 | .0245 | .0160 | .0105 |
| 30 | .7419 | .5521 | .4120 | .3083 | .2314 | .1741 | .1314 | .0994 | .0754 | .0573 | .0334 | .0196 | .0151 | .0116 | .0070 | .0042 |
| 40. | .6717 | .4529 | .3066 | .2083 | .1420 | .0972 | .0668 | .0460 | .0318 | .0221 | .0107 | .0053 | .0037 | .0026 | .0013 | .0007 |
| 50 | .6080 | .3715 | .2281 | .1407 | .0872 | .0543 | .0339 | .0213 | .0134 | .0085 | .0035 | .0014 | .0009 | .0006 | .0003 | .0001 |
| 60 | .5504 | .3048 | .1697 | .0951 | .0535 | .0303 | .0173 | .0099 | .0057 | .0033 | .0011 | .0004 | .0002 | .0001 | .0000 | .0000 |

compounded quarterly) and the 3 percent interest rate column (12 percent payable quarterly is 3 percent per quarter). The number is .3066. In this example, therefore, I would lend you $1,533 ($5,000 × .3066).

Spend some time perusing Tables 10–1 and 10–2, and you will see why Albert Einstein described compound interest as man's greatest invention. At fairly low interest rates, the future value of $1 does not rise very rapidly as the number of periods increases. But as the interest rate gets higher, a dollar grows to staggering amounts with the passage of time. By the same token, a dollar payable many years from now is worth very little today at high discount rates such as have been common in recent years.

# ■ DIVIDEND DISCOUNT MODELS

The concept that a common stock is worth the present value of future dividends is expressed in the following equation:

$$P_o = \frac{d_1}{(1 + k)} + \frac{d_2}{(1 + k)^2} + \cdots \frac{d_n}{(1 + k)^n}$$

$$= \sum_{t=1}^{\infty} \frac{d_t}{(1 + k)^t}$$

where:

$P_o$ = the worth of the stock today,

$d_1, d_2 \ldots d_n$ = the expected annual dividend stream,

$k$ = the discount rate (rate of return) deemed appropriate for the uncertainty of the dividend estimates (annual compounding will be assumed in this and all subsequent calculations in this chapter).

From this generalized statement, three types of dividend streams can be considered:

1. Dividends are expected to remain unchanged.
2. Dividends are expected to grow at a constant rate ($g$). (We will not deal with declining dividend streams, but the basic mathematics would not be different.)
3. Dividends are expected to grow at a variable rate ($g_1$, $g_2$ . . .)

Similarly, the discount rate ($k$) can be assumed to remain constant or to change over time. Within the framework of the Capital Asset Pricing Model, the discount rate would reflect the magnitude of: (*a*) the risk-free rate, (*b*) the risk premium of stocks as an asset class versus risk-free assets, and (*c*) any additional uncertainties inherent in forecasting the cash flows of the particular stock.

## *The Zero Growth Model*

If dividends are expected to remain unchanged at today's rate ($d_o$), and the discount rate also is expected to remain constant, the basic valuation equation reduces to:

$$P_o = \frac{d_o}{k}$$

This formula is applicable only to the valuation of preferred stocks, which have fixed dividend rates, or to the common stocks of very mature companies such as big-city electric utilities, whose dividends are likely to show little, if any, secular growth. As the formula indicates, such stocks are evaluated by dividing the indicated dividend rate ($d_o$) by an appropriate dividend yield ($k$). The appropriate yield usually is derived from the recent relationship between the yield on the particular stock and the yield on high-grade bonds. For example, the stocks of mature electric utilities usually sell at prices which provide dividend yields approximately equal to U.S. Treasury bond yields. Therefore, they may be considered undervalued ("cheap") when their dividend yields exceed Treasury bond yields and overvalued ("expensive") when their dividend yields are below Treasury bond yields.[6]

## *The Constant Growth Model*

If dividends are expected to grow at a constant rate ($g$), the stream of dividends will be: $d_o(1 + g)$, $d_o(1 + g)^2$ . . . $d_o(1 + g)^n$. Assuming a constant discount rate ($k$), the basic valuation formula would be:

$$P_o = \frac{d_o(1 + g)}{(1 + k)} + \frac{d_o(1 + g)^2}{(1 + k)^2} + \cdots \frac{d_o(1 + g)^n}{(1 + k)^n}$$
$$= \sum_{t=1}^{\infty} \frac{d_o(1 + g)^t}{(1 + k)^t}$$

---

[6]Strictly speaking, there is an implication that *some* dividend growth is expected. Otherwise, the dividend yield on a utility stock should exceed the yield on a Treasury bond since the latter has no default risk while the former has a risk of declining dividends if not outright bankruptcy. Preferred stock dividend yields, interestingly, usually are *below* high-grade bond yields; but this is because their income is largely tax-exempt to corporate buyers. On a "taxable-equivalent" basis, preferred stock yields are higher than bond yields.

As long as it is assumed that $k$ is greater than $g$ (a reasonable assumption since a continuous growth rate in excess of the discount rate would produce an infinite present value), the equation can be simplified to:[7]

$$P_o = \frac{d_1}{(k - g)}$$

This formula is most applicable to the valuation of the overall market (as represented by, say, the Standard & Poor's 500 Composite Stock Price Index) or of very large, broadly diversified companies. In these cases, it is possible to envision growth extending over a great number of years at a rate which can be described as constant despite the presence of cyclical fluctuations around the underlying trend.

A simple transformation of the formula gives it another interesting property. Since

$$P_o = \frac{d_1}{(k - g)}, \text{ then } (k - g) = \frac{d_1}{(P_o)}$$

Therefore, $(k - g)$ can be viewed as a normalized dividend yield. That is, given assumptions about $k$ and $g$, a constant-growth stock or group of stocks would be considered fairly valued at a price that produces a dividend yield equal to $k$ minus $g$.

Furthermore, it can be seen that:

$$k = \frac{d_1}{P_o} + g$$

From this latter expression, it follows that an investor who has an idea about the likely constant dividend growth rate of a stock can estimate the total rate of return that will be produced from a purchase by adding the estimated growth rate to the first year's dividend yield. For example, a dividend yield of 6 percent and a long-term growth rate of 6 percent will produce a *long-term* total return of 12 percent.[8]

***Constant Growth Model Applied to the Overall Market.*** In July 1985, the S&P 500 Index reached a new record high in excess of 190, having gained about 90 percent from the level to which it had fallen three years earlier during a cyclical downturn. For an investor trying to determine the reasonableness of the new high price level of the market, the constant growth dividend discount model ($P_o = d_1/(k - g)$) might have been quite helpful.

At the time the S&P Index reached its new high, the majority view of economists regarding the long-term economic outlook was that real GNP would grow at a rate of about 3 percent (consisting of about $1\frac{1}{2}$ percent growth rate in employment and $1\frac{1}{2}$ percent productivity growth) and that inflation would average about 6 percent, for total long-term GNP growth of about 9 percent per annum.[9] Since corporate

---

[7]For a mathematical proof of this simplification, together with an extensive discussion of other valuation formulas, see J. Fred Weston and Eugene F. Brigham, *Essentials of Managerial Finance*, 5th ed. (Hinsdale, Ill.: Dryden Press, 1979), chapter 14.

[8]Emphasis is placed on the words *long-term*. If the stock is purchased at a dividend yield of 6 percent and sold a couple of years later at a substantially lower (or higher) dividend yield, the total return for the holding period will be quite different from 12 percent.

[9]See, for example, Alan Murray, "Extent of Future U.S. Growth," *The Wall Street Journal*, December 13, 1984.

sales, earnings, and dividends had grown more slowly than GNP for many years,[10] an investor in mid-1985 might reasonably have forecast long-term dividend growth (g) at a rate of about 8 percent per annum versus 9 percent for GNP. This same investor, had he or she been a student of history, would have known that the stock market had produced a real rate of return (i.e., net of inflation) of about 7 percent over extended time periods.[11] Therefore, with a 6 percent inflation rate, a reasonable rate at which to discount corporate dividends (k) might be about 13 percent. Finally, the investor would have noted that in mid-1985, dividends on the S&P 500 Index were running at a rate of almost 8.00.[12] Therefore, the trend rate of dividends a year forward ($d_1$) might be about 8.50.

Substituting these variables in the valuation equation, ($P_o = d_1/(k - g)$), the investor might have concluded that the intrinsic value of the S&P 500 Index in mid-1985 was: 8.50/(.13 − .08), or about 170. At an actual price level of over 190, the stock market might have appeared to be a bit high relative to long-term economic prospects.

On the other hand, our investor might have focused on two nonconventional views of the economic outlook. One nonconventional view, associated with supply-side economists, was that incentive-oriented fiscal and monetary policies would increase productivity, real GNP, and corporate profitability without aggravating inflation. According to this view, dividend growth (g) would be about 10 percent per annum, so that the value of the S&P 500 Index would be approximately: 8.50/(.13 − .10), or 283, and the market could rise a great deal further before becoming overpriced. But another nonconventional view, the "stagflation school," was that continuing huge federal deficits would sap much of the vitality of the private economy and lead to much higher rates of inflation. This view might have put real GNP growth at only 2½ percent, inflation at over 9 percent, total GNP growth at 12 percent, dividend growth at 10 percent, and the common stock discount rate at 16 percent. The value of the S&P 500 Index would be approximately: 8.50/(.16 − .10), or 142, thus posing serious downside risk from the 190 level of mid-1985.

The various views could be summarized as in Table 10–3, with sample probabilities assigned to each. The conclusion would probably have been that the market was fairly priced even at its record high level.[13]

---

[10]For a good analysis, see Dale N. Allman, "The Decline in Business Profitability," *Economic Review of the Federal Reserve Bank of Kansas City,* January 1983.

Dividends grew even more slowly than earnings mainly because, in an inflationary environment, the replacement cost of plant and equipment rose faster than internal cash generation, so that a shrinkage of dividend payout ratios, along with an increase in debt, was needed to finance capital outlays.

[11]The most widely quoted study of historical asset returns has been Roger G. Ibbotson and Rex A. Sinqfield, *Stocks, Bonds, Bills and Inflation: The Past and The Future* (Charlottesville, Va.: Financial Analysts Research Foundation, 1982).

[12]Data on the index are published by Standard & Poor's in *The Analysts Handbook.*

[13]It will be noted in the table that different assumptions regarding k and g, in different economic environments, produce different normalized dividend yields (k − g). There is, however, a body of theory which argues that (k − g) should be a constant, at least in the long run. The argument is that the major factor causing changes in k is changes in the expected rate of inflation; but changes in expected inflation, it is claimed, should equally impact the expected growth rate of earnings and dividends (g) since corporations tend to pass on inflationary and disinflationary forces to their customers. Much of the argument contends that measured profits during inflation do not account for the real economic profits that accrue from a reduction in real corporate liabilities. These views have been presented forcefully in Franco Modigliani and Richard A. Cohn, "Inflation, Rational Valuation and

**TABLE 10–3   Hypothetical Valuation Criteria for S&P 500 Index in Mid-1985**

| Viewpoint | Inflation | Dividend Growth(g) | Discount Rate(k) | Normalized Dividend Yield(k − g) | S&P Value* | Subjective Probability |
|---|---|---|---|---|---|---|
| Consensus | 6% | 8% | 13% | 5% | 170 | .5 |
| Supply-side | 6 | 10 | 13 | 3 | 283 | .3 |
| Stagflation | 9 | 10 | 16 | 6 | 142 | .2 |
| Probability-weighted average† | 6½ | 9 | 13½ | 4½ | 198 | |

*These values assume that the normalized dividend level one year forward ($d_1$) was 8.50 in all three cases, which would not be quite correct but seems adequate for exposition purposes.

†For simplicity, the weighted averages are expressed in round numbers.

## The Variable Growth Model

While continuous growth in excess of the discount rate ($g > k$) is an unreasonable assumption because it produces infinite present values, many companies do exhibit very rapid growth for 5, 10, or more years. Ultimately, usually as a result of product obsolescence or competition, the growth slows. Indeed, if it did not, the company would eventually swallow up the entire economy. Analysts deal with such cases by assuming that growth will pass through one or more stages of deceleration until finally settling down at a constant growth rate equal to that of the average company. The constant-growth formula is applied to determine the value of the stock at that point, and that assumed terminal price is discounted to the present and added to the present value of the dividends paid during the rapid-growth period. That is:

$$P_o = \text{Present value of dividends prior to constant-growth period}$$
$$\text{plus}$$
$$\text{Present value of assumed terminal price of stock}$$

***Illustration.***   Suppose that we were trying to place a value on the stock of Texas Instruments in July 1985. The price of the stock was about $100 per share, having ranged from $150 to $90 during the prior 18 months. The dividend rate was $2.00 per share compared with cyclically volatile earnings that had averaged about $5.50 per share over a five-year period.

Suppose we assumed that Texas Instruments' future growth would pass through two stages. The first stage would be a 10-year period in which earnings per share grew at a fairly rapid rate, somewhat in excess of 15 percent, and dividends grew at an even more rapid 20 percent, having started at a relatively low level. The second stage would see growth permanently stabilized at an average of about 10 percent.

the Market," *Financial Analysts Journal,* March–April 1979; and in Burton Malkiel, *The Inflation-Beater's Investment Guide* (New York: W. W. Norton, 1980). Not only does the empirical evidence tend to contradict these theoretical arguments, the theory itself has some deficiencies, as described by Martin Feldstein in "Inflation and the Stock Market," *American Economic Review,* December 1980. On the other hand, there is some evidence that the "inflation passthrough" argument may apply to assets like commercial real estate. See Leon G. Cooperman, Steven G. Einhorn, and Meyer Melnikoff, *The Case for Pension Fund Investment in Property* (New York: Goldman Sachs, June 1983).

Thus:

$$g_1 = 20 \text{ percent and lasts for 10 years } (n = 10)$$
$$g_2 = 10 \text{ percent and persists thereafter.}$$

Further, suppose we assume that an appropriate discount rate for this stock is 14 percent, except that the uncertainty of the forecast of an extra-rapid growth rate for the first 10 years suggests a larger discount rate during that period, perhaps 18 percent.
Thus:

$$k_1 = 18\%; \ k_2 = 14\%.$$

The value of Texas Instruments' stock in this example would be somewhat under $90 per share, derived as shown in the equation and Table 10–4 below. If the as-

---

**TABLE 10–4   Two-Stage Growth Valuation**

1. Present Value of Dividends During Initial Growth Period (20 percent annual growth for 10 years, discounted at 18 percent annual rate)

| Period($n$) | (1) Value of Dividends ($d_t$) (See Table 10–1) | (2) Present Value Factor (See Table 10–2) | Present Value of Dividends (Columns 1 × 2) |
|---|---|---|---|
| 0 | $ 2.0000 | — | — |
| 1 | 2.4000 | .8475 | $ 2.0340 |
| 2 | 2.8800 | .7182 | 2.0684 |
| 3 | 3.4560 | .6086 | 2.1034 |
| 4 | 4.1472 | .5158 | 2.1392 |
| 5 | 4.9766 | .4371 | 2.1752 |
| 6 | 5.9720 | .3704 | 2.2120 |
| 7 | 7.1664 | .3139 | 2.2496 |
| 8 | 8.5996 | .2660 | 2.2874 |
| 9 | 10.3196 | .2255 | 2.3270 |
| 10 | 12.3834 | .1911 | 2.3664 |
| | | | $21.9626 |

$$\sum_{t=1}^{10} \frac{2.00(1.20)^t}{(1.18)^t} = \$21.9626$$

2. Present Value of Assumed Terminal Price

$$\frac{d_{11}}{k_2 - g_2} = \frac{\$12.3834 \times 1.10}{.14 - .10} = \frac{\$13.6215}{.04} = \$340.54$$

$$\frac{1}{(1 + k_1)^{10}} = \frac{1}{(1.18)^{10}} = \frac{1}{5.2338} = .1911*$$

$$\$340.54 \times .1911 = \$65.08$$

---

*See Table 10–2 for verification.

sumptions underlying this valuation were approximately correct, the stock's price of $100 per share in July 1985 was reasonable, being fairly close to its intrinsic value. But at the earlier high of $150, the stock was substantially overpriced.

$$
\begin{aligned}
P_o &= \left[ \sum_{t=1}^{n} \frac{d_o(1 + g_1)^t}{(1 + k_1)^t} \right] + \left[ \frac{d_{n+1}}{(k_2 - g_2)} \times \frac{1}{(1 + k_1)^n} \right] \\
&= \left[ \sum_{t=1}^{10} \frac{2.00(1.20)^t}{(1.18)^t} \right] + \left[ \frac{d_{11}}{(.14 - .10)} \times \frac{1}{(1.18)^{10}} \right] \\
&= \$21.96 + \$65.08 \\
&= \$87.04
\end{aligned}
$$

## Three-Stage Variable Growth Models

The Texas Instruments illustration, just presented, assumed a sudden change in the 11th year from a rapid 20 percent growth rate to an average 10 percent growth rate. However, many security analysts who employ dividend discount models consider it more realistic to assume that above-average growth rates gravitate toward average in a more gradual, three-stage fashion. This is illustrated in Figure 10–1, which shows the earnings and dividends stream of a company that grows rapidly and then gradually slows down.

**FIGURE 10–1  The Three-Stage Growth Framework**

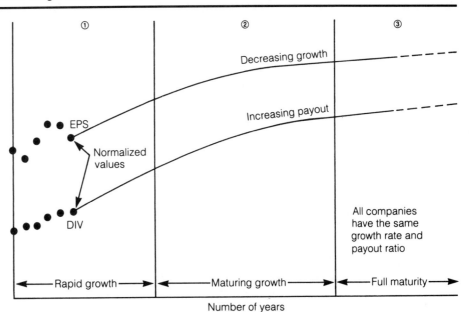

SOURCE: Drexel Burnham Lambert.

Utilizing this framework, computer programs have been developed which call for specification of the following variables:

1. Normalized earnings and dividends for the current year—that is, the earnings and dividends that would likely prevail if the business environment were neither cyclically high nor low.
2. The number of years in stage 1—that is, the number of years during which the analyst can confidently forecast that the company will exhibit well-above-average earnings growth.
3. The specific earnings growth rate expected during stage 1.
4. The dividend payout ratio expected by the end of stage 1. (The first year's payout ratio is implied by the normalized dividends and earnings per share specified for the current year.)
5. The number of years in stage 2—that is, the period during which the earnings growth rate will decelerate toward the average growth rate and during which the payout ratio will rise toward the average payout ratio.
6. Whether the growth rate and payout ratio transition in stage 2 will proceed in a straight line or curvilinear manner. (Figure 10–1 assumes a curvilinear transition path. Actually, if the transition period is 10 or more years, both linear and curvilinear assumptions produce fairly similar results.)
7. Stage 3—that is, the "forever after"—earnings growth rate and payout ratio.

Given this information, the computer calculates each year's dividends up to the point where constant growth to infinity is assumed. At this point, dividend valuation computer programs differ considerably in complexity. In the simplest case, the current price of the stock is specified, and the computer calculates the discount rate which equates the stream of dividends with the current price. This "implied discount rate" is the rate of return which will be earned by an investor who buys at the current price and holds "forever," assuming that the growth rate, payout, and time period assumptions are correct. The investor can then decide if this rate of return is greater or less than he or she requires for the risks involved, in which case the stock is either considered underpriced or overpriced.

Most sophisticated computer programs go beyond merely calculating the implied discount rate. They rely on the capital asset pricing equation, which specifies that the expected rate of return for a stock $(R_s)$ is a function of the risk-free rate $(R_f)$, the rate of return expected for the market in aggregate $(R_m)$, and the stock's systematic risk, or beta $(B)$. Specifically, the user specifies $R_f$, $R_m$, and $B$, in the equation $R_s = R_f + B (R_m - R_f)$, and the computer calculates $R_s$, which can be called the required discount rate.[14] The required discount rate is then compared with the im-

---

[14]Some models assume there is a capital market *plane* rather than a *line*, in which $R_s$ is also, in part, a function of the stock's relative dividend yield. The reason for taking dividend yield explicitly into account is that the component of $R_s$ which comes from current income has usually been taxed at a different rate than the component which comes from growth. See William M. Bethke and Susan E. Boyd, "Should Dividend Models be Yield-Tilted?" *Journal of Portfolio Management,* Spring 1983.

For a description of how to program a dividend discount model on a hand-held programmable computer see Russell J. Fuller, "Programming the Three-Phase Dividend Discount Model," *Journal of Portfolio Management,* Summer 1979.

plied discount rate and the degree of over- or underpricing is expressed as a positive or negative risk-adjusted excess return, referred to as *alpha* in portfolio theory.

For example, suppose the current price of a stock equates with the expected dividend stream at an implied discount rate of 17.4 percent, while the capital asset pricing equation suggests a required rate (risk-adjusted) of 16.2 percent. The computer will show that purchase of the stock will produce an annualized risk-adjusted excess return, or alpha, of +1.2 percent. This can be done for every stock being analyzed, and the computer can print out a listing of all the stocks ranked from the most positive to the most negative alpha.

Another version of the same basic approach is for the computer, after calculating the required discount rate, to then discount the dividend stream at that rate and derive an intrinsic present value. The current stock price can then be compared with this intrinsic value, and a percentage over- or underpricing is calculated. Using the previous example, suppose that the intrinsic value at the required 16.2 percent discount rate is $50 per share.[15] And suppose the current price (with an implied discount rate of 17.4 percent) is $40 per share. The price/value ratio is 40/50, or 80 percent. A similar ratio can be calculated for every stock being analyzed, and a list can be produced which ranks the stocks from lowest (most undervalued) to highest (most overvalued) price/value ratio.[16]

***Illustrations.***    Many brokerage firms offer their institutional clients monthly valuation tabulations and graphs derived from computer programs such as we have been describing, and many financial institutions have developed their own in-house versions.[17]

One of the more creative formats for presenting valuation data is published by Morgan Stanley. In addition to providing its clients with valuations for individual stocks, Morgan Stanley attempts to see if there are any mispricings of broad groupings of stocks. Charts show the relationships, at different points of time, between the price/value ratios produced by the Morgan Stanley model and expected growth rates, betas, quality ratings (Morgan Stanley classifies stocks into six quality categories), and company size (they have 10 size groups ranging from largest to smallest capitalization).

Figure 10–2, for example, focuses on the relationship between value and quality at two points in time—July 1985 (solid line) and June 1973 (dashed line). Both time periods, in Morgan Stanley's view, were characterized by slow economic growth and disinflation. The chart shows that in July 1985 higher-quality stocks were undervalued relative to lower-quality stocks whereas the reverse was true in the earlier period.

---

[15]In this illustration, the required discount rate is derived using the stock's current beta value. Some computer programs take account of the likelihood that if the character of the company's growth does, indeed, change from its present path to that of the average company, the stock's beta will gradually converge toward 1.0. These programs, in effect, use a different required discount rate at each stage of growth to calculate the intrinsic value, and the overall required return is a weighted average of the returns in each stage.

[16]There is not a precise mathematical correspondence between excess return and price/value ratio. That is, two stocks may both have excess returns of 1.2 percent but different price/value ratios. However, the *ranking* of stocks tends to be fairly similar using both measures.

[17]See Barbara Donnelly, "The Dividend Discount Model Comes Into Its Own," *Institutional Investor,* March 1985.

**FIGURE 10–2    Quality Rating and Relative Value (equally weighted averages)**

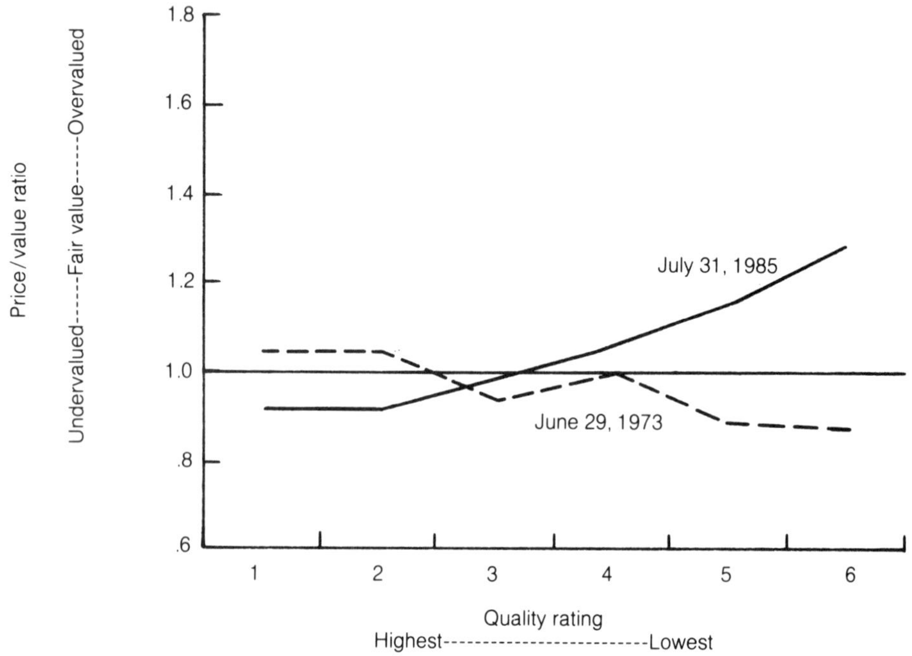

SOURCE: Morgan Stanley, *Investment Perspectives,* August 27, 1985.

Morgan Stanley highlighted this difference because, in their opinion, the earlier relationship was more representative of what the value-versus-quality relationship should be in a slow-growth, disinflationary economic environment. Therefore, they recommended that their clients switch out of lower-quality stocks and into higher-quality issues in order to benefit from the change in valuations that they expected to take place.

As another illustration of the usefulness of dividend discount models, consider Figure 10–3. This chart tracks the performance of a simple three-stage model applied to the largest 250 stocks in the S&P 500 Index over a 12-year period. Each year, the 250 stocks are divided into quintiles from lowest to highest rate of return implicit in the beginning-of-year market prices of the stocks (given consensus expectations regarding each of their dividend growth patterns.) The cumulative wealth actually produced by one dollar invested in the top two and bottom two quintiles at the start of the period is shown in the chart, along with the cumulative wealth produced by the S&P 500 Index. Note that the two top-ranked quintiles produced remarkably good results, while the lowest-ranked quintiles underperformed the overall market.

**Complications.**    Despite its proven usefulness, many professional investors shy away from the dividend discount framework of analysis because of a number of inherent complexities. First, it is recognized that assumptions about corporate developments in stage 3 (15 or more years in the future) are extremely tenuous. Second, even small differences in key assumptions regarding stages 1 and 2 produce large

**FIGURE 10–3**  *Cumulative Wealth Derived from $1 Invested in 1972
(discounted dividend valuation quintiles versus S&P 500 Index)*

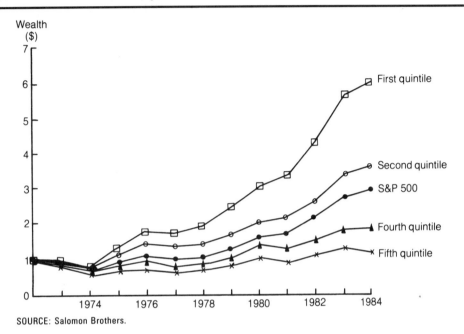

SOURCE: Salomon Brothers.

differences in calculated intrinsic values.[18] Finally, many rapidly growing companies pay little or no dividends, and speculation on when such payments will begin is felt to be futile.

# ■ PRICE/EARNINGS RATIOS

Because of the complications in using dividend discount models, and notwithstanding their proven usefulness, most practicing security analysts continue to use the less sophisticated concept of price/earnings (P/E) ratios.

## Price/Earnings Ratio of the Market

Table 10–5 shows the average annual P/E ratio of the Standard & Poor's 500 Index since 1948. Note that right after World War II, when many people believed that another economic depression was likely, the ratio was only 6 or 7. As fears of another depression diminished, perhaps as a result of the stimulus provided by the Korean War, the market's P/E ratio rose to a level of 10 to 11.

---

[18]For example, in a model that has been utilized by the Prudential Insurance Company, every change of one percentage point of growth assumed in stage 1 produces, on average, a change of 10 percent in intrinsic value. A change in assumed beta of 0.15 produces, on average, a 10 percent change in value. Similar alterations in value occur from changes in assumptions about the time span of stage 1 or stage 2.

**TABLE 10–5   P/E Ratio of Standard & Poor's 500 Composite Stock Price Index**

| | | | | | |
|---|---|---|---|---|---|
| 1948 | 7 | 1958 | 16 | 1973 | 13 |
| 1949 | 7 | 1959 | 17 | 1974 | 9 |
| 1950 | 6 | 1960 | 17 | 1975 | 11 |
| | | 1961 | 21 | 1976 | 10 |
| 1951 | 9 | 1962 | 17 | 1977 | 9 |
| 1952 | 10 | 1963 | 17 | 1978 | 8 |
| 1953 | 10 | 1964 | 18 | 1979 | 7 |
| 1954 | 11 | 1965 | 17 | 1980 | 8 |
| 1955 | 11 | 1966 | 15 | 1981 | 8 |
| | | 1967 | 17 | 1982 | 9 |
| 1956 | 14 | 1968 | 17 | 1983 | 12 |
| 1957 | 13 | 1969 | 17 | 1984 | 10 |
| | | 1970 | 16 | 1985 | 12 |
| | | 1971 | 17 | | |
| | | 1972 | 17 | | |

Beginning in the mid-1950s, the investment world became convinced that corporate earnings growth would be strong and persistent, notwithstanding the occasional interruptions of mild recessions. Average price/earnings ratios rose from 11 in 1955 to 21 in 1961. But a 21 ratio for the overall market was an aberration. Except for 1961, there was a 15-year period, from 1958 to 1972, of remarkable P/E stability centered around a level of 17. Utopia had arrived. An investor seemingly had a guide for making reliable P/E judgments.

Most peculiarly, the stock market had maintained a level of stability at the very time when the social fabric of the United States was being torn as a result of the Vietnam War. Ultimately, reality caught up with the market, and its utopia proved no more lasting than others in the history books. As the long-term inflationary impact of Vietnam began to sink into the consciousness of economy-watchers, OPEC came along and levied its severe tax on the Western World. Price/earnings ratios collapsed under the burden—dropping to 13 on the S&P in 1973, and to 9 in 1974. A brief rally brought the market P/E level in 1975 and 1976 back to the 10–11 range of the early 1950s. But later in the decade, rampaging inflation caused interest rates to soar and earnings quality to deteriorate, which in turn drove P/E ratios down again to nearly the lows of 1948–50. Even after inflation subsided in the early 1980s, runaway federal deficits perpetuated the fear that inflation was not dead. This fear kept interest rates high, and P/E ratios could not break decisively above a 10–12 level.

Several generalizations seem to flow from this history:

1. When investors as a group are fearful of economic depression or rampant inflation, the market's P/E level is likely to be in the 7–9 range.
2. When investors look to the future with confidence, the market's P/E level is likely to be around 15–18.
3. When market sentiment oscillates rapidly between fear and confidence, its P/E level is likely to oscillate between 10 and 14.

**Relationship of P/E and Dividend Yield.** These empirical generalizations can be tied back to our earlier theoretical presentation of the constant-growth dividend discount model. It will be recalled that the model was: $P_o = d_1/(k - g)$. When we applied this model to the problem of evaluating the S&P 500 Index, we concluded that a reasonable range of estimates for $(k - g)$ was .03 to .06.

Since, as we pointed out, $(k - g)$ is the normalized dividend yield, we can ask the question: What normalized P/E ratio range is consistent with a normalized dividend yield range of .03–.06? Assuming that the dividend payout ratio of the S&P Index centers around the 45 percent level in the future, as it has in recent years, we can derive the answer to this question with simple algebra. As shown in Table 10–6, a dividend yield of .03 translates into a P/E of 15; and a dividend yield of .06 translates into a P/E of 7.5.[19]

**TABLE 10–6   Derivation of Price/Earnings Range from Dividend-Yield Range**

| | High End of Range | Low End of Range |
|---|---|---|
| | $P_o = \dfrac{d_1}{.03}$ | $P_o = \dfrac{d_1}{.06}$ |
| | Assume:  $d_1 = .45e_1$ | Assume:  $d_1 = .45e_1$ |
| | Then:  $P_o = \dfrac{.45e_1}{.03}$ | Then:  $P_o = \dfrac{.45e_1}{.06}$ |
| | $\dfrac{P_o}{e_1} = \dfrac{.45}{.03}$ | $\dfrac{P_o}{e_1} = \dfrac{.45}{.06}$ |
| | $\dfrac{P_o}{e_1} = 15$ | $\dfrac{P_o}{e_1} = 7.5$ |

# Price/Earnings Ratios of Industries and Companies

Most investors try to estimate an appropriate P/E ratio for a stock by tracing its historical relationship to the P/E of the overall market. However, it frequently is helpful to do this in two steps: (1) examine the P/E ratio of the industry relative to that of the S&P 500 Index, (2) examine the P/E of the company relative to its industry.[20] Since the S&P 500 Composite Stock Price Index is divided into several dozen industry subindexes, each of which has accompanying earnings and P/E data, this is

---

[19]Note that $e_1$ refers to normalized earnings of the *next 12 months*, whereas the historical P/E record is based on the *same year* earnings. With earnings trending upward, $e_1 > e_0$ and $P_o/e_o$ would be higher than $P_o/e_1$. For further elaboration see Frank K. Reilly, Frank T. Griggs, and Wenchi Wong, "Determinants of the Aggregate Stock Market Earnings Multiple," *The Journal of Portfolio Management*, Fall 1983.

[20]Of course, if the stock is of a company that is not part of a clearly definable industry, the two-step procedure is not possible. The importance of isolating industry influences on P/Es is discussed in David A. Goodman and John W. Peavy III, "Industry Relative Price-Earnings Ratios as Indicators of Investment Returns," *Financial Analysts Journal*, July–August 1983.

easily accomplished.[21] One simply divides the industry P/E (e.g., 15) by the market P/E (e.g., 10) to derive an industry relative P/E (1.5 in this example, meaning that the industry P/E is 50 percent higher than the market P/E) and then the stock P/E by the industry P/E to derive a stock/industry relative P/E. Price, earnings, and P/E data for individual stocks are available in the many sources described in Chapter 3.

*Illustration.*     In illustrating the dividend discount approach to a stock's evaluation, we used the example of Texas Instruments and calculated a mid-1985 value of somewhat under $90 per share. Let us now examine the P/E history of that stock. In July 1985, as described earlier, the stock's price was about $100 per share, having ranged between $150 and $90 during the prior 18 months. Earnings per share had been even more volatile than the stock's price, however. In 1983, the company ran a deficit of $6 per share; in 1984 earnings soared to $13 per share; and in 1985 they plunged once again.

Clearly, when the earnings of a company are so volatile, it is often meaningless to calculate a price/earnings ratio by dividing price by a recent 12-month earnings number. Some attempt must be made to "normalize" earnings. One way to do this is to calculate an average of the prior year's earnings, the current year's probable earnings, and the following year's expected earnings. Table 10–7 shows that Texas Instruments' P/E in 1985 was 18, using as the denominator a normalized earnings figure calculated in this manner and using the average of the stock's high and low price as the numerator. For years prior to 1985, the table shows the P/E ratio of the stock using its high-low mean average price and a centered three-year moving average of earnings. The same procedure is used to determine the average annual P/E of the S&P Electronic Components industry group.[22] The P/E for the S&P 500 Index, taken from Table 10–5, uses average annual prices and contemporaneous earnings rather than smoothed earnings because aggregate corporate earnings are not as volatile as for electronics companies.

Table 10–7 shows the annual ratio of the Electronics group's P/E to the S&P 500 P/E, and the ratio of Texas Instruments' P/E to the group P/E. These data reveal that the stocks of major companies producing electronic components have tended to carry P/E ratios about twice the level of the overall market's P/E, and that Texas Instruments' P/E usually has been a bit higher than the group's P/E. Past history thus would have suggested that the average prices of electronics stocks in 1985 were on the low side of normal, at a 1.5 P/E relative to the market, and that Texas Instruments was selling a bit on the low side relative to its group. With the overall market at a P/E level of about 12, electronics stocks and Texas Instruments might normally be expected to trade at a P/E level near 25. If the normal earning power of Texas Instruments were estimated at about $6 per share, a stock price of about $150 per share might have been considered normal. Interestingly, $150 is at the top of the 1984–85 price range of the stock ($90–$150). But, also interesting, the dividend discount approach produced a valuation near the $90 low end of the price range. So

---

[21]The data are published by Standard & Poor's in annual and monthly volumes entitled *Analysts Handbook*. In addition to prices and earnings per share, other earnings statement and balance sheet data are published for each industry.

[22]The group consists of AMP, Intel, Motorola, National Semiconductor and Texas Instruments. Fairchild was included until 1979, when it was acquired by Schlumberger.

**TABLE 10–7   P/E Relationships: Texas Instruments, Electronics Group, and Overall Market**

| | Average P/E Ratios | | | P/E Relatives | |
| --- | --- | --- | --- | --- | --- |
| | S&P 500 | S&P Electronic Components | Texas Instruments | Electronic Components Relative to Market | Texas Instruments Relative to Electronic Components |
| 1971 | 17 | 32 | 31 | 1.9 | 1.0 |
| 1972 | 17 | 29 | 31 | 1.7 | 1.1 |
| 1973 | 13 | 29 | 33 | 2.2 | 1.1 |
| 1974 | 9 | 22 | 26 | 2.4 | 1.2 |
| 1975 | 11 | 22 | 25 | 2.0 | 1.1 |
| 1976 | 10 | 24 | 28 | 2.4 | 1.2 |
| 1977 | 9 | 14 | 17 | 1.6 | 1.2 |
| 1978 | 8 | 11 | 12 | 1.4 | 1.1 |
| 1979 | 7 | 11 | 12 | 1.6 | 1.1 |
| 1980 | 8 | 15 | 16 | 1.9 | 1.1 |
| 1981 | 8 | 17 | 15 | 2.1 | 0.9 |
| 1982 | 9 | 21 | 72 | 2.3 | N.M. |
| 1983 | 12 | 32 | 32 | 2.7 | 1.0 |
| 1984 | 10 | 22 | 44 | 2.2 | N.M. |
| 1985 | 12 | 18 | 18 | 1.5 | 1.0 |
| | | | Median: | 2.1 | 1.1 |

perhaps the $120 mid-point of the price range was about as fair a price as an efficient market would be likely to produce, and the July 1985 price of $100 might have been viewed as somewhat cheap.[23]

# Determinants of Relative Price/Earnings Ratios

Table 10–8 shows the relative P/E ratios of a representative group of industries at three different times—September 1972, when a bull market had been in progress for over two years and the P/E level of the S&P 500 Index was about 20; March 1980, when the market was suffering from a great deal of investor uncertainty and the P/E level of the S&P 500 was a little over 7; and July 1985, when the S&P Index had reached a new record high price level but its P/E was a relatively modest 12. Two very interesting observations emerge from this tabulation:

1. While many industries had roughly the same relative P/E in all three periods, despite the different overall market climates and P/E levels, many other industries had markedly different relative P/E ratios from one period to another.

2. The range of relative P/E ratios was greatest in 1972, when absolute P/Es were at their highest level. At that time, relative P/E ratios of 1.5 and higher were not

---

[23]Optimists on the stock might even have argued that normalized earnings in 1985 were closer to $10 per share than to $6. The $10 could be derived from the fact that the stock's year-end 1984 book value was $63 and that the long-term median return on equity had been about 16 percent. A 16 percent return on a $63 book value would produce earnings per share of about $10. See Chapter 12 for a detailed discussion of Texas Instruments' return on equity and book value.

*TABLE 10–8    A Sample of Industry Relative P/E Ratios*

| Industry | P/E of Industry ÷ P/E of S&P Composite Index | | |
|---|---|---|---|
| | **September 1, 1972** | **March 31, 1980** | **July 31, 1985** |
| Aerospace | 0.7 | 1.1 | 0.8 |
| Airlines | 0.9 | 1.0 | 1.0 |
| Aluminum | 1.3 | 0.6 | 1.1 |
| Automobile | 0.6 | 0.6 | 0.5 |
| Banks | 0.7 | 0.7 | 0.7 |
| Beverages | 1.5 | 1.3 | 1.3 |
| Building supplies | 0.8 | 0.7 | 0.9 |
| Chemicals | 0.9 | 0.9 | 1.0 |
| Cosmetics | 1.5 | 1.3 | 1.0 |
| Drugs | 1.7 | 1.6 | 1.1 |
| Electrical equipment | 1.1 | 1.1 | 1.0 |
| Electronics | 1.7 | 1.8 | 1.5 |
| Foods | 0.7 | 0.9 | 1.0 |
| Forest products | 0.9 | 1.0 | 1.1 |
| Machinery | 0.9 | 1.1 | N.M. |
| Office equipment | 1.6 | 1.5 | 1.1 |
| Oils | 0.8 | 0.9 | 0.8 |
| Paper | 1.0 | 0.8 | 0.9 |
| Publishing | 1.0 | 1.3 | 1.5 |
| Railroads | 0.5 | 0.9 | 0.8 |
| Retail | 0.7 | 0.9 | 0.9 |
| Rubber | 0.5 | 0.8 | 0.9 |
| Soaps | 1.1 | 0.9 | 1.0 |
| Steel | 0.7 | 0.6 | 0.8 |
| Textiles | 0.6 | 0.8 | 0.9 |
| Tobacco | 0.7 | 1.0 | 0.8 |
| Utilities: | | | |
| Electric | 0.5 | 0.9 | 0.6 |
| Gas | 0.6 | 1.1 | 0.8 |
| Telephone | 0.6 | 0.9 | 0.8 |

SOURCE: First Boston Corporation; Standard & Poor's; Shearson Lehman Brothers.

uncommon, while many industries were as low at 0.5. Since then, few industries have had P/E relatives in excess of 1.5, and none in this sample was below 0.6.

Table 10–9 shows that even among high P/E stocks, the dispersion of P/Es has varied considerably over time. The table shows the number of stocks in each of six P/E categories among the 50 highest P/E stocks at various points in time. Note that in December 1972, all 50 of the darlings of Wall Street carried P/Es in excess of 25. But in September 1974 the P/Es of the 50 highest P/E stocks ranged from below 14 to 26 and higher, while in February 1978 all were 16 or lower.

What factors might account for differences in P/E ratios among different companies or industries at a given point in time? What factors might account for changes in the relative P/E of a given company or industry over an extended period of time? And what might explain compressions or expansions of the whole range of P/E ratios in the marketplace?

**TABLE 10–9  P/E Distribution of "Top 50" at Important Stock Market Points**

| P/E | Point of Greatest P/E Expansion 12/72 | Trough of 1973–74 Bear Market 9/74 | Point of Tightest P/E Compression 2/78 | Peak of 1980–81 Market Cycle 11/80 | Trough of 1981–82 Market Cycle 7/82 | 12/84 |
|---|---|---|---|---|---|---|
| Below 14 | 0 | 5 | 32 | 0 | 12 | 0 |
| 14–16 | 0 | 21 | 18 | 0 | 28 | 16 |
| 17–18 | 0 | 8 | 0 | 0 | 6 | 14 |
| 19–22 | 0 | 11 | 0 | 19 | 3 | 14 |
| 23–25 | 0 | 2 | 0 | 13 | 1 | 2 |
| 26+ | 50 | 3 | 0 | 18 | 0 | 4 |

SOURCE: Kidder Peabody.

*The Role of Growth.*    Unquestionably, the price-earnings ratio should be higher for an industry or company which is expected to have rapid earnings growth than for one which is expected to grow more slowly. A simple example shows why this is so.

Suppose company A is currently earning $1 per share and that its earnings can be expected to grow at 20 percent per annum for five years. Meanwhile, company B, which also has current earnings per share of $1, is expected to have earnings growth of 10 percent per annum for five years. Thereafter, both companies are expected to grow at an equal rate.

Given these assumptions, A's earnings per share at the end of five years will be $1 multiplied by $(1.20)^5$, or $2.49, while B's earnings will be $1 multiplied by $(1.10)^5$, or $1.61. Therefore, the stock of company A could sell today at $25, or a P/E ratio of 25, while the stock of company B could sell today at $16, or a P/E ratio of 16, yet both would be selling at 10 times the earnings expected five years hence, when future growth rates equalize. It would not seem reasonable for both companies to sell at the same P/E ratio today in view of the great difference in expected earnings growth for the next five years.

*Other Factors.*    While it is clear, however, that company A, with rapid expected earnings growth, should sell at a higher P/E than company B, with much slower expected growth, it is not at all clear how much higher the rapid-growth company's P/E should be. The simple arithmetic which suggested that a 25:16 relationship would be appropriate is too simple for a variety of reasons, including the following:

1. The 10 percent growth expectation may be held with a higher degree of confidence than the 20 percent expectation. This should temper the amount of P/E premium accorded to the higher growth company (just as *k,* the discount rate discussed earlier, is a function of risk).

2. The difference in expected growth rate may be explained by different factors. Company A's earnings growth may be higher because of more rapid unit sales growth, more rapid selling price growth, a low or zero dividend payout policy, a highly leveraged capital structure, a favorable income tax status, or even an ultra-liberal set of accounting practices. It would seem reasonable to expect that, in setting P/E ratios, the marketplace takes into account not only the amount and certainty of earnings growth but also the sources of earnings growth.

3. Recent earnings may have accelerated or decelerated in relation to the longer term normal growth rate. Since investors are very much influenced by cyclical, as well as secular, earnings patterns, near-term earnings presumably affect P/E ratios.

4. Aside from growth and growth-related factors, other characteristics that might affect P/E ratios include the liquidity of the trading market of one stock versus another and the charisma of one company's management versus another.[24]

***Multiple Regression Analysis.***    It is not possible to derive theoretically the appropriate influence that each of these factors should have on relative price/earnings ratios. Therefore, a number of researchers have sought to answer the riddle empirically, using multiple regression analysis.[25] For example, suppose a researcher hypothesizes that price/earnings ratio differences among companies are mainly attributable to (1) differences in expected long-term earnings growth rate, (2) differences in the cyclical variability of earnings, (3) differences in normal dividend payout ratio, and (4) differences in financial leverage. To test the hypothesis, the researcher might select a sample of, say, 100 companies in a variety of industries and for each company gather the following data:

1. Relative price/earnings ratios at recent bull market peak and bear market trough dates (excluding companies with deficits or nominal earnings for which P/Es would be meaningless).

2. Three-to-five-year expected earnings growth rates published by, say, the Value Line Survey at each of the dates chosen for measuring price/earnings ratios. (Perhaps the most troublesome aspect of empirical research in this field is that the market's consensus growth expectations cannot be measured directly. Different researchers use different methods of measurement. Some extrapolate actual past data; some use the published data of one or more investment services; and some use the unpublished data of one or more financial institutions.)

3. The standard deviation of the past 10 years' percentage changes of earnings per share, or some other measure of variability of earnings.

4. The average dividend payout ratio for, say, the five years prior to each price/earnings ratio measurement date.

5. The debt-to-assets ratio at the balance sheet date nearest to each price/earnings ratio measurement date, or some other measure of financial leverage.

Using a computerized multiple regression program, the researcher would input the data and, for the peak and trough periods, would produce an equation of the form:

$$X_1 = b_1 X_2 + b_2 X_3 + b_3 X_4 + b_4 X_5 + a$$

The various $b$ values would indicate the influence on $X_1$, the relative price/earnings ratio, of $X_2$, $X_3$, $X_4$, and $X_5$, the hypothesized explanatory factors of expected earn-

---

[24]For a survey of professional security analysts' views regarding P/E determinants, see Lal C. Chugh and Joseph W. Meador, "Stock Valuation Process: The Analysts' View," *Financial Analysts Journal,* November–December 1984. The influence of management's charisma is related amusingly in "The CEO Factor," *Financial World,* June 15, 1981.

[25]Reviews of the literature are contained in Frank K. Reilly, *Investment Analysis and Portfolio Management* 2nd Edition (Hinsdale, Ill.: Dryden Press, 1985), chapters 12–15, and in William Beaver and Dale Morse, "What Determines Price-Earnings Ratios?" *Financial Analysts Journal,* July–August 1978.

ings growth, historical earnings stability, dividend payout, and leverage. ($X_1$ is referred to as the dependent variable and $X_2$, etc. are the independent variables.) The final factor of the equation, $a$, is the so-called constant factor which causes the average of the calculated values of $X_1$ to equal the average of the actual values of $X_1$. In this example, the constant would cause the average of the calculated values of $X_1$ to be approximately 1.0, which is the average of all of the P/E relatives of any broad cross section of companies. The computer also would produce other regression statistics such as the coefficient of determination ($R^2$) and so-called $t$ statistics which indicate the significance of each $b$-value. For example, the computer might have produced the following information for the bull market peak date and the bear market trough date.[26]

| Explanatory Factor | Bull Market Peak | | Bear Market Trough | |
|---|---|---|---|---|
| | *b* Value | *t* Statistic | *b* Value | *t* Statistic |
| Earnings growth . . . . . . . . . . . . . . | 0.1 | (4.8) | 0.05 | (2.4) |
| Earnings variability . . . . . . . . . . . | −0.01 | (1.1) | −0.01 | (3.3) |
| Dividend payout . . . . . . . . . . . . . | 0.003 | (0.7) | 0.005 | (1.1) |
| Leverage . . . . . . . . . . . . . . . . . . | −0.02 | (0.3) | −0.03 | (0.7) |
| . . . . . . . . . . . . . . . . . . . . . . . . | $R^2 = .40$ | | $R^2 = .32$ | |

This information would suggest the following conclusions:

1. At the bull market peak, every 1 percent of expected earnings growth rate gave rise, on average, to a relative P/E of 0.1. Moreover, this finding carried a high degree of statistical significance because $t$ statistics in excess of 3.0 are not likely to occur randomly. (A $t$ statistic of 2.0 to 3.0 is also considered quite significant; 1.0 to 2.0 is moderately significant; and under 1.0 is not generally considered significant). On the other hand, at the bear market trough the marketplace accorded a relative P/E of only 0.05 to each 1 percent of expected earnings growth, and this finding, too, was statistically significant.

2. The higher the historical variability of earnings, other things being equal, the lower a company's relative P/E was both at the bull market peak and bear market trough. The $b$ value of $−0.01$ means that relative P/E went down 0.1 for each 10 percent standard deviation of earnings change. However, the $t$ statistics suggest that one can be more confident that earnings variability will influence P/E in bear markets than in bull markets.

3. Dividend policy did not have a strong relationship to relative P/E in either period (the $t$ statistics were fairly low), but such influence as existed was positive. At the bull market peak, a 50 percent payout ratio would have added, on average, a relative P/E of 0.15 (.003 × 50) while a similar payout ratio at the bear market trough would have added a relative P/E of 0.25 (.005 × 50). Presumably, the higher influence of payout in a bear market, together with the lower influence of expected growth, reflects investors' feelings, at such times, that "a bird in hand is worth two in the bush."[27]

---

[26]While the data presented here are merely illustrative, they are fairly typical of the actual research findings which have been published over the years.

[27]Statisticians would urge caution in interpreting the meaning of the $b$ values for this type of multiple regression study because of the existence of what is called *multicollinearity*. This term refers to

4. Leverage was, in general, viewed negatively by the market (note the negative *b* value), but it was not very significant (note the low *t* statistics).

5. Many other factors must have affected relative P/E ratios. The $R^2$ values of the two periods mean that the four measured factors explained only 40 percent and 32 percent, respectively, of the relative P/E differences among the sampled companies.

***Importance of the Current Earnings Cycle.***     While regression equations can be useful in quantifying the impact of certain basic financial factors on *normal* P/E ratios, they are not very helpful in tracing the influences on short-term P/E variations around their normal values. Among the most important of these short-term influences is the acceleration or deceleration of a company's earnings around its longer-term growth rate. For example, Figure 10–4 shows a close relationship between the movement of Texas Instruments' quarterly average stock price and its quarterly earnings per share. Clearly, an investor who has in mind a normal relative P/E for Texas Instruments equal to about double the overall market's P/E, should recognize that the stock's P/E at any instant in time will be greatly influenced by the current stage of the company's earnings cycle.[28]

# ■ OTHER VALUATION GUIDELINES

Thus far in this chapter we have reviewed the two most widely used measures of common stock valuation—the classic theoretical dividend discount approach and the more pragmatic relative price/earnings ratio approach. While these are the most widely used measures of stock values, it should be recognized that the period of rampant inflation during the late 1970s shook the foundations of these measures. High rates of inflation caused investors increasingly to question whether normal ac-

---

the fact that the explanatory factors tend not to be independent of each other. For example, a company's earnings growth rate is influenced by its dividend and leverage policies. Consequently, a multiple regression analysis of the influence on P/E ratios of earnings growth, dividend policy, and financial leverage must confront the multicollinearity problem. For when multicollinearity exists, the *b* values derived from the analysis are far less reliable than if the explanatory factors were truly independent. Textbooks on econometrics devote considerable space to methods of trying to overcome or minimize the multicollinearity problem.

In addition, it should be noted that the equation assumed a *linear* relationship between P/E and each explanatory variable, whereas some of the relationships may be *curvilinear*. Finally, mention should be made of a technique known as discriminant analysis, which is being used increasingly in econometric research. The objective of discriminant analysis is similar to that of multiple regression analysis—namely, to quantify the influence of a group of variables on another variable. Discriminant analysis is used, however, when the dependent variable cannot itself be quantified. For example, if the problem is to determine the impact of financial leverage, cash flow, and company size on the probability of whether or not a company will go bankrupt, the dependent variable is qualitative in nature—yes or no; bankrupt or not bankrupt—rather than the more typical type of variable which can be measured on a quantitative scale. The independent variables in discriminant analysis may be either quantitative or qualitative.

[28]It follows from this that an ability to *forecast* the earnings cycle would be extraordinarily valuable in forecasting stock P/Es and prices. But since accurate earnings forecasts are extremely difficult to make, several researchers have investigated the usefulness of current "earnings surprises" in forecasting stock prices. The research reveals that earnings surprises do have price-predictive value. See Robert D. Arnott, "The Use and Misuse of Consensus Earnings," and Charles P. Jones, Richard J. Rendleman, and Henry A. Latané, "Earnings Announcements: Pre- and Post-Responses," *Journal of Portfolio Management,* Spring 1985.

**FIGURE 10–4   Texas Instruments—Cyclical Pattern of Stock Price and Earnings per Share**

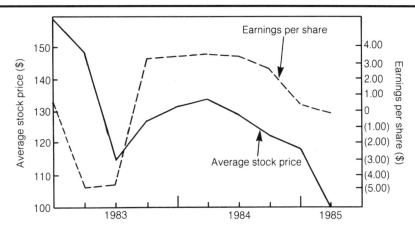

counting statements of corporate earnings were meaningful (see Chapter 9) and whether dividends were being paid from true earnings or were simply a return of capital, a disguised liquidation of the business. Reflecting these concerns, at least two supplementary guidelines to valuation came into fairly widespread use, price-to-asset ratios and price-to-sales ratios.

## The Role of Asset Values

In a report dated May 15, 1985, Mr. Francis H. M. Kelly, research director of the brokerage firm of Oppenheimer & Co., made the following statement to the firm's institutional investment clients:

> We have begun a new series of reports under the title of *Asset Transfer Values*. In contrast with the typical Wall Street preoccupation with earnings growth or earnings valuation, these reports attempt to measure the value of a corporation as seen through the eyes of a businessman. In short, we are concerned with the value of the business as a business rather than the value of an equity as a fractional share of reported earnings. Frequently these two measures of value vary widely from each other, for each involves value elements that are not carried over to the other. Many corporate assets are hidden on the balance sheet and are not immediately connected with earning power, for example LIFO reserves, ownership of real estate or assignable long-term leases, trade names and over-funded pension liabilities. In these cases, a narrow focus on earning power can seriously understate the value of a corporation. Similarly, periodic fads in equity evaluation, as in the case of growth investing in the early 1970s or technology new issues in 1983, can capitalize a company's worth well above levels that any sober businessman would recognize.
>
> Why have we undertaken this exercise? Because we believe there is a wide demand for alternative ways of thinking about corporate values. An assortment of circumstances has channeled a great deal of credit into the purchase of entire corporations—$70.0 billion in completed cash offers last year. Equity investors who refused to think in broader valuation terms were unable to come to grips with the most vigorous, novel, and concentrated form of equity buying in a generation. The forces behind this buying wave include:
> 1. The growing maturity of major goods-producing industries and the pickup in free cash flow that comes from holding down capital outlays.

**FIGURE 10–5**   *Market Price to Replacement Cost of Book Value, S&P 400*

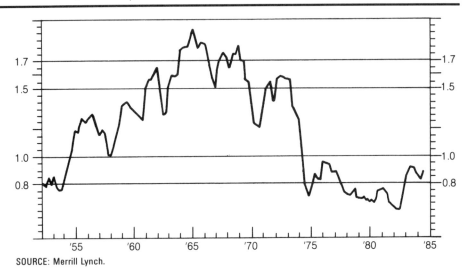

SOURCE: Merrill Lynch.

2. The obsolescence of historical cost accounting in accurately portraying the impact of a decade or more of inflation on asset values and liabilities.
3. The positive effect on cash flow of the 1981 liberalization of depreciation.
4. The effect of deregulation on industrial restructuring and concentration.
5. The benign attitude of the Justice Department toward a majority of announced large mergers.
6. The exceptional availability of fixed-income financing to implement planned company purchases.
7. The willingness of leading financial institutions and Wall Street banking firms to facilitate hostile acquisitions.

Was Mr. Kelly arguing that corporate assets per se have some intrinsic value aside from the earnings and dividends they are capable of generating? Not at all. What he was arguing was that assets (properly measured) will ultimately be utilized by astute managers to produce a stream of earnings and dividends. Therefore, analysts who focus on assets may be able to gain an advantage over analysts who focus on historical and projected earnings trends.[29]

Based on a similar line of reasoning, several efforts have been made to evaluate the overall level of the stock market by reference to true net asset values, using various capital goods and inventory price indexes to adjust reported book values. The results of one such effort, by Merrill Lynch, are displayed in Figure 10–5, showing the ratio of the Standard & Poor's Industrial Stock Price Index to Merrill Lynch's estimates of the replacement cost of the book values of the 400 companies

---

[29]A number of analysts focus on stocks selling at less than net-net working capital per share—defined as current assets minus current liabilities minus long-term debt and preferred stock minus intangible assets, divided by number of shares. *Forbes* magazine periodically publishes lists of such stocks under the heading, "Loaded Laggards."

included in that index. It will be noted that this method of valuation showed the stock market to be very dear in the mid- to late-1960s and very cheap from 1978 through 1982.

## Price/Sales Ratios

In our discussion of price/earnings ratios, an important problem was noted, namely that many companies have extremely volatile earnings patterns. For such companies, there is a need to normalize earnings in order to calculate a meaningful P/E ratio. The difficulty with normalizing earnings, however, is that there is no agreed-on method of doing this. Some analysts may use an average of historical earnings; some may use an average of past and estimated future earnings; some fit a trend line to past earnings and extrapolate the trend a year or two forward; and some use very subjective methods.

One approach to this problem, which has inspired a considerable following as a result of an interesting book espousing it,[30] is to examine price/sales (P/S) ratios (the stock's price divided by the latest 12-months' revenues per share). The author of the book pointed out that the price/sales ratio of most large companies usually falls in a range of about 0.4 to 0.8. Ratios significantly above that range usually suggest that a stock is overpriced.[31] Ratios below that range should be taken as a signal that further investigation of the company's financial condition is warranted, since companies with low P/S ratios often have dangerously high debt levels.

If a balance sheet analysis of a low P/S stock indicates a low probability of bankruptcy, the stock is probably a good candidate for purchase. A major exception would be the stocks of companies in high-turnover businesses with very low profit margins per dollar of sales, such as supermarket chains. For such companies, very low price/sales ratios are not necessarily indicative of good values. At the other extreme, young "emerging growth" companies often have P/S ratios of 2 or more without being overpriced. A ratio above 3, however, is probably too high according to advocates of this valuation method.

## ■ SUMMARY

If the history of the stock market teaches one anything, the lesson is that no single valuation method works best at all times. Given this lesson, most wise investors use more than one method, looking for stocks which appear to be bargains from several different perspectives.[32] In this chapter, we have described several different ways of measuring stock values.

[30]Kenneth L. Fisher, *Super Stocks* (Homewood, Ill.: Dow Jones-Irwin, 1984).

[31]In the January 28, 1985, issue of *Forbes* magazine (p. 126), Fisher wrote, "Merck and IBM are financial fortresses but also sell at price/sales ratios about 1.5. Only a few stocks have ever rendered above-average, long-term results from such levels."

[32]It is important, however, that the perspectives be truly different, one from the other. A combination of essentially the same valuation methods will not be better than any one method alone. For an excellent discussion of multiple valuation models, see Robert D. Arnott and William A. Copeland, "The Business Cycle and Security Selection," *Financial Analysts Journal,* March–April 1985.

We began by presenting the basic theory that a stock's value is equal to the sum of its probable future dividends, discounted to the present using an interest rate that appropriately reflects the risks of being wrong about future dividend amounts. Illustrations were offered of how this theory can be applied in practice, both to the valuation of individual stocks and to the valuation of the level of the overall stock market.

Notwithstanding evidence that classic valuation theory can be applied to everyday investment practice, we pointed to reasons why many security analysts do not take kindly to dividend discount models. The most common alternative valuation method, utilizing price/earnings ratios, was itself described from different perspectives. Illustrations were presented of how the P/E history of the overall market and of individual stocks and industry groups can be a guide to the choice of an appropriate P/E in any given situation. We also showed how one might try to determine appropriate P/Es by elaborate statistical analyses.

Both dividend discount methods and P/E ratios rely heavily on earnings data published in corporate financial reports. But the accuracy of earnings data was increasingly questioned during periods of rapid inflation or expected future inflation. Consequently, there developed a growing tendency to supplement the traditional earnings-based measures of stock value with alternatives that focus on asset values and sales revenues. The chapter concluded with a description and illustration of such supplementary measures, with a reiteration that the best type of valuation analysis is multifaceted.

# SUGGESTED READINGS

Bernstein, Peter L. "Capital Market Expectations: The Macro Factors," in *Managing Investment Portfolios*. Boston: Warren, Gorham & Lamont, 1983.

Dreman, David. *The New Contrarian Investment Strategy: The Psychology of Stock Market Success*. New York: Random House, 1983.

Farrell, James L., Jr. *Guide to Portfolio Management*. New York: McGraw-Hill, 1983, Chapters 4–6.

*Financial Analysts Journal,* November–December 1985. (A special edition devoted to valuation models.)

Fisher, Kenneth L. *Super Stocks*. Homewood, Ill.: Dow Jones-Irwin, 1984.

Hawkins, David F., and Walter J. Campbell. *Equity Valuation: Models, Analysis and Implications*. New York: Financial Executives Research Foundation, 1978.

Ibbotson, Robert G., and Rex A. Sinquefield. *Stocks, Bonds, Bills, and Inflation: The Past and The Future*. Charlottesville, Va.: Financial Analysts Research Foundation, 1982.

Leuthold, Steven C. *The Myths of Inflation and Investing*. Chicago: Crain Books, 1980.

Malkiel, Burton. *The Inflation-Beater's Investment Guide*. New York: W. W. Norton, 1980.

# CHAPTER

# *Industry Analysis*

*Observe always that everything is the result of a change.*

Marcus Aurelius

As suggested in the previous chapter, common stock value judgments often are best made in a "top-down" fashion—starting with an overview of the aggregate market level, then relating industry group values to the overall market, and finally considering individual companies in relation to the industry (or industries) in which they participate. Since value judgments relate strongly to the outlook for corporate sales, earnings, and dividends, a concomitant of the top-down approach to valuation is to view a company's sales and earnings as a progression from the overall economy to the industry to the company.

Broad economic trends and cycles, including both real and price components, have been discussed in earlier chapters. In this chapter, we provide some tools for analyzing the trends and cycles of industry sales and earnings. The following chapter moves from the industry to the company level.

## ■ *UNDERLYING TRENDS: THE INDUSTRIAL LIFE CYCLE*

A useful framework for analyzing industry trends is a concept known as the industrial life cycle. The idea, which is analogous to the three-stage dividend discount valuation model, is that most industries' product lines, and even modes of marketing, go through stages of development resembling those of a human being. In the early part of their lives they grow at a very rapid rate. After a time the growth rate slows down; while expansion continues, it is at a more moderate pace. Finally, they stop growing and either live a relatively stable existence for a long time—or die. The validity of this frame of reference has been sufficiently established to suggest that the analysis of a company should begin with an examination of the developmental stages of each major activity in which the company engages. After positioning each activity in its life cycle, the analyst can go on to appraise the particular company's prospective market shares of, and profits from, those activities.

## The Basic Life-Cycle Model

A simple version of the industrial life cycle is portrayed in Figure 11–1. On the vertical scale are unit sales of the industry (or product line), and on the horizontal scale is time. Note that the graph is semilogarithmic, the vertical scale being logarithmic and the horizontal scale arithmetic. On a logarithmic scale, equal distances represent equal percentage changes. For example, when unit sales grow from 2 (thousand, million, or whatever) to 3, the line rises less steeply—covers less vertical distance—than when sales grow from 1 to 2. Thus, Figure 11–1 portrays·an accelerating rate of sales growth in stages 1 and 2, a gradually decelerating growth rate in stage 3, and a sharp deceleration of growth (perhaps leading to decline) in stage 4.

It also must be noted that the length of the time periods (the horizontal distances) of the various growth stages shown on the graph is merely illustrative. There is no uniformity of elapsed time for the growth phases of different industries. For example, some new products encounter a brief but explosive burst of growth, whereas others

**FIGURE 11–1   The Basic Life Cycle Model**

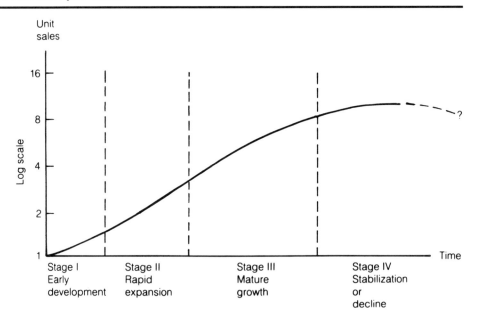

build market acceptance more slowly. Likewise, the span of stages 2 and 3, the period of expansion and gradual maturation, is quite variable among different products. But time cannot be ignored. Indeed, harking back to the idea that stocks are worth the present value of future cash flows, it is almost as important to assess correctly the probable time spans of as yet incompleted growth stages as it is to predict correctly the actual rates of growth during each stage.

**The Initial Growth Stage.** Observers of the industrial life cycle note that the first stage of a product's development usually is characterized by a high rate of growth of the market with perceived opportunities for large profits. These perceptions, however, often give rise to fierce competition and a high rate of bankruptcies. The automobile industry provides a dramatic example of this phenomenon. Between 1900 and 1908, more than 500 automobile companies were organized. Of these, about 300 quickly went out of business, either voluntarily or involuntarily. By 1917, 76 companies were active in the industry, but 10 produced three quarters of the total output. Today, of course, only a handful of U.S. and foreign companies dominate the auto industry. Other examples of rampant competition in new fields when they were in their early development stage include air conditioners, television manufacturing, transistors, and electronic calculators.

It should be recognized, however, that new industries are not necessarily pioneered by large numbers of small companies which kill each other off in a bitter competitive struggle. The synthetic fiber industry, for example, was largely pioneered by a single giant company—duPont—, and vigorous competition did not emerge until many years after the original introduction of nylon. Electrostatic copying of documents (Xerox) and instant photographic processing (Polaroid) are other illustrations. In any event, the focus of discussion in this chapter will be on the phases of growth that follow the early development stage because most publicly traded companies have already emerged from their infancy.

**The Follow-Through.** The second stage of growth is labeled "rapid expansion" in Figure 11–1. It refers to the fact that after some years, through consolidations and internal expansion, a relatively few companies usually take over a fairly large percentage of a young industry's total volume of business. They broaden the market by improving the quality and reducing the price of the product or service. Growth is very rapid but with fewer risks of disaster than in the early development stage.

The transition from accelerating growth in stage 2 to decelerating—but still quite rapid—growth in stage 3 (labeled "mature growth") is subtle, and some may doubt that it is worthwhile to delineate the two stages. Let it merely be noted that as an industry or product line ages, it begins to be confronted by the inroads of newer products and services competing for the same basic market. Also, the market itself gets nearer to its saturation point, and it becomes more difficult to broaden that market via price reductions or quality improvements.

In a recent article, *Forbes* magazine posed the question of why it happens so often in a promising new industry that the participants fail to make the transition from a rapid burst of growth to a lesser but more enduring period of mature growth.[1] Using

---

[1] Geoffrey Smith and Paul B. Brown, "Emerging Growth Stocks: Why So Many Peak So Early," *Forbes*, January 28, 1985.

a number of real-world examples, *Forbes* identified as a common denominator a failure to develop follow-on lines of business that build on the market for the product or service that sparked the initial success. Ironically, the problem often is not that managements fail to see that need for these follow-on lines, but quite the opposite. They frequently see *too many* opportunities and end up in businesses which they really don't know well enough to operate successfully.

***Stabilization or Decline.***   Even if a growth industry manages to develop follow-on lines of business successfully, in most cases this is a self-limiting process. The final stage of growth is difficult to label because the industrial life-cycle concept departs from a strictly anthropomorphic analogy at this point. Aged human beings inevitably deteriorate and ultimately die. Aged industries, on the other hand, may follow one of three paths: *(a)* slow growth, especially in relation to the rest of the economy; *(b)* level output, which meets replacement demand but neither grows nor declines to any significant degree; or *(c)* an actual decline and ultimate disappearance of the industry.

What must happen to prevent an industry in the stabilization stage of the life cycle from dying? The noted management consultant Peter F. Drucker believes that the key is for the managements of the companies in that industry to focus on productivity improvement.[2] Rather than go off on ill-conceived diversification binges, they should adopt as an operating philosophy: "If we cannot become bigger, we must become better." Sound advice, all too often ignored.

***Speed of Transition.***   Most recent observers of the industrial life cycle have a sense that the time span of the growth stages has been speeding up, particularly for the first two stages. For example, the aluminum industry was born in 1888. Its formative period lasted for two decades. By its third decade (1910–20), U.S. aluminum production was still in the rapid expansion stage, growing at a 15 percent per annum rate. Maturation, with a slower but still relatively rapid 6 percent growth rate, persisted throughout the 1920s and even through the Great Depression. Growth actually speeded up again in the 1940s and 50s under the impetus of the war and the rise of the heavy aluminum-consuming aerospace industry. And during the 1960s, aluminum clearly remained in stage 3 of its life cycle, growing at double the rate of real GNP. Not until the 1970s, when growth slowed to less than 4 percent per annum, could one begin to wonder whether a transition to stage 4 was occurring.

The history of the electronics industry in the United States provides some vivid illustrations of the speedup of the first two life-cycle stages of new products and contrasts strongly with the very extended transition of the aluminum industry. The discrete transistor segment of the electronics industry doubled every year from 1955 to 1960 (early development stage) and grew more than 35 percent per annum from 1960 to 1965 (rapid expansion stage). The transistor's mature growth stage then set in, with volume increases of about 12 percent per annum from 1965 to 1975. The stabilization stage has not yet arrived, as transistor growth persists at a rate of some

---

[2]An illustration of his reasoning is outlined in "Making Room in No-Growth Firms," *The Wall Street Journal,* December 30, 1983.

**TABLE 11-1  Life Cycle Characteristics of Five Types of Retailing**

| Retailing Type | Introduction Period | Period of Maximum Market Share | Elapsed Time |
|---|---|---|---|
| Downtown department store . . . . . . . . . . . . | 1860 | 1940 | 80 years |
| Variety store . . . . . . . . . . . . . . . . . . . . . . | 1910 | 1955 | 45 |
| Supermarket . . . . . . . . . . . . . . . . . . . . . . | 1930 | 1965 | 35 |
| Discount store . . . . . . . . . . . . . . . . . . . . | 1950 | 1970 | 20 |
| Home improvement center . . . . . . . . . . . . . | 1965 | 1980 | 15 |

SOURCE: William R. Davidson, Albert D. Bates, and Stephen J. Bass, "The Retail Life Cycle," *Harvard Business Review,* November-December 1976, p. 94.

6 percent.[3] Nevertheless, the speed of transition from stage 1 to stage 3 is in marked contrast to the aluminum industry's history.

The integrated circuit segment of the electronics industry went through a similarly rapid early transition—100 per annual growth from 1965 to 1970, dropping to a 30 percent rate during the 1970s and 20 percent thereafter. However, maturation, stage 3, does not yet appear in sight to most experts.

As a final illustration of the speedup of the industrial life cycle, we might cite the household appliance industry. Morgan Stanley has noted that "the span of time between the introduction of a new household appliance and the peak of production declined from 34 years for those appliances introduced before 1920 to eight years for products introduced between 1929 and 1959. For the video cassette recorder and the personal computer, the period would be two to three years."[4]

**Service Industry Life Cycles.**  While most discussions of the industrial life cycle deal with goods-producing industries, it is important to note that service industries are also amenable to analysis within the same framework. For example, an article in the *Harvard Business Review* showed how the history of the retailing industry over 120 years could be described as a sequence of new modes of marketing, each with its own life cycle. Interestingly, as illustrated in Table 11-1, each new marketing innovation aged more rapidly than the prior innovation.

## Analysis of End-User Markets

An important guide to whether an industry is in the process of moving to a new stage in its life cycle is an appraisal of the major markets for the industry's products or services. An industry can sustain an above-average growth rate in three ways, (1) by maintaining a stable penetration of rapidly growing markets, (2) by achieving a growing penetration of markets which have average growth rates, and (3) most dynamically, by achieving a growing penetration of rapidly growing markets. Similarly,

---

[3]This rate is a composite of very rapid growth of power and optical transistors, which together comprise about 50 percent of the market, and negative growth of more traditional discrete transistors.

[4]*Investment Perspectives,* June 11, 1985, p. 5.

***TABLE 11–2    Semiconductor Growth Patterns***

| | Worldwide Market ($ billions) | | | Growth Rates | |
|---|---|---|---|---|---|
| | 1980 | 1985 Estimate | 1990 Forecast | 1980–1985 | 1985–1990 |
| Integrated circuits  . . . . . . | $ 9.5 | $20.3 | $51.8 | 17% | 20% |
| Discrete devices  . . . . . . . | 4.5 | 5.3 | 8.2 | 4 | 8 |
| Total . . . . . . . . . . . . . | 14.0 | 25.6 | 60.0 | 13 | 18 |

**Forecast End-Use Growth Rates**

| | |
|---|---|
| Telecommunications  . . . . . . . . . . . . . . . . . . . . . . . . . . | 20% |
| Office automation . . . . . . . . . . . . . . . . . . . . . . . . . . . | 20 |
| Computers . . . . . . . . . . . . . . . . . . . . . . . . . . . . . . . | 15 |
| Automotive instruments . . . . . . . . . . . . . . . . . . . . . . . . | 15 |
| Other instruments . . . . . . . . . . . . . . . . . . . . . . . . . . . | 20 |

SOURCE: Montgomery Securities (San Francisco, California) Second Annual Semiconductor Conference, January 23–25, 1985.

an industry's growth will slow down or decline if its user-markets are declining or its penetration of those markets is giving way to competing products.

There are many ways to delineate an industry's markets—for example, by geographic area, by age or income bracket of individual consumers of its products, by the various lifestyles of consumers, or most commonly, by consuming industry. Trade associations and brokerage houses devote considerable effort to compiling data which analyze the sales of various industries in terms of their end-user markets.[5] One such analysis, relating to the semiconductor industry, was prepared recently by the brokerage firm, Montgomery Securities.

As summarized in the top portion of Table 11–2, the worldwide (non-Communist) semiconductor market was estimated at about $25 billion in 1985,[6] having grown at a compound annual rate of about 13 percent from 1980. Of this total, integrated circuits grew at about a 17 percent annual rate. Growth for the 1985–90 period was estimated at 18 percent for the industry as a whole and 20 percent for integrated circuits. As shown in the lower portion of the table, this growth was seen to stem from the continued pervasive application of integrated circuits throughout the industrial and service sectors of the world economy.

In telecommunications and office automation as end-user markets for semiconductors, we have an example of the most dynamic type of growth. Semiconductors are taking a growing share of rapidly growing markets. The computer market is an ex-

---

[5]The most comprehensive data on market breakdowns of consuming industries are compiled by U.S. Department of Commerce in a national accounting system known as input-output tables. Unfortunately, budgeting constraints have created such lengthy time lags in the publication of these data that they have become rather useless for investment analysis purposes. Another problem is that the data are based on the Commerce Department's Standard Industrial Classification System. While this system identifies almost 150 *manufacturing* industries and subindustries, it identifies fewer than 70 *service* industries; yet the service sector has become far more important than the manufacturing sector in the United States as a source of employment and income. An extensive description of input-output data and their application is contained in the fourth edition of this text, pp. 438–43.

[6]The figure is a trend value. Actual 1985 sales of semiconductors were below trend.

ample of somewhat less dynamic growth, since semiconductors represent a fairly stable share of the growing market for computers. In the case of automotive end-uses, the auto industry is itself a very mature market, but semiconductors are being used increasingly in each automobile. The conclusion of this analysis of end-uses of semiconductors was that the "stabilization phase" of the semiconductor industry's life cycle was nowhere near emergence as of 1985.

# The Life Cycle of Profits

The most common use of the industrial life-cycle concept has been in the analysis of sales volume. Figure 11–2 represents what we believe to be the composite opinion of management scientists about the typical pattern of profit margins and earnings in relation to revenues during the course of an industry's life cycle.

The following characteristics of the profit life cycle are noteworthy:

1. The growth path of revenues has a shape similar to that of unit sales—rising sharply for a time, then rising somewhat more slowly, and finally leveling off.
2. The profit margin is negative until the industry's revenues reach a critical mass. At that point, margins rise rapidly along with rapidly growing revenues, causing the level of earnings to soar.
3. Profit margins continue to expand until the mature growth stage, when they level out. Sometime during this stage, but before the stabilization stage of revenues is reached, margins begin to decline.
4. Despite the gradual tapering off of profit margins during stage 3, the actual level of earnings continues to rise during most of the period because revenue growth, while slowing, is sufficient to offset the deteriorating margins.
5. Finally, revenue and profit margin trends either offset each other and earnings stabilize, or earnings actually decline as falling revenues and deteriorating profit margins have a cascading effect.

**Evidence of "Gravitation Toward The Mean."** Some theoretical underpinnings of these ideas date back to the classical economist, John Stuart Mill. He believed that rates of return on investment should tend over time to equalize among industries in a competitive market system. If above-average returns exist in a particular industry, new entrants to the business will be attracted, and the increased competition will drive down rates of return. Similarly, if below-average returns are being earned in an industry, new investments will tend not to be made in that industry, resulting in a reduction of supply relative to demand and, ultimately, in a more normal rate of return.

Of course, the real world does not conform precisely to this theory. Various rigidities exist which retard new entrants into highly profitable industries (e.g., large capital requirements, technological complexities, and patents) and which perpetuate investments in low-profit industries (e.g., entrenched managements, labor union resistance, and government subsidies). Nevertheless, there is evidence that interindustry and even intercompany rates of return do tend over time to converge toward the average.

**FIGURE 11–2   The Life Cycle of Profits**

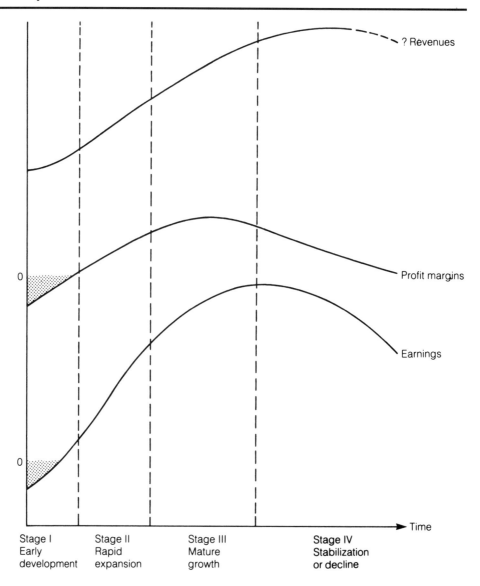

For example, Mr. Tony Estep of Salomon Brothers selected 100 companies in a cross-section of industries for which rate-of-return data were readily available. In one study, covering the period 1962–78, he calculated the average return on equity (ROE) for each company for the first five years of the period 1962–66. The companies were then ranked from highest to lowest 1962–66 ROE and were divided into quintiles accordingly. The average ROE for each quintile of companies was then calculated annually for the entire time span, as shown in the upper panel of Figure 11–3. A similar study was done for the period 1975–84 (except that 1975 alone represented

**FIGURE 11–3  Changes in Return on Equity of Five Groups of Companies (mean ROE each year = 100)**

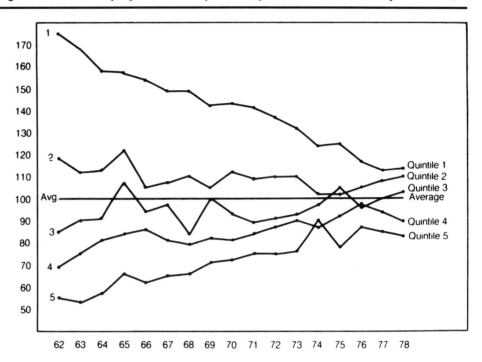

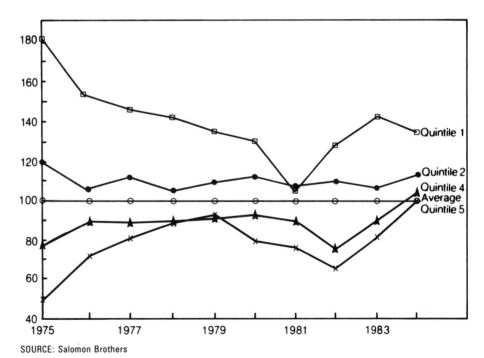

SOURCE: Salomon Brothers

the base period rather than the average of 1975–79), with results shown in the lower panel. The graphs of the data clearly support the notion that interindustry and intercompany rates of return tend toward equality over time. The initially high ROE companies subsequently tend to have declining returns, while the low ROE companies tend to have rising returns.[7]

The key to the specific shape of the profit life cycle of an industry is the relationship between unit costs and unit selling prices as volume proceeds from stage to stage. This relationship reflects two main factors: (1) the impact of economies of scale on unit costs and (2) the pricing strategies of the leading companies in the industry. While a detailed examination of these two subjects is beyond the scope of this chapter, a general review of some critical concepts is in order.

***Unit Costs—The Experience Curve.***    It has long been observed that as the output of a new good or service expands, various economies of scale begin to appear. Heavy start-up costs (for example, research and development, tooling, employee hiring, and training), which drag profits down in the earliest phase of a new product's life cycle, start to be spread over many units. Workers become more productive as they gain familiarity with their tasks. Plant layouts, equipment, and methods are improved. There is less waste and less redoing of work to correct defects.

A quantification of the impact of economies of scale is known as an experience curve, also called a learning curve. It relates average costs of incremental units of output to cumulative total output. Unit costs are usually expressed in real or constant-dollar terms, so as not to allow the impact of general inflationary forces to obscure the basic cost-versus-output relationship.

Suppose, for example, that the first year's output of a new product is 1 million units, followed by 2 million units in the second year, then 3 million, 4 million, and 5 million (in the fifth year). Cumulative output would, then, be 1 million, 3 million, 6 million, 10 million, and 15 million units. Research in a number of industries suggests that during the early development and rapid expansion stages of a product's growth, each doubling of cumulative output results in a 10 percent to 30 percent reduction in the average cost of incremental units.[8] In our example, the average cost per unit of the first 1 million units might have been $100, and the average unit cost of the next 1 million units might have been $80 (not counting any economywide inflationary impacts). This would suggest an experience curve factor of 80 percent— a doubling of cumulative output from 1 million to 2 million units resulting in costs of the second million units dropping to 80 percent of the initial unit cost level.

If 80 percent were, indeed, the correct experience factor, then by the time cumulative output reached 4 million units (early in the third year), average unit costs would have dropped to $64 (80% × $80). Cumulative output of 8 million units would drop average costs to $51 (80% × $64 = $51.20), and cumulative output of 16 million units (at the start of the sixth year) would result in average unit costs of about $41.

---

[7]For some contrary evidence see Barbara M. Fraumeni and Dale W. Jorgenson, "Rates of Return by Industrial Sector in the United States, 1948–76," *American Economic Review,* May 1980.

[8]See, for example, Pankaj Ghemawat, "Building Strategy on the Experience Curve," *Harvard Business Review,* March–April 1985.

*FIGURE 11-4   Semiconductor Memory Experience Curve*

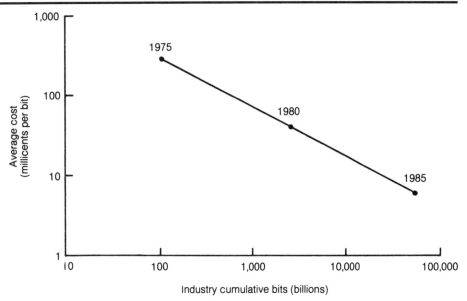

SOURCE: Derived from various industry statistics.

If this information were put onto a graph on which both scales were logarithmic, a straight line with a slope of −20 percent would result. That is, with cumulative output on the horizontal scale and average unit costs on the vertical scale, each 100 percent increase moving horizontally would produce a 20 percent decrease moving vertically.

A real-life illustration of this phenomenon is presented in Figure 11-4.[9] Here it is estimated that semiconductor memory devices for computers have an experience factor of about 75 percent. That is, costs are estimated to drop about 25 percent for each doubling of output.

Clearly, there are limits to the ability of an industry to achieve continuing economies of scale. In the first place, when the industry matures (which the semiconductor industry has not yet done), it takes longer and longer for output to double. Therefore, even if the experience curve was still impacting costs, the time period for achieving the economies of scale would be stretching out ever further. Moreover, to the extent that raw material inputs represent an important component of costs (which they do not in the semiconductor industry), there is no reason to believe that these can keep falling as output rises. At some point, volume discounts and other purchasing efficiencies cannot be expanded. Similarly, employee and capital efficiency eventually get stretched as far as possible. Indeed, as the industry grows, diseconomies of scale begin to creep in, such as large administrative staffs and complex cost accounting and inventory systems. Thus it is that products or services which have been

---

[9]The scales of the graph are delineated in 10-fold changes, such is the dynamic of the industry.

around for many years are said to be near the bottom of the experience curve. Instead of a straight line continuing downward, the experience curve becomes truly a curve and declines at a decelerating rate, eventually flattening out.

The main problem posed for the investment analyst who tries to determine the shape of an industry's experience curve is lack of data. Most companies operate in more than one industry, and although published revenue and earnings breakdowns by major activity have become increasingly prevalent, cost- and unit-volume break-downs by product line are too sketchy to permit experience curves to be calculated with much accuracy. Therefore, the analyst must be content to draw inferences from articles in trade journals, from interviews with corporate officials, and from observing the pricing behavior of different competitors in an industry, the subject to which we turn next.

***Pricing Strategies.***    More often than not, it is reasonable to assume that a company's market share is a good proxy for its cumulative experience relative to that of other companies in the same industry. Therefore (although there are many exceptions to the rule), a good starting assumption for considering pricing strategies is that the higher a company's market share is, the lower its unit costs are relative to the costs of its competitors—irrespective of where the industry in aggregate stands on the experience curve. For example, if company A has a higher market share than B which, in turn, has a higher share than C, D, and other companies in the industry, comparative unit costs at a given point in time might be something like those shown in Figure 11–5.

This type of cost structure happens to be rather typical of most American industries. And because it is, the pricing strategies adopted by companies A and B, the low-cost producers, can have a profound impact on the specific shape of the industry's life cycle of profitability. It also can provide some important clues regarding the beliefs of the leading companies' managements about the growth prospects of the industry and the nature of the competitive environment. The clues can be outlined as follows:[10]

1. If the pricing behavior of the market leaders can be described as umbrella pricing or rate-of-return pricing, it is reasonable to infer that they view the industry as having good growth prospects with little likelihood of rampant competition. With umbrella pricing, companies A and B tend to set their prices at a level slightly above their estimate of the unit costs of the higher cost producers. The result is that prices do not change frequently; the low-market-share producers earn a modest rate of return; and the high-market-share producers make very high rates of return.

Presumably, if A and B have adopted this strategy (as evidenced by relative price stability and a high rate of return by the market leaders), they must expect that it will enable them to grow satisfactorily without needing to gain additional market share. Therefore, they must anticipate *(a)* that the overall market will be a growth

---

[10]The discussion in this section is, admittedly, somewhat simplistic. It does not take into account the fact that each of the competitors in an industry tries to differentiate its own product (for example, by quality or service to customers). Obviously, the more successful a company is in differentiating its product, the less an outsider can infer from its pricing decisions anything about the basic nature of the industry. See, for example, Earl L. Bailey, ed., *Pricing Practices and Strategies,* (New York: The Conference Board, 1978).

*FIGURE 11–5*   **Relationship Between Market Share and Unit Costs**

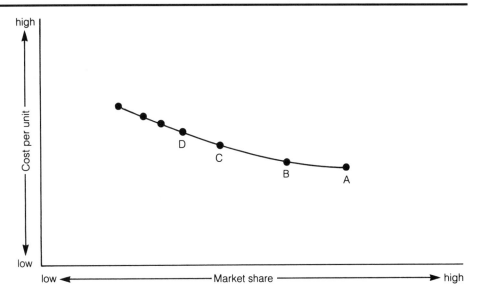

market and *(b)* that the costs of entry by new competitors or the costs of gaining market share by the existing competitors are too high to make such competitive assaults likely. (Costs, in this context, would include capital requirements, technical skills, advertising and promotion, establishing distribution channels, and so forth.) Of course, A and B may be wrong in their assumptions, and a good investment analyst must consider that possibility. But clues to the thinking of the market leaders, from what they do rather than merely from what they say, is valuable investment information.

2. If the pricing behavior of companies A and B can be described as experience-curve pricing, it is reasonable to infer that they view the industry as having good growth prospects but are concerned about competitive inroads. With experience-curve pricing, the low-cost producers reduce prices steadily over time as their unit costs fall with cumulative experience. This has two effects: *(a)* it helps to speed up the broadening of the market, and *(b)* if the higher-cost producers wish to stay in the market, they must follow prices down. The result is that A and B earn satisfactory rates of return (although not as high as with umbrella pricing), while the low-market-share producers are under continuous profit pressure and are financially unable to invest in enough new capacity to sustain their market share. Similarly, potential new entrants into the industry are discouraged from doing so.

Observation of the behavior of many growth industries during the past 30 years suggests that umbrella pricing has largely given way to experience-curve pricing. The electronics industry offers a good illustration. During the 1950s, when transistor growth was proceeding rapidly, the market leaders did not reduce prices as much as unit costs were falling. Profits soared, bringing new entrants flooding into the business and depressing profits thereafter. On the basis of this lesson, manufacturers of integrated circuits have been much more aggressive in cutting prices along with costs. (Indeed, this policy has recently come into conflict with their own capital requirements for expansion.) The moral is clear: experience-curve pricing behavior is a clue to the investor that managements foresee substantial volume growth opportunities in an industry, but it also is a warning to the investor to be very cautious in predicting the long-term success of weak competitors in the industry.

3. If pricing in an industry appears to reflect mainly the changing cyclical balance between the market's demands for its product and the industry's productive capacity, rather than a considered strategy of umbrella pricing or experience-curve pricing, investment analysts usually have a signal that managements believe the industry is in, or is nearing, the stabilization phase of its life cycle. The aluminum industry provides a good illustration of this statement. For after many decades of steadily reducing prices (at least in relation to the general price level if not in absolute terms) and broadening the uses of aluminum, the managements of aluminum companies in recent years have made great efforts to limit capacity expansion and to raise prices whenever demand permits.[11] Only when demand falls sharply relative to existing productive capacity do they cut prices. It seems reasonable to infer that their focus on keeping prices and profit margins high reflects their belief that volume growth can no longer be relied upon to provide good earnings gains.

Investment analysts must recognize that this type of pricing runs the risk of encouraging aluminum users to switch to substitute materials, which would aggravate the natural slowing of demand.[12] The key to whether the strategy boomerangs or not is the so-called price elasticity of demand for the product—the percentage change in quantity demanded per percentage change in price. As one writer puts it: "Just as some industries have supply characteristics that make them very good at raising production, some industries have demand characteristics that make them superb at raising prices . . . people will buy about the same amounts of its products at virtually any price." He notes, however, that "it helps if there is . . . a cartel to constrain supply and to insure price discipline."[13]

# ■ ANALYSIS OF CYCLICAL VARIATIONS AROUND TRENDS

## Information Required

An adequate study of the cyclical behavior of an industry should cover a period long enough to encompass several recessions and should provide an overview which includes:

1. A comparison of the sales of the industry with one or more broad economic measures such as gross national product, personal consumption expenditures, producers' durable equipment outlays, and so forth. A convenient source of industry sales data is Standard & Poor's *Analysts Handbook*, which contains earnings statement and balance sheet information for the dozens of industries included in S&P

---

[11]See John Merwin, "Too Big to Quit, Too Rich to Fail," *Forbes,* February 25, 1985.

[12]See Geoffrey Smith, "The New Alchemists," *Forbes,* April 9, 1984.

[13]James Gipson, "Growth on the Demand Curve: The New Kind of Growth," *Journal of Portfolio Management,* Winter 1980.

stock price indexes.[14] Macroeconomic data are published in the *Survey of Current Business*.

2. A similar comparison to the above, but in physical unit rather than dollar terms. Many trade associations publish unit volume data for their industries, but in general such data are not directly available for most industries. A useful proxy can be one or more of the industry components of the Federal Reserve Board's Industrial Production Index (although it must be recognized that production and sales often differ over short time periods due to inventory accumulation or liquidation). The production indexes are published in the *Federal Reserve Bulletin* and supplementary releases. As for the broad economic measures, these are published in real (constant-dollar) terms, in addition to current-dollar terms, thus facilitating industry volume comparisons with overall economic volume data. In addition, the composite FRB Industrial Production Index is itself an excellent monthly indicator of the aggregate movement of economic activity.

3. A comparison of the selling prices of the industry with aggregate price behavior. Here the analyst can use the Bureau of Labor Statistics' Producer Price Index or the Consumer Price Index. Both of these series measure not only aggregate price behavior but also disaggregate the data into dozens of different product indexes. The figures are published in the *Monthly Labor Review* and supplementary releases.

4. A comparison of the response of profit margins of the industry (for example as published by Standard & Poor's in the *Analysts Handbook*) to changes in sales volume and selling prices.

For greatest insight into cyclical patterns it is best to utilize monthly or quarterly data, rather than annual data, since business cycles typically overlap calendar years. Moreover, it is best to use seasonally adjusted data since the operations of many industries are influenced by a recurring seasonal pattern in the demand for their products or in their mode of production. While many of the industrial production indexes and price indexes mentioned above are published in seasonally adjusted form, many are not; and corporate sales and earnings data are not. Of course, computer programs are available which enable the security analyst to make such adjustments, but this may be too much of a chore. If it is, and if observation of the raw data leads the analyst to believe that there is a strong seasonal pattern in the industry under review, it may be helpful to express each month's or quarter's figure as a percentage increase or decrease from the same period in the prior year (which presumably was affected by the same seasonal factors) rather than just focus on the raw data.

## Ratio Analysis of the Data

Once the necessary data are assembled, one of two simple analytical techniques may be used to determine the nature of the industry's cyclical behavior. The first technique is ratio analysis. The industry data are divided by the aggregate data, and the

---

[14]Admittedly, the S&P industry groups include only large publicly owned firms and thus may not be completely representative of the whole industry. (Of course, since these are the firms of major investment interest, the data may be even more relevant than if the coverage was more comprehensive.) Another factor which may make the S&P data less than ideal is the multi-industry nature of many large companies that are classified in a particular industry grouping.

**FIGURE 11–6    Ratio of Electronic Components Production to Total Industrial Production**

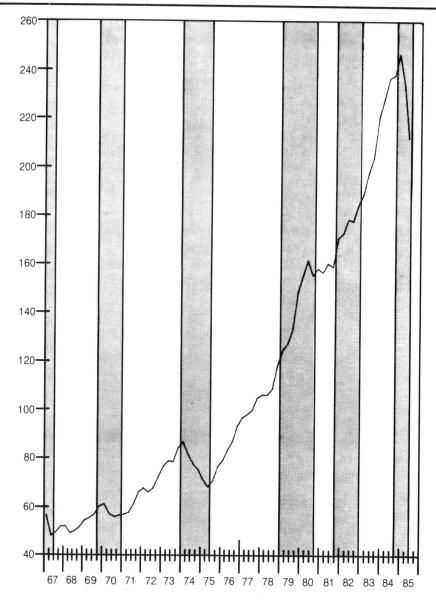

direction of movement of the ratio indicates whether the industry is doing better or worse than the aggregate with which it is being compared. For example, Figure 11–6 shows the ratio of the FRB index of electronic components production to the aggregate industrial production index. The shaded areas on the chart represent periods when the aggregate index was level or declining—that is, when the overall economy was in "minirecession" or full-blown recession.

This chart reveals that the output of electronic components has been in a strong secular uptrend relative to the total economy. However, this secular trend has been

**FIGURE 11–7   Prices of Semiconductors Relative to Producer Prices of All Goods**

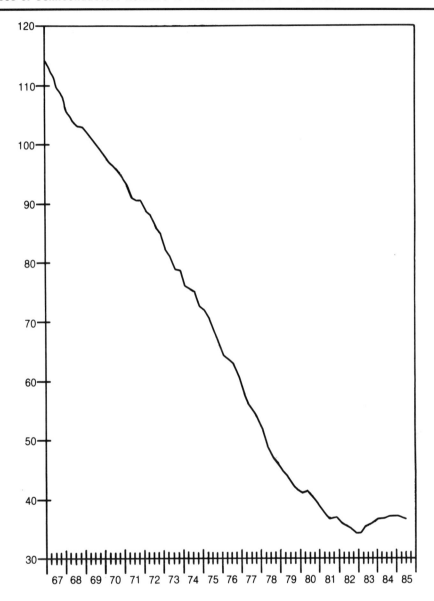

pierced repeatedly by relative downturns, sometimes quite severe, during periods of general economic weakness.[15]

---

[15]A relative downturn does not necessarily mean that electronic component output actually falls. A relative downturn can also occur if the rate of growth of components slows markedly. Note also that the electronic components industry did quite well during the 1979–80 and 1982 economic slowdowns, although it was devastated in 1985.

Figure 11–7 plots the ratio of the producer price index of semiconductors to the aggregate producer price index. The chart reveals, until quite recently, a classic pattern of experience-curve pricing. Except for a few brief periods, semiconductor prices dropped steadily as unit costs dropped. The more recent change in this pattern may be accounted for by several factors, according to knowledgeable industry sources. Most importantly, domestic semiconductor manufacturers have been trying to shift their product mix to higher-priced, higher-margined products due to the onslaught of Japanese competition in commodity-type products. These industry observers generally expect a resumption of aggressive relative price reductions.

In summary, Figures 11–6 and 11–7 reveal a pronounced sensitivity of electronic component unit volume to the overall business cycle, but the dominant influence on the industry's pricing has been production costs and business strategy rather than the general economy's cycle.

# Scatter Diagrams and Regression Analysis

In addition to the ratio analysis technique, the relationship between an industry and the macroeconomy (or indeed the relationship between any two sets of data) can be observed with the use of scatter diagrams and regression analysis. The scatter diagram gives a visual image of the relationship, and the regression analysis quantifies the relationship.

Figure 11–8 is a scatter diagram relating quarterly sales of the companies in Standard & Poor's Semiconductor Stock Price Index to quarterly Gross National Product. The semiconductor data are in sales per index share terms, while GNP is in trillions of dollars at seasonally adjusted annual rates. The period covered is 1978 through 1984. The dot for any given quarter represents the point at which the value for GNP that quarter (the horizontal scale) intersects the value for semiconductor sales that quarter (the vertical scale). The line drawn through the dots is a line of regression which was calculated using a standard computer program. (Analysts not wishing to bother with precise computations usually can do almost as good a job by simply drawing in a freehand line which seems to fit the data.)

The equation of the regression line is:

$$\text{Semiconductor sales per share} = (3.66 \times \text{GNP}) - 1.09$$
$$R^2 = 91\% \text{ and the } t\text{-statistic for the GNP coefficient is } 16.6$$

This equation suggests a normal relationship of S&P semiconductor sales to GNP as follows:

| GNP<br>($ trillions; annual rate) | Semiconductor Sales per Share<br>(quarterly rate) |
|---|---|
| 2.0 | 6.23 |
| 2.5 | 8.06 |
| 3.0 | 9.89 |
| 3.5 | 11.72 |

It will be noted that most of the dots are fairly close to the regression line; $R_2$ is a rather high 91 percent; and the GNP coefficient has a strongly significant $t$-statistic.

**FIGURE 11–8   Semiconductor Industry Sales versus GNP (1978–1984)**

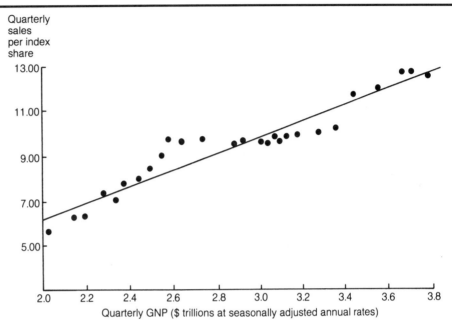

Indeed, the overall relationship is so high that an investor might be tempted to use it as the basis for short-term semiconductor sales forecasting.

For example, in the fourth quarter of 1984, GNP was $3.76 trillion, at an annual rate, and semiconductor sales (per index share) were 12.72—almost exactly what they should have been based on the regression line (12.67). Suppose the investor at that time had an economic forecast in hand (for example, from a brokerage firm's research department) which predicted that GNP would grow very slowly in the coming year and would be only $3.95 trillion by the fourth quarter of 1985—a gain of only 5 percent, or little more than the rate of inflation. In other words, the prediction was that 1985 would be a minirecession year.

Armed with the line of regression, the investor might predict that semiconductor sales would grow from the actual figure of 12.72, in the fourth quarter of 1984, to a normal 13.37 (3.66 × 3.95 − 1.09) in the fourth quarter of 1985. If the investor made such a seemingly plausible forecast, he or she would be making one of the most widespread *misuses* of this type of regression analysis.

The close relationship of semiconductor sales and GNP to a large degree reflects the fact that they both have had upward-trend rates of growth. Therefore, a regression of the two data series should be used mainly to predict the *trend values* of semiconductor sales but not *short-term cyclical variations around trend*. Since, as was shown in the earlier ratio analysis, unit sales of electronic components usually decelerate sharply during recessions and minirecessions and since unit prices have followed a fairly steady downtrend, it would be normal to expect fourth quarter 1985 semiconductor sales to be well below trend in view of the relatively bearish GNP forecast. (Indeed, this actually turned out to be the case.)

**FIGURE 11–9** *Semiconductor Industry Profit Margins versus Sales Changes (1978–1984)*

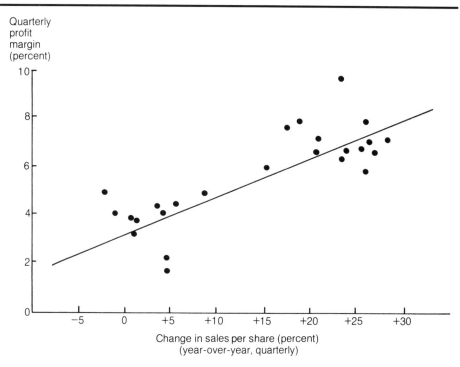

As for semiconductor *profits* during the course of the business cycle, Figure 11–9 shows how quarterly profit margins (net income as a percent of sales) of the S&P Semiconductor group rose and fell with quarterly changes in sales (year-over-year percentage changes each quarter) of the group from 1978 through 1984.

The equation of the regression line is:

$$\text{Profit margin} = (.16 \times \text{sales change}) + 3.2$$
$$R^2 = 64\% \text{ and the } t\text{-statistic for the sales coefficient is } 6.5$$

This means that when sales are growing rapidly, say at a rate of 20 percent year-over-year, profit margins will typically be in excess of 6 percent (.16 × 20 + 3.2). But when sales growth slows, for example to less than 5 percent, during recessions, profit margins are likely to plunge to less than 4 percent; indeed, profits may well disappear during such periods (and, indeed, did in 1985).

# ■ SUMMARY

An adequate understanding of an industry from an investment viewpoint requires judgments about the industry's probable trend rate of growth and about probable cyclical variations around the trend. We have described methods of investigating both the trends and cycles of an industry.

A first approach to trend analysis involves the concept of industrial life cycles, whereby industries evolve from early development to rapid expansion of the surviving companies, leading ultimately to maturity and even decline. In most industries, there has been a marked speedup in the transition from one life cycle stage to another.

In order to judge what state in the life cycle an industry will be operating in during the years ahead, and therefore what its trend rate of growth is likely to be, it helps to view the industry in terms of the uses for its products and services. We showed how the supplying industry's growth trends can be inferred from the growth trends of the users of its output and from the degree to which it has penetrated its user markets.

An important adjunct to life cycle analysis, which has traditionally been *sales* oriented, is to try to understand the implications of sales trends for trends in *profitability*. Here, we have tried to convey the importance of appreciating the interaction of pricing strategies and costs of production. An investigation of the pricing strategies of the leading companies in an industry can provide a clue to what the managements of those companies themselves believe to be the probable trends of growth in the industry.

Once the investor has made a judgment about probable trends, cyclical variations around the trends must be considered. To do this, it is best to separate the cyclical influences on unit volume, prices, and profit margins. Methods of examining the cycles in these factors by ratio analysis and regression analysis were illustrated.

---

## SUGGESTED READINGS

*Annual Encyclopedia of Business Information Services*. Detroit: Gale Research.

Brownstone, David M., and Gorton Carruth. *Where to Find Business Information*. New York: John Wiley & Sons, 1979.

Fruhan, William E., Jr. *Financial Strategy*. Homewood, Ill.: Richard D. Irwin, 1979.

Ghemawat, Pankaj. "Building Strategy on the Experience Curve." *Harvard Business Review,* March-April 1985.

Porter, Michael E. *Competitive Advantage: Creating and Sustaining Superior Performance*. New York: The Free Press, 1985.

———— . *Competitive Strategy: Techniques for Analyzing Industries and Competitors*. New York: The Free Press, 1980.

Reekie, W. Duncan. *Industry, Prices and Markets*. New York: John Wiley & Sons, 1979.

Wheelwright, Steven C., and Spyros Makridakis. *Forecasting Methods for Management*. 3rd ed. New York: John Wiley & Sons, 1980.

# CHAPTER

## 12

# *Company Analysis*

*Shallow men believe in luck, wise and strong men in cause and effect.*

Ralph Waldo Emerson

Having dealt, in the previous chapter, with relationships between macroeconomic developments and industry trends and cycles, we move now to the individual company level. First, we show how investment analysts can draw upon their understanding of industry dynamics to reach a preliminary judgment about the sales and earnings potential of a company. Next, an analytical framework is presented for translating this preliminary and rather generalized judgment into a more precise statement about the company's prospects, including a framework for analyzing risk aribtrage opportunities. Finally, we shift from the sometimes deceptive accuracy of numerical analysis to a qualitative consideration of the company's management style. This final step can often affect the degree of confidence which analysts will have in the company's ability to translate its potential into a reality.

## ■ *COMPANY PROSPECTS BASED ON PRODUCT-LINE ANALYSIS*

A very helpful first step in company analysis is to determine the industry distribution of the company's revenues and to make a judgment about the stage of the industrial life cycle in which each major industry segment is positioned. Many companies have the bulk of their operations in one industry. These include, for example, the major oil companies, automobile producers, retailers, utilities, etc. However, in the increasingly complex business world of recent years, more companies than ever have diversified beyond the industry of their origin. A recent article in *The Economist* magazine of England stated:

> According to Professor Derek Channon of the Manchester Business School, who keeps track of such things, 80 percent of the top 200 manufacturing and service companies in America (versus 30 percent in 1950) and 65 percent in Britain (25 percent in 1950) are now in more than one line of business. Of these companies, he reckons a third in America and a quarter in Britain are sufficiently diversified to be called conglomerates. In 1960, only about 5 percent in either country could be so described.[1]

Consider the company we have used earlier to illustrate various procedures of security analysis—Texas Instruments. The annual reports of that company document the following distribution of gross revenues (before deducting intracompany transfers):

|  | 1976 | 1980 | 1984 |
|---|---|---|---|
| Components (e.g., integrated circuits) ...................... | 39% | 39% | 46% |
| Digital products (e.g., mini- and microcomputers) .............. | 24 | 26 | 19 |
| Government electronics (e.g., surveillance systems) ............ | 20 | 19 | 24 |
| Metallurgical materials (clad metals) ....................... | 9 | 5 | 4 |
| Services (seismic data for oil exploration) .................. | 8 | 11 | 7 |
| Total revenues ..................................... | 100 | 100 | 100 |

Clearly, only a professional business or security analyst would have the resources to evaluate the life-cycle status of each of these major product categories of Texas Instruments. However, based on a general knowledge acquired from a regular reading of *The Wall Street Journal, Business Week, Fortune*, etc., supplemented by a trip to the library to read, say, the material contained in Standard & Poor's *Industry Surveys*, even nonprofessionals can make some reasonable judgments. For example, they might reach the following general conclusions:

> Components—Continued rapid growth, but highly cyclical.
> Digital products—Above-average growth, but maturing and cyclical.
> Government electronics—Steady, somewhat-above-average growth.
> Metallurgical—Slow growth and highly cyclical.
> Seismic services—Slow growth, perhaps speeding up in the 1990s.
>     Total:  Above-average growth, but cyclical.

# ■ ANALYSIS OF EARNINGS GROWTH COMPONENTS

After an overall judgment has been made about the prospective growth and cyclical nature of a company's major lines of business, a deeper understanding can be gained by taking a different perspective on the sources of its earnings. A simple, but analytically powerful, truism is that a company's earnings per share is equal to the

---

[1]*The Economist*, June 15, 1985, p. 76.

company's rate of return on stockholders' equity multiplied by the per share value of stockholders' equity.[2] That is:

$$\frac{\text{Net income}}{\text{per share}} = \frac{\text{Net income}}{\text{Stockholders' equity}} \times \frac{\text{Stockholders' equity}}{\text{Number of common shares}}$$

$$= \frac{\text{Net income}}{\text{Number of common shares}}$$

It follows from this relationship that growth of net income per share can stem from either an increase in stockholders' equity per share, or from an increase in return on stockholders' equity, or from some combination of the two. The principal source of growth of stockholders' equity is earnings retention—that is, paying out only a portion of net income in cash dividends to common stockholders and retaining and reinvesting the balance. The contribution of earnings retention to growth of net income per share can be illustrated by a numerical example. Assume that a company is earning 15 percent on stockholders' equity—that is, $1.50 of net income per common share for every $10 of stockholders' equity per share. And assume, further, that the company has a dividend payout ratio of 40 percent—that is, it pays dividends of $0.40 per share for every $1 of available earnings. Its retention rate, then, is 60 percent—$0.60 plowed back into the business out of every $1 earned ($0.90 plowed back on $1.50 earned).

Now, if the company continues to earn 15 percent on the old capital and, in addition, is able to put the new, plowed-back funds to work at a 15 percent return, its earnings per share will grow by 9 percent. This may be shown as follows:

$$
\begin{aligned}
\text{Earnings on old capital} &= 15\% \times \$10.00 = \$1.50 \text{ per share} \\
\text{Earnings on new capital} &= 15\% \times \$\ 0.90 = \underline{\ \ .135} \text{ per share} \\
\text{New level of earnings per share} &= \qquad\qquad\qquad \$1.635 \\
\text{Growth of earnings per share} &= \$1.635/\$1.50 \quad = 9\%
\end{aligned}
$$

An alternative way of stating the relationship is:

$$
\begin{aligned}
\text{Earnings growth} &= \text{Return on equity} \times \text{Retention rate,} \\
&= \text{Return on equity} \times (1 - \text{Payout ratio}), \\
&= 15\% \times (1 - 40\%) = 15\% \times 60\%, \\
&= 9\%
\end{aligned}
$$

Thus, earnings growth and dividend growth are determined by the simultaneous interaction of return on equity and dividend policy. Security analysts place great emphasis on the product of rate of return and retention rate. It is known as the internal growth rate, and will be examined in depth in the sections which follow, with particular emphasis on:

Operating Profit Margins,
Asset Utilization,
Financial Policies, and
Income Taxes.

---

[2]Stockholders' equity, also referred to as book value, equals the balance sheet value of common stock and surplus items or, alternatively, total assets minus liabilities and preferred stock.

## *Internal Growth Rate Components of Semiconductor Companies*

To illustrate the key concepts, we shall continue to use Texas Instruments as an example and will compare its financial statistics to those of three of its leading competitors—Advanced Micro Devices, Intel, and Motorola. The first two are engaged almost exclusively in the semiconductor industry and the third is, like Texas Instruments, more diversified. Table 12–1 shows the internal growth rate components for these four companies during the decade 1975–84. Also shown for each component is the median for the period. For simplicity, all data in this and subsequent tables are taken directly as reported by the companies, without making allowances for the many accounting problems described in Chapter 9. Also, values for asset and equity accounts are averages of beginning-of-year and end-of-year amounts, to allow for earnings plowback and new financing during the year. Thus, for example, the return on equity refers to earnings relative to average of beginning- and end-of-year equity.

The data in Table 12–1 reveal the following:

The pure semiconductor companies, Advanced Micro Devices and Intel, had much higher median rates of return on equity (23 to 25 percent) than their more diversified competitors, Motorola and Texas Instruments (14 to 16 percent). All except Motorola exhibited a very high year-to-year variability around the median return, and all except Motorola did less well in the latter half of the ten-year period than in the earlier years.

The pure companies plowed back all of their earnings into the business (that is, paid no dividends), whereas the diversified companies appeared to have a policy of paying out about 25 percent and retaining about 75 percent.

The combined result of earnings rate and retention was that Advanced Micro Devices and Intel had internal growth rates in excess of 20 percent, on average (although trending downward), while Motorola and Texas Instruments had internal growth rates of 11 to 12 percent.

These data confirm the overall outlook resulting from the life-cycle analysis of Texas Instruments' product lines, presented earlier, which was for above-average growth, although cyclical. Still further confirmation of this conclusion can be obtained by more detailed earnings component analysis, as described below.

## *Components of Return on Equity*

Many years ago, the duPont Corporation recognized that its operations could be managed best if its executives were provided with data that decomposed the return on equity into a number of critical variables. The duPont analytical technique has since become widely adopted by both corporate managers and investment analysts. Several statistical services publish data for investors which isolate the major components of the return on equity of hundreds of different companies.[3] Each has a somewhat different format, but the general idea should become clear from the following discussion.

---

[3]For example, see the Standard & Poor's Corporation publication, *Financial Dynamics*.

**TABLE 12–1    Internal Growth Rate Components, Major Semiconductor Companies**

| | Advanced Micro Devices | | | Intel | | |
|---|---|---|---|---|---|---|
| | Return on Average Equity | Retention Rate | Internal Growth Rate | Return on Average Equity | Retention Rate | Internal Growth Rate |
| 1975 | 13% | 100% | 13% | 26% | 100% | 26% |
| 1976 | 31 | 100 | 31 | 28 | 100 | 28 |
| 1977 | 16 | 100 | 16 | 24 | 100 | 24 |
| 1978 | 21 | 100 | 21 | 35 | 100 | 35 |
| 1979 | 32 | 100 | 32 | 31 | 100 | 31 |
| 1980 | 24 | 100 | 24 | 26 | 100 | 26 |
| 1981 | 7 | 100 | 7 | 6 | 100 | 6 |
| 1982 | 13 | 100 | 13 | 6 | 100 | 6 |
| 1983 | 31 | 100 | 31 | 14 | 100 | 14 |
| 1984 | 37 | 100 | 37 | 16 | 100 | 16 |
| Median | 23 | 100 | 23 | 25 | 100 | 25 |
| | Motorola | | | Texas Instruments | | |
| 1975 | 7% | 52% | 4% | 11% | 63% | 7% |
| 1976 | 14 | 76 | 10 | 16 | 75 | 12 |
| 1977 | 14 | 75 | 11 | 17 | 72 | 12 |
| 1978 | 15 | 74 | 11 | 18 | 71 | 13 |
| 1979 | 16 | 75 | 12 | 19 | 74 | 14 |
| 1980 | 17 | 76 | 13 | 20 | 78 | 16 |
| 1981 | 14 | 71 | 10 | 9 | 57 | 5 |
| 1982 | 11 | 65 | 7 | 11 | 67 | 7 |
| 1983 | 13 | 75 | 10 | (11) | N.M. | N.M. |
| 1984 | 18 | 81 | 15 | 23 | 85 | 20 |
| Median | 14 | 75 | 11 | 16 | 73 | 12 |

***Return on Assets.*** If we examine the structure of corporate earnings statements we find, in essence:

1. Sales (or revenues).
2. Minus: Operating expenses (cost of goods sold, depreciation, selling, general and administrative expenses).
3. Plus or minus: Other income or expense items.
4. Minus: Interest charges.
5. Minus: Income taxes.
6. Equals: Earnings.

The best measure of operating earnings in this structure is line 1 minus line 2. However, for convenience one can also deduct (or add) line 3, the company's various nonoperating items, unless these are very large and should be viewed separately. The net of lines 1, 2, and 3 is known as EBIT—earnings before interest and taxes. When EBIT is expressed as a percentage of sales, we have an excellent measure of operating efficiency. This measure is not affected by a company's mode of financing or by taxation, as is the more familiar net profit margin (earnings after interest and taxes, divided by sales).

The EBIT margin measures a company's effectiveness in minimizing expenses in relation to sales. It does not measure a company's effectiveness in minimizing the amount of assets (current and fixed) necessary to support its level of sales. A measure of this characteristic of a company's operations is known as asset turnover, sales divided by assets.[4]

Isolating these two measures—the EBIT margin and the asset turnover—has another useful property. When the two measures are multiplied by each other, the result is the ratio EBIT/assets. This is the company's pretax, preinterest return on assets. It is a comprehensive measure of profitability which can be used to study a given company's performance over time and, perhaps more importantly, can be used to compare and contrast the profitability of many different companies because it is independent of differences in modes of financing and differences in applicable tax laws.[5] To restate the relationship algebraically:

$$\frac{EBIT}{Sales} \times \frac{Sales}{Total\ assets} = \frac{EBIT}{Total\ assets}$$

(Pretax, preinterest × (Asset turnover) = (Pretax, preinterest
profit margin)                                    return on assets)

Turning again to the four semiconductor companies in our illustration, Table 12–2 shows the components of their return on assets from 1975 to 1984. The data reveal the following:

The typical EBIT/sales margin for the diversified companies has been about 10 percent. For the purer semiconductor companies, EBIT margins were higher, tending to fall in a 10 to 20 percent range. Intel's margins in excess of 20 percent from 1975 to 1980 were quite atypical for the industry.

Asset turnover for the industry, as evidenced by these four companies, has typically been about 1.5, but Texas Instruments' turnover has rather consistently been significantly higher than that of its competitors. As a result, Texas Instruments' return on assets was generally higher (although more variable) than that of its diversified competitor, Motorola, but not as high as the purer semiconductor companies because of its lower margin on sales.

What appears to have happened is that Texas Instruments has aggressively pushed sales of low-margin products. Its challenge, therefore, is to shift its sales mix toward higher-margin products without negatively impacting turnover—a challenge that the

---

[4]As with equity, the average of beginning- and end-of-year assets is used.

[5]There are limits, however, to how far one should push such comparisons. For example, it would not be very meaningful to compare the return on assets of a bank with that of a manufacturing company.

**TABLE 12–2   Return on Asset Components, Major Semiconductor Companies**

| | Advanced Micro Devices | | | Intel | | |
|---|---|---|---|---|---|---|
| | EBIT/ Sales | Sales/ Average Assets | EBIT/ Average Assets | EBIT/ Sales | Sales/ Average Assets | EBIT/ Average Assets |
| 1975 . . . . . . . . . . . . | 8% | 1.4 | 12% | 24% | 1.5 | 37% |
| 1976 . . . . . . . . . . . . | 14 | 1.8 | 26 | 23 | 1.7 | 40 |
| 1977 . . . . . . . . . . . . | 10 | 1.6 | 16 | 22 | 1.5 | 33 |
| 1978 . . . . . . . . . . . . | 14 | 1.6 | 23 | 22 | 1.4 | 30 |
| 1979 . . . . . . . . . . . . | 17 | 1.6 | 28 | 23 | 1.5 | 35 |
| 1980 . . . . . . . . . . . . | 13 | 1.6 | 20 | 23 | 1.3 | 30 |
| 1981 . . . . . . . . . . . . | 3 | 1.2 | 3 | 7 | 1.0 | 7 |
| 1982 . . . . . . . . . . . . | 6 | 1.3 | 8 | 5 | 0.9 | 5 |
| 1983 . . . . . . . . . . . . | 17 | 1.4 | 25 | 17 | 0.8 | 14 |
| 1984 . . . . . . . . . . . . | 20 | 1.5 | 29 | 19 | 0.9 | 17 |
| Median . . . . . . . . . . | 14 | 1.6 | 22 | 22 | 1.4 | 30 |
| | Motorola | | | Texas Instruments | | |
| 1975 . . . . . . . . . . . . | 8% | 1.3 | 10% | 9% | 1.4 | 13% |
| 1976 . . . . . . . . . . . . | 12 | 1.4 | 16 | 11 | 1.6 | 18 |
| 1977 . . . . . . . . . . . . | 12 | 1.4 | 17 | 11 | 1.7 | 18 |
| 1978 . . . . . . . . . . . . | 11 | 1.4 | 16 | 10 | 1.8 | 19 |
| 1979 . . . . . . . . . . . . | 11 | 1.5 | 17 | 10 | 1.9 | 19 |
| 1980 . . . . . . . . . . . . | 10 | 1.5 | 16 | 10 | 1.9 | 20 |
| 1981 . . . . . . . . . . . . | 9 | 1.5 | 14 | 5 | 1.8 | 9 |
| 1982 . . . . . . . . . . . . | 7 | 1.4 | 11 | 6 | 1.8 | 10 |
| 1983 . . . . . . . . . . . . | 8 | 1.4 | 12 | (6) | 1.7 | (11) |
| 1984 . . . . . . . . . . . . | 9 | 1.5 | 14 | 9 | 1.9 | 17 |
| Median . . . . . . . . . . | 10 | 1.4 | 15 | 10 | 1.8 | 18 |

experience of its competitors suggests cannot be met. Its historical median EBIT/ assets return of 18 percent is probably the best it can do in the future.[6]

***Leverage and Taxes.***   At this point, the analyst must take account of the fact that companies do not finance themselves solely with equity—that is, common stock and retained earnings. They regularly utilize both short-term and long-term debt. (Some companies also issue preferred stock which, though technically equity, is usually thought of as quasi debt.) Much of this debt is interest-bearing, for example, bank loans and bonds; but much is not, for instance accounts payable.

The ratio interest/assets measures the joint impact of (*a*) the proportion of assets financed with interest-bearing debt and (*b*) the average interest rate on this debt. The ratio assets/common equity, which rises as the total amount of debt supporting a

---

[6]A professional security analyst would examine each expense component of the EBIT/sales ratio and each asset component of the sales/asset ratio before reaching final conclusions. For example, it is helpful to trace the history of cost of goods sold/sales, other expense/sales, sales/fixed assets, sales/ inventory, etc. For illustrations see William E. Fruhan, Jr., *Financial Strategy* (Homewood, Ill.: Richard D. Irwin, 1979). Also see the third edition of this text, pp. 312–19.

company's assets rises, is a more comprehensive measure of financial leverage[7] than the measure used in bond analysis, namely long-term debt/total capital (see Chapter 13).

If we now subtract from the EBIT/assets return the amount of interest burden (interest/assets) and multiply by the financial leverage factor (assets/common equity), we have the pretax return on common equity.[8]

$$\left[ \frac{\text{EBIT}}{\text{Assets}} - \frac{\text{Interest}}{\text{Assets}} \right] \times \frac{\text{Assets}}{\substack{\text{Common} \\ \text{equity}}} = \frac{\text{Net income before taxes}}{\text{Common equity}}$$

$$\left[ \substack{\text{(Pretax, preinterest} \\ \text{return on assets)}} - \text{(Interest burden)} \right] \times \left( \substack{\text{Financial} \\ \text{leverage}} \right) = \text{(Pretax return on equity)}$$

Finally, a company's income tax rate (income taxes/net income before taxes) must be reflected. As described in Chapter 9, there are many reasons which may cause the tax rate of one company to be different from that of another company, even in the same industry.

If we multiply the pretax return on equity by the so-called tax retention rate (100 percent minus the tax rate), we come full circle to the original return on equity which we set out to analyze:

$$\frac{\text{Net before taxes}}{\text{Common equity}} \times \left[ 100\% - \frac{\text{Income taxes}}{\text{Net before taxes}} \right] = \frac{\text{Net income}^9}{\text{Common equity}}$$

(Pretax return on equity) ×      (Tax retention rate)      = (Return on equity)

***Putting It Together.*** Table 12–3 shows the median interest burden (1.5 percent), leverage ratio (1.9), and tax retention rate (55 percent) for Texas Instruments, along with the other return on equity components discussed previously.[10] The bottom line suggests that a 17 percent average ROE is a reasonable expectation for the company, somewhat higher than the 16 percent median ROE achieved from 1975 through 1984 and well above the ROE of the average industrial corporation in the United States.

---

[7]The term *financial leverage* differs from *operating leverage*. The latter refers to the relationship of fixed costs to variable costs. Where the fixed-cost proportion (depreciation and overhead as well as financial charges) is high, the volume of sales needed to break even is high. But once this breakeven point is exceeded, earnings rise more rapidly than sales. Conversely, losses are magnified at sales levels falling short of the breakeven point. For a good concise discussion of operating leverage, financial leverage, and the relationships between the two see chapters 5 and 15 of J. Fred Weston and Eugene F. Brigham, *Essentials of Managerial Finance,* 5th ed. (Hinsdale, Ill.: Dryden Press, 1979).

[8]Once again, we remind the reader that the data used to measure these relationships are based on average of beginning- and end-of-year assets and equity.

[9]Note that if the company has preferred stock outstanding, this net income figure will be before deducting preferred dividends. Therefore, to be accurate, a final step would be to deduct such dividends. Alternatively, preferred dividends could be included in the interest/assets ratio.

[10]A simpler version of the return on equity components analysis presented here short circuits explicit consideration of interest on debt. Instead of beginning with the EBIT margin, it begins with the pretax margin *after* interest has already been deducted, i.e., net before taxes/sales. Thus:

$$\frac{\text{Net before taxes}}{\text{Sales}} \times \frac{\text{Sales}}{\text{Assets}} = \frac{\text{Net before taxes}}{\text{Assets}}$$

(Pretax margin) × (Asset turnover) = (Pretax return on assets)

**TABLE 12–3   Components of Texas Instruments' Return on Equity**

|  | | |
|---|---|---|
| | EBIT margin (EBIT/sales) | 10.0% |
| × | Asset turnover (sales/assets) | × 1.8 |
| = | EBIT return on assets. | = 18.0% |
| − | Interest burden (interest/assets) | − 1.5% |
| = | Pretax return on assets | = 16.5% |
| × | Leverage (assets/equity) | × 1.9 |
| = | Pretax return on equity | = 31.0% |
| × | Tax retention rate (100% − (tax/net before tax)) | × 55.0% |
| = | Estimated return on equity | = 17.0% |

# Sources of Book Value Growth

Having examined the components of return on equity, we turn now to the other major source of growth in earnings per share, namely growth in book value per share. For most companies, book value per share increases mainly as a result of earnings retention. In addition, if the common stock of a company has a market price in excess of book value per share, the sale of additional shares at that price can create an increment to the book value of the existing shares. The prospects for each source of increasing book value per share should be considered by the investment analyst.

*Earnings Retention.*   Studies of corporate policies regarding the payment of dividends versus retention of earnings suggest that many interacting factors are at work in any given situation:

1. Most managements and boards of directors make an effort to project future requirements and new opportunities for investment in plant, equipment, and working capital. Against these projected uses of funds, they consider the probable availability and costs of alternative sources of funds—retained earnings, increased borrowing, sale of additional stock. Based on these estimates, they make judgments, at each quarterly dividend meeting, as to how much of the company's earnings to pay out and how much to retain.

2. These judgments are conditioned also by subjective attitudes toward debt, by a balancing of the desires and tax status of the principal stockholders against the desires and tax status of the other stockholders, and by the dividend payout ratios of competing companies.

3. In the background of all the calculations and judgments is a recognition that once a dividend rate is established, the stock market will take very unkindly to a

$$\frac{\text{Net before taxes}}{\text{Assets}} \times \frac{\text{Assets}}{\text{Common equity}} \times \left[100\% - \frac{\text{Income taxes}}{\text{Net before taxes}}\right] = \frac{\text{Net income}}{\text{Common equity}}$$

$$\begin{pmatrix}\text{Pretax return}\\ \text{on assets}\end{pmatrix} \times \begin{pmatrix}\text{Financial}\\ \text{leverage}\end{pmatrix} \times \ \ (\text{Tax retention rate}) \ \ \ = (\text{Return on equity})$$

While this version is simpler and in rather widespread use, it should be recognized that the pretax margin is less useful in comparing one company against another than the EBIT margin. The former reflects financial policies while the latter does not. To the extent that one seeks to measure *operating* efficiency through a profit margin calculation, the EBIT margin does this more effectively.

subsequent cut. Therefore, dividend rate increases tend to lag behind earnings increases and, once declared, tend to be maintained even when earnings decline. Thus, students of investments refer to "the information content of dividend changes." Dividend increases are viewed as a signal that management expects future earnings to be high enough to support a higher new dividend plateau, and dividend cuts are viewed as a signal that management expects a lower level of earnings for the foreseeable future.

Recognizing that these many factors influence corporate dividend and earnings-retention policies, the investment analyst should not assume that past payout and retention percentages will continue in the future before first considering whether there may be reasons for a change. In the case of the major semiconductor companies, we have seen that the pure companies, with very rapid growth rates, have followed a policy of plowing all earnings back into the business. The more diversified companies, Motorola and Texas Instruments, with many product lines in slower growth phases than semiconductors and thus less in need of constant capital infusions, have tended to pay out about 25 percent of earnings as cash dividends and to retain about 75 percent. There appear to be no reasons to expect any major changes in this policy in the near future, although a gradual increase of payout ratios is likely as the semiconductor industry itself begins to mature.

***Effects of Selling New Stock.*** Suppose a company's return on equity is 15 percent, its book value is $200 million, and it has 10 million shares outstanding. Book value per share is $20 and earnings per share $3 (15% × $20).

Suppose the company now raises $20 million of capital by selling 500,000 additional shares at two times book value, or $40 a share. Total book value rises 10 percent to $220 million and total shares outstanding 5 percent to 10.5 million. Book value per share is raised to $220/10.5, or $20.95 per share, an increase of almost 5 percent from the previous $20. This provides a basis for an equivalent 5 percent growth of earnings per share if the rate of return on equity can be maintained. That is, earnings per share would be 15% × $20.95, or $3.14 per share, an increase of almost 5 percent.

The potential impact on growth of earnings per share when new stock is sold at a premium over book value can be shown more generally, as follows:[11]

1. Let *P/BV* equal the ratio of the selling price of the new shares to the book value of the existing shares.

2. The percentage growth in dollar book value equals the percentage growth in number of shares multiplied by *P/BV*.

3. The percentage growth in per share book value, and therefore of earnings per share if rate of return on equity remains constant, equals:

$$\left[\frac{1 + \text{Percent growth in dollar book value}}{1 + \text{Percent growth in number of shares}}\right] - 1.0$$

---

[11]While the context of our discussion deals with substantial one-time sales of new shares, a number of companies sell small amounts of new shares on a more or less continuous basis, via employee stock option and savings plans. Over time, the aggregate of such sales can become quite large and can contribute meaningfully to the issuer's growth. Intel Corporation is a good example.

**4.** Substituting statement (2) in the numerator of statement (3), we have the growth rate of book value and earnings per share equal to:

$$\left[ \frac{1 + (\text{Percent growth in number of shares})(P/BV)}{1 + \text{Percent growth in number of shares}} \right] - 1.0$$

Further consideration of the last statement should make it apparent that another way book value per share can be increased is by retiring shares at a discount from existing book value. For example, suppose that a company has 10 million shares outstanding with a book value of $50 per share. And suppose that the company's stock is selling in the open market for $30 (a *P/BV* of 0.60). If the company has $60 million of excess cash which it uses to buy in 2 million shares at $30, the book value per share will be increased from $50 (500/10) to $55 (440/8), or by 10 percent. This can be shown, using our formula, as follows:

$$\left[ \frac{1 + (-20\%)(.60)}{1 + (-20\%)} \right] - 1.0 = \left[ \frac{1 - 12\%}{1 - 20\%} \right] - 1.0 = \left[ \frac{.88}{.80} \right] - 1.0 =$$
$$1.10 - 1.0 = .10$$

In addition to the sale of new stock for cash, when one company merges with another through an exchange of shares, the acquiring company in effect sells its stock for the assets of the acquired company. If the book value of the acquired assets exceeds the book value of the stock given up by the acquiring company to the shareholders of the acquired company, the result is that the book value per share of the surviving company will exceed that of the acquiring company. The result is exactly analogous to a sale of stock for cash. Whether the earnings per share of the surviving company increase proportionately to the increase in book value, or indeed whether they increase at all, depends, of course, on the rate of return earned by the surviving company.

Turning again to Texas Instruments, the historical record indicates that its stock generally trades at a significant premium over book value. For example, book value per share at the end of 1984 was $63, while the stock's price range in 1984–85 was $90–$150. Therefore, growth opportunities through the sale of new shares at a premium over book value (sale either for cash or via mergers) clearly exist for the company. This reinforces the conclusion of both the life-cycle and earnings component analyses that Texas Instruments, notwithstanding periodic severe cyclical downturns, is a company with above-average long-term earnings growth prospects.

# ■ *SPECIAL SITUATIONS AND RISK ARBITRAGE*

Aside from the price-to-book value and earnings per share relationships described above, mergers and other capital restructurings often create investment opportunities known as special situations. Special situations have three characteristics:

**1.** A unique corporate development is occurring which makes certain securities of the company, or of a related company, attractive apart from general economic, industry, or securities market conditions.

2. This corporate development is noncontinuing in nature. If not seized upon when it appears, the specific investment opportunity may be lost. The securities may continue to be worthwhile investments, but not as special situations.
3. The investment is amenable to fairly precise measurement of the magnitude of possible gains and losses. The probabilities of such gains and losses are less precisely measurable, but they are, nonetheless, capable of being estimated.

Special situations most often arise from the following types of corporate development:

*Tenders*. A company or an outsider desiring to gain control of the company offers to buy a stated number of shares, usually a a price above the current market.

*Mergers and Acquisitions*. Special situation opportunities can arise whether the merger is via cash or via an exchange of shares.

*Liquidations*. A company disposes of its assets and distributes the proceeds to its shareholders.

*Spin-offs*. A company decides to divest itself of a particular division or subsidiary by distributing shares in that entity to existing shareholders.

*Reorganizations*. When a company emerges from bankruptcy, the resulting reorganization may create opportunities to exchange old securities, bought at panic prices, for new securities with higher potential values.

*Recapitalizations*. Administrative changes in the capital structure of a company may involve a realignment of relationships among the company's securities with attendant profit possibilities.

Special situations arising from these corporate developments frequently are referred to as risk aribtrage opportunities, for reasons that will be apparent from the example given below.[12] It should be noted, however, that the term *special situation* often is used by financial advisory services and stockbrokers in a broader context to include unique investment opportunities arising from such factors as:

Hidden earnings or hidden assets
New technological developments
New management
New markets
Litigation
Tax rulings

**Example.** Columbia Pictures agreed to be acquired by the Coca-Cola Company. For each share of Columbia Pictures (then trading at $58), Coca-Cola (then trading

---

[12]One of the most famous risk arbitrageurs of our time has written a book on the subject. See Ivan F. Boesky, *Merger Mania* (New York: Holt, Rinehart & Winston, 1985).

at $33) would pay either cash or stock, at the Columbia Pictures owner's option, according to the following formulas:

**a.**   Cash of $32 ⅝ plus an amount equal to 1.2 times Coca Cola's average closing price during the 15 trading days prior to the effective date of the merger.

**b.**   1.2 shares of Coca Cola plus additional shares having a market value of $32 ⅝ based on the same average price as in (a).

The reason for offering either cash or stock stemmed basically from tax considerations. Putting taxes aside, the value of the exchange offer was $32 ⅝ plus 1.2 times Coca-Cola's future average price. But one did not have to know, or even guess at, that future price to have an investment opportunity because the spread could be locked in by the following arbitrage:

| | |
|---|---:|
| BUY 100 Columbia Pictures at $58 | |
| Cost: $5,800 plus commissions .............................. | ($5,850.00) |
| SELL SHORT 120 Coca-Cola at $33 | |
| Proceeds: $3,960 minus commissions ......................... | $3,900.00 |
| Receivable on merger date ............................... | 3,262.50 |
| Spread .......................................... | $1,312.50 |

***Rate of Return Factors.***   Having calculated that a spread of some $1,300 can be achieved, the next question is: What annualized rate of return does that spread represent? Several factors must be considered to answer the question—capital requirements and costs, time likely to elapse between the arbitrage and the consummation of the merger, and taxation of the profit.

The minimum amount of capital that will be required to establish the arbitrage will depend on the official margin requirements at the time. Assuming that both purchases and short sales require the posting of 50 percent margin, approximately $4,900 will be required in this arbitrage (50 percent of: ($5,800 + $3,960)). In addition, the margin purchase will involve a debit balance on which interest will have to be paid, thus reducing the spread to somewhat below $1,300, let's say to $1,250.[13] Thus, return to the investor will be approximately $1,250/$4,900, or about 25 percent.

But this 25 percent return is without reference to the time that will be needed to complete the merger. The faster the negotiations proceed, the higher will be the arbitrageur's *annualized rate of return.* Suppose, in this case, it is estimated that four months will elapse between the arbitrage date and the merger date. The annualized rate of return would then be three times 25 percent, or 75 percent.

Finally, depending on how the arbitrage is structured, the elapsed time, and which of the Coca-Cola options (cash or stock) is ultimately accepted, the profit may be taxed either as short-term income or as some combination of short-term and long-term capital gain. Clearly, the *net* realized rate of return will be importantly affected by tax considerations.

---

[13]These figures are applicable to trades by small individual investors. Professional arbitrageurs, dealing in large volume, have substantially lower capital requirements and capital costs. For example, they recapture most of the interest earned on the investment of the escrowed proceeds of their short sales.

To summarize, the reward variables in a special situation (whether an arbitrage or a more broadly defined special situation) include:

1. The workout values of the securities purchased and sold.
2. The amount and cost of capital invested.
3. The time elapsed between the transactions and the ultimate settlement.
4. The tax liability.

**Risk Variables.**   Whatever the estimated net rate of return, we know there is no free lunch in our economic system. What kinds of risks do special situations such as this involve? Several will readily come to mind:

1. The antitrust authorities may object and seek an injunction against the merger.
2. Key groups of investors may object to the deal and try to undo it.
3. Another company may make a different bid.
4. As the two companies' managements work out the details of the transaction, one of them may find out things about the other that they don't like and threaten to call the deal off.

Any or all of these developments will, at the very least, cause a lengthy time delay, and time delay reduces rate of return. Failure of the whole deal, moreover, would leave the investor exposed to the impact of market price fluctuations in the securities bought or sold short. No longer would there be a locked-in spread. Hence the appellation *risk arbitrage*.

# ■ MANAGEMENT: THE QUALITATIVE FACTOR

Professional security analysts have mixed views on the investment significance of the quality of a company's management. Some argue that management quality should not be considered as an independent factor in a stock's evaluation. Management's actions, according to this view, are already reflected in the company's sales growth, in its rate of return on assets and on equity, in the soundness of its balance sheet, and in all of the other "numbers" that influence the market value of the company's stock.

Another view is that an independent appraisal of management quality is very important when judging the value of a stock. According to this view, today's numbers often reflect decisions made by earlier generations of management, while tomorrow's numbers will reflect decisions made by current management. Since a stock's value should, at least in principle, be more a function of tomorrow's numbers than of today's or yesterday's, an appraisal of management quality should assist the valuation process.

Empirical evidence lends support to both views. On the one hand, many examples can be cited of "the knight-in-shining-armor CEO whose arrival suddenly recharges a sagging multiple" or "the wheeler-dealer CEO whose unpredictable moves give investors the jitters."[14] On the other hand, stock price data on hypothetical portfolios of companies receiving awards as best-managed suggest that lower returns are earned

---

[14]"The CEO Factor," *Financial World*, June 15, 1981, p. 19.

on these portfolios than on control portfolios of other companies in the same industries.[15] But perhaps this is because best-management awards tend to be given to companies whose past earnings results have been outstanding—a fact already impounded in the companies' stock prices at the time of the awards. If so, the moral is not that management quality shouldn't be appraised by investment analysts; rather, it is that management quality needs to be appraised by criteria independent of the company's past earnings record and related financial statistics.

Obviously, an outside investor is not privy to a company's inner workings. But there are clues, we think, which may signal to an investor whether a company's managerial style is likely to influence future earnings trends positively or negatively.

## Attributes of Managerial Excellence

Several years ago a best-selling book, *In Search of Excellence,*[16] tried to pinpoint the factors that distinguish successful business management. The major criterion of success was a demonstrated ability to respond appropriately to changes in the external operating environment. That ability appeared, to the authors, to depend on whether the company possessed several of eight managerial characteristics. Since some of these characteristics are more visible to outside observers than others, we have classified them accordingly. They are as follows:

Quite Visible, Even from Outside:

1. The company has intimate knowledge of its customers' needs and puts those needs at the forefront of its activities; its products and services are widely reputed to be of high quality, and they are modified as customers' needs change.
2. The company has a well-articulated and widely understood set of corporate values. Product quality may be one such value; other examples include innovation or low cost of production.
3. The company does not go into businesses far from its realm of expertise and tends to expand, and even diversify, from within rather than by acquisition.

Partially Visible from Outside:

1. The company fosters entrepreneurship. Autonomy is pushed down the line, and innovation is well rewarded.
2. Administrative staffs are lean; organizational structure is simple; lines of responsibility are clear.
3. Each individual employee is made to feel that he or she is crucial to the company's success.

Not Directly Visible from Outside:

1. The decision process is action-oriented. Task forces are formed as needed and then disbanded; standing committees are discouraged.

---

[15]Andy Granatelli and John D. Martin, "Management Quality and Investment Performance," *Financial Analysts Journal,* November-December 1984.

[16]Thomas J. Peters and Robert H. Waterman, Jr., *In Search of Excellence: Lessons from America's Best-Run Companies* (New York: Harper & Row, 1982).

**2.** A "loose-tight" synergy exists whereby firm central direction and maximum individual autonomy reinforce each other naturally and without rulebooks.

The fact that the latter two characteristics of excellence are not directly observable by outsiders is not too troubling. Indeed, the loose-tight characteristic can be viewed as simply an amalgam of the other seven rather than as one separate and distinct. And the use of task forces rather than standing committees is not the only clue to whether a company's decision process is action-oriented. More troubling is the observation by some critics of the analysis that there must be something wrong with the list because many companies cited in the book as excellent have fallen on hard times recently. And a study of those companies reveals some problems with the characteristics of excellence themselves.[17] Consider, for example, two of the first three characteristics outlined above. While corporate values can be a unifying force and lead to greatness, they can become obsolete and represent a drag on the company's future progress. Moreover, sticking to the business one knows best makes sense, but it may also mean sticking to a business that is becoming obsolete.

"Not so," argues the sequel to *In Search of Excellence,* entitled *A Passion for Excellence.*[18] This latter book focuses on two of the eight characteristics as *most* critical: exceptional attention to the needs of customers and exceptional attention to the creative potential of each individual employee. This dual attentiveness, it is argued, will make a company's managers aware of pending obsolescence of products, markets, and even corporate values and will give rise to the innovations needed to meet the challenge of obsolescence.

We suspect that the authors of *In Search of Exellence* and *A Passion for Excellence* have the better side of the argument. The critics' citation of well-managed companies that subsequently fell from grace merely proves, if anything, that managers are human and that human beings can make serious mistakes of judgment no matter how they are organized, no matter what their values are, and no matter how much attention they pay to their customers and employees. The only thesis one has to accept is that falls from grace are less likely if companies possess these characteristics of managerial excellence than if they do not. And the evidence in support of the thesis outweighs the evidence against it.[19]

## Some Danger Signals

Investors who feel that they simply do not have the resources to make more than a cursory study of the management factor should at least be alert for a number of danger signals, such as:

> A product line that is pretty much the same from one year to the next. While some companies have succeeded by maintaining a constancy of product for

---

[17]See, for example, "Who's Excellent Now?" *Business Week,* November 5, 1984.

[18]Thomas J. Peters and Nancy Austin, *A Passion for Excellence* (New York: Random House, 1985).

[19]It is interesting, we think, though the authors do not dwell on it, that Japanese companies exhibit many of the characteristics of excellence described in these books.

long periods of time (e.g., Mercedes), such constancy more often indicates a management that is out of touch with the changing needs of its customers.

A history of repeatedly going outside of a company's own management ranks to select chief executive and chief operating officers. This usually is evidence of lack of attention to personnel development throughout the company.

A much higher level of compensation for the chief executive officer than for the other officers whose salaries are shown in a company's proxy statements and other shareholder reports. This may indicate a one-man rule situation.

A board of directors consisting mainly of company officers rather than outside members. Although some companies have done very well with inside boards, they tend to be too parochial in perspective and too much under the thumb of the CEO. (Directors' affiliations are published in annual proxy statements.)

A low percentage of sales directed to research and development (R&D) expenditures compared with competitors. Innovation doesn't usually just spring forth from the minds of innovative people. Money has to be spent on R&D support. (Data on R&D spending are contained in 10-K reports and are summarized for large companies in an annual "R&D Scorecard" published in *Business Week.*)

A large number of lawsuits alleging environmental pollution, age or race discrimination, and the like. Managements which treat matters of social responsibility cavalierly are likely to treat customers' needs and employees similarly. (The Investor Responsibility Research Center, a nonprofit Washington, D.C., organization, provides subscribers with impartial, concise, timely information on the social and environmental questions raised in shareholder resolutions proposed to major corporations and publishes in-depth reports on social issues and public policies that affect corporations and investors.)

## *What Went Wrong at Texas Instruments?*

On July 27, 1985, during a period of sharply declining earnings, Texas Instruments announced that its president and chief executive officer, J. Fred Bucy (age 56), had resigned and been replaced by Jerry R. Junkins (age 47). Mark Shepherd, Jr. (age 62), would continue as chairman and chief corporate officer, according to the announcement.

Since Mr. Bucy, who had been president only since 1976 and chief executive officer only since 1984, was not near retirement age and was apparently in good health, the financial community assumed that his resignation had been requested. But since his replacement was a 26-year veteran of Texas Instruments and an engineer like most of his predecessors, and since Mr. Shepherd had a reputation for being a very strong-willed manager (he had added the title chief corporate officer to his chairmanship at the same time that he had added the title chief executive officer to Mr. Bucy's presidency), the financial community wondered whether the appointment of Mr. Junkins was merely an effort to appear to be "doing something" during a period when earnings were falling sharply, or whether some changes for the better were really in the offing.

For the better in what sense? In an article describing the change in the Texas Instruments' management, *Fortune* magazine noted that:

> Texas Instruments had suffered severe setbacks during recent years in two major consumer markets, digital wrist watches and personal computers. This suggested that Messrs. Shepherd and Bucy may have been long on engineering know-how but short on marketing know-how. Yet Mr. Junkins had no record of marketing experience.
>
> Both Messrs. Shepherd and Bucy had a reputation for a highly centralized management style. Would Mr. Junkins be willing (and able with Mr. Shepherd's presence) to loosen the reins and encourage lower-level innovations?[20]

It is most interesting that the *Fortune* article focused on the very two managerial ingredients—attentiveness to customers and attentiveness to employees—that *A Passion for Excellence* focuses on. In both dimensions, the *Fortune* researchers concluded, Texas Instruments had been falling far short of managerial excellence.

# ■ SUMMARY

In this chapter, a company's future prospects were viewed from three perspectives. First we considered the status of each major product line in terms of the industrial life-cycle framework that had been outlined in the prior chapter. Next, we decomposed the sources of earnings growth into a series of financial ratios and examined the significance of each. The key ratios and key relationships were:

| | |
|---|---|
| Internal growth rate | = Return on equity × Retention rate. |
| Return on assets | = EBIT margin on sales × Asset turnover. |
| Return on equity | = Return on assets adjusted for leverage, interest, and income taxes. |
| Retention rate | = Dividend policy. |
| Other growth sources | = Sale of shares at premium (or redemption at discount) relative to book value. |

The section on other growth sources was followed by a discussion of so-called special situation and risk arbitrage investment opportunities frequently arising from mergers, tenders, and other unique corporate developments. Finally, we stepped back from numerical relationships and considered the subject of managerial excellence or lack thereof. While somewhat ephemeral, management quality is as much a corporate resource as working capital or plant and equipment. Although harder to quantify, it cannot be ignored by intelligent investors.

---

[20]Brian O'Reilly, "Texas Instruments: New Boss, Big Job," *Fortune*, July 8, 1985. Also see J. Robert Lineback, "Can Jerry Junkins Get It Back On Track?" *Electronics*, August 12, 1985. For a "yes" answer regarding Mr. Jenkins' willingness and ability to loosen the reins see Todd Mason, "Texas Instruments: Off The Roller Coaster?," *Business Week*, April 28, 1986.

# SUGGESTED READINGS

Abell, Derek F. *Defining the Business: The Starting Point of Strategic Planning.* Englewood Cliffs, N.J.: Prentice-Hall, 1980.

Bernstein, Leopold A. *Financial Statement Analysis: Theory, Application and Interpretation.* 3rd ed. Homewood, Ill.: Richard D. Irwin, 1983.

Boesky, Ivan F. *Merger Mania.* New York: Holt, Rinehart & Winston, 1985.

Drucker, Peter F. *Managing in Turbulent Times.* New York: Harper & Row, 1980.

Fruhan, William E., Jr. *Financial Strategy.* Homewood, Ill.: Richard D. Irwin, 1979.

Peters, Thomas J., and Nancy Austin. *A Passion for Excellence.* New York: Random House, 1985.

Peters, Thomas J., and Robert H. Waterman, Jr. *In Search of Excellence: Lessons From America's Best-Run Companies.* New York: Harper & Row, 1982.

Porter, Michael E. *Competitive Advantage: Creating and Sustaining Superior Performance.* New York: The Free Press, 1985.

————. *Competitive Strategy: Techniques for Analyzing Industries and Competitors.* New York: The Free Press, 1980.

# CHAPTER

## 17

# *Investor Policies*

*Progress is impossible without change, and those who cannot change their minds cannot change anything.*

George Bernard Shaw

A substantial body of research clearly indicates that most investors, not only individuals but also financial institutions, do not manage their portfolios effectively. That is, investors do not construct or manage their portfolios in a manner that reflects their attitude toward risk, nor do they recognize the likely financial consequences of disappointing investment performance. It is therefore appropriate to consider how the strong points of modern portfolio theory (MPT) can be incorporated into actual investment practices in order to improve results. The focus of our discussion rests on three critical elements that should be central to every rational investor's deliberations: (1) defining investment objectives clearly and realistically, (2) determining an appropriate asset-mix strategy for achieving these objectives, and (3) adopting operating tactics that will effectively implement the broad strategic plan. It is also important to stress the dynamic nature of investor decision-making in the real world. Capital market conditions are ever-changing, and diligent adjustment to important trends is necessary to achieve determined goals consistently over long time periods. Few investors do. Let's first look at the needs and constraints of different investor groups and review their behavior patterns—differentiating what they should do and what they really do.

# ■ INVESTOR OBJECTIVES

## Individual Investor Objectives

Portfolio objectives for an individual investor are probably influenced by a wide variety of factors, but the two most important are thought to be *(a)* the investor's stage in the life cycle and *(b)* psychological makeup or capacity to withstand the stress and tensions of risk.

For example, consider three key stages in the life cycle of an individual: *(a)* the young investor, *(b)* an individual at midstream, and *(c)* a person on the verge of retirement.

Most financial counselors believe that young investors should not take very large risks since they are new at the game and probably would be quite distressed by the loss of a significant share of initial, hard-earned capital accumulation. But the overall risk of common stocks is quite tolerable, especially if an "emergency" savings fund has been established and a well-designed life insurance program has begun. Over time, there will, of course, be setbacks either in corporate earnings or in the securities market as a whole, but in the longer run, quality shares tend to rise as dividends and earnings grow. Time is the one thing youth has in abundance!

The average business or professional person is probably moving into the prime of life from 40 to 50. Although earnings are perhaps not at the highest level that will be attained, they find themselves in these years with greater financial mobility than previously. Generally the house is paid for, or almost so, insurance programs are well under way, and a comfortable cash balance is available in the bank for any emergency that may arise. The investor is financially more mature and sophisticated. It is during this period that funds can be used more aggressively. The whole gamut of investment possibilities may be considered. These include a speculative capital gains portfolio or trading in performance stocks—the market favorites of the time— or moving into cyclical stocks at the appropriate stage of the business cycle. Investors can buy on margin to enhance profitability, sell short, look into special situations, consider convertible bonds or warrants, or trade in options. They can switch from stocks to bonds to take advantage of interest rate trends. In light of their tax position, they can consider tax-exempt state and municipal bonds, tax-sheltered investments, oil and gas royalties, real estate, or stock gifts to children, even commodities and financial futures.

Investors are also in a better position to know their own psychological makeup at this stage of their career. The capacity to take risks varies among individuals. Some, aiming at preservation of capital, perhaps painfully accumulated, are content with a low anticipated return involving little risk. Others, confident of their earning capacity and their ability to replace any losses, will aim at higher returns commensurate with higher risks.

As the individual investor moves along in years to the verge of retirement, we would expect his or her risk aversion to become greater. For the investor between 55 and 65, it makes less sense to take speculative chances in the pursuit of capital gains and high returns. Since the prime earning years are about over, there is not much time left to rebuild capital and recoup possible speculative losses. Presumably, then,

**FIGURE 17–1   Financial Strategies for Three Stages of Life**

|  | Young Single | Young Couple | Couple Mid 50s |
|---|---|---|---|
|  | Income, $40,000<br>Assets, $10,000 | Joint income, $85,000<br>Assets, $80,000 | Joint income, $175,000<br>Assets, $250,000 |
| Primary investment objectives | Wealth accumulation via regular monthly savings; Investment program intended to achieve long-term capital gains; Maintain liquidity. | Reduction of current income taxes; Capital accumulation on a tax-advantaged basis; Maintain sufficient liquidity for potential purchase of home. | Preservation of capital; Reduction of current taxes; Retirement planning; Provide for orderly distribution of estate. |
| Basic living expenses | $18,000 | $38,000 | $70,000 |
| Federal and state taxes | $ 9,000 | $22,000 | $58,000 |
| Marginal tax bracket | 36% | 44% | 50% |
| Insurance | Appropriate levels of life and disability insurance should be reviewed periodically, weighing such factors as life style and number of dependents. | | |
| Emergency fund | $2,000 money-market fund with checking account privilege. | $6,000 money-market fund with checking account privilege. | $10,000 money-market fund with checking account privilege. |
| Investment portfolio | $5,000 growth mutual fund for capital appreciation and professional portfolio management<br><br>$3,000 tax-managed trust for tax-deferred compounding and growth. | $30,000 diversified stock portfolio or growth mutual fund for capital appreciation.<br><br>$20,000 tax-managed trust for tax-deferred compounding and liquidity.<br><br><br><br>$10,000 developmental oil and gas limited partnership for reduction of current tax liability and tax-advantaged cash flow.<br><br>$10,000 real estate limited partnership for capital appreciation and tax-sheltered income. | $50,000 diversified high-quality common stock portfolio.<br><br>$30,000 tax-managed trust for tax-deferred compounding and liquidity.<br><br>$100,000 municipal bonds, staggered maturities with maximum of 10–12 years.<br><br>$30,000 developmental oil and gas limited partnership for reduction of current tax liability and tax-advantaged cash flow.<br><br>$25,000 real estate limited partnership for capital appreciation and tax-sheltered income. |
|  | Use excess cash flow for monthly additions to mutual fund and tax-managed trust. | $4,000 IRA contribution (husband-wife).<br><br>Use excess cash flow for monthly additions to tax-managed trust and stock portfolio. | $4,000 IRA contribution (husband-wife).<br><br>Use excess cash flow for monthly additions to tax-managed trust and stock portfolio. |

NOTE: As of this writing, comprehensive changes in the Federal Tax Code will make some of these investments obsolete.
SOURCE: Janney Montgomery Scott Inc.

**FIGURE 17–2     Risk-return Positions of Individuals at Various Life Cycle Stages**

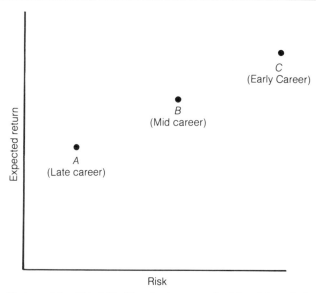

SOURCE: John L. Maginn and Donald L. Tuttle *Managing Investment Portfolios,* A Dynamic Process (New York: Warren Gorham & Lamont, 1983), p. 133.

the investor on the eve of retirement will want to shift the portfolio to provide income to augment social security and other possible retirement benefits. The objective becomes mainly the highest income commensurate with safety rather than speculative or even long-term capital gains.

Figure 17–1 is an example of how one financial planner views the shifting life cycle concept. Within the context of portfolio theory, as described in Chapter 4, the risk-return position of individual investors at various points in the life cycle is shown in Figure 17–2. As Robert D. Milne appropriately points out: "Exactly where each investor fixes his or her risk-return tradeoff at various life-cycle stages depends on individual circumstances and individual risk-taking attitudes. Given two mid-career individuals, for example, the extremely cautious investor might be significantly to the left of, and below, point *B,* whereas a more aggressive individual might be substantially to the right (and, hopefully, above)."[1]

## Individual Investment Behavior

Until recently, very little was known about the actual investment behavior of individuals. However, a variety of extensive studies now provide an incisive view as to how individuals have been managing their funds and why. These findings refute much conventional wisdom about individual investors and present a great deal of fascinating material on the expectations of investors and their attitudes toward risks and rewards.

---

[1]Robert D. Milne, "Determination of Portfolio Policies: Individual Investors," *Managing Investment Portfolios, A Dynamic Process,* John L. Maginn and Donald L. Tuttle, (New York: Warren Gorham & Lamont, 1983), p. 133.

**TABLE 17–1  Risk Variance Among Individual Investors**

| | | Non-Affluent | | Affluent | | All Non-Affluent | All Affluent |
|---|---|---|---|---|---|---|---|
| | | **Male** | **Female** | **Male** | **Female** | | |
| Substantial risk | 1 | 8% | — | 4% | 3% | 4% | 3% |
| | 2 | 27 | 13 | 17 | 8 | 21 | 14 |
| | 3 | 32 | 36 | 51 | 47 | 34 | 49 |
| | 4 | 21 | 26 | 18 | 24 | 24 | 21 |
| Minimum risk | 5 | 11 | 23 | 7 | 18 | 16 | 12 |
| Not ascertained | | 1 | 2 | 3 | — | 1 | 1 |
| Total | | 100 | 100 | 100 | 100 | 100 | 100 |

*Non-Affluent* = Income between $15,000 and $49,999 (Number of cases = 145)
*Affluent* = Income $50,000 or more (Number of cases = 287)
Based on all respondents who made at least one type of securities transaction in the past year.
SOURCE: Gallup Consumer Financial Services Monitor, April 1985.

For example, a study by Gallup Financial Services Monitor shows that most individual investors are neither very aggressive nor very conservative but maintain a middle-of-the-road attitude towards risk.[2] See Table 17–1. It is interesting that female investors tend to be, on balance, more conservative than their male counterparts. Other studies show that risk-taking behavior has been found to be positively related to income and negatively related to age.

A study by the New York Stock Exchange shows that 49 percent of stockholders held only one common stock in their portfolios and another 20 percent only two. (See Table 17–2). Twenty-two percent of shareholders studied held between three and seven issues, while only 9 percent held eight or more. Thus, 91 percent of all the individual investors surveyed had portfolios of less than eight separate issues, making the portfolios substantially more risky than warranted by the previously noted survey of investor attitudes. A further irony is that most investors, when surveyed on another occasion, agreed that portfolio diversification was a good idea. We will return to this apparent inconsistency of individual investor behavior in the next chapter.

**TABLE 17–2  Number of Common Stocks Held by All Adult Shareholders**

| Number | Percent |
|---|---|
| 1 | 49% |
| 2 | 20 |
| 3–7 | 22 |
| 8 or more | 9 |
| Total | 100% |
| (Base) | (753) |

SOURCE: New York Stock Exchange, mid-1985.

[2]Study findings of this nature are highly responsive to the investors' most recent experience. That is, following periods of poor capital market performance, investors tend to become more conservative. Conversely, they become more risk-oriented when returns have been favorable.

**TABLE 17–3    (A) Individual Investor Behavior, 1972–1985 ($ billions)**

| Year | (1)<br>Direct Household Acquisition of Equities Plus Equity Mutual Funds | (2)<br>Direct Household Acquisition of Equities | (3)<br>Net Acquisition of Equity Mutual Funds | (4)<br>Direct Household Acquisition of Equities Plus Mutual Funds* | (5)<br>Net Acquisition of<br>Bond Mutual Funds | (6)<br>Net Acquisition of<br>Money Market Mutual Funds |
|---|---|---|---|---|---|---|
| 1972 | $ (7.1) | $ (5.3) | $ (1.8) | $ (5.4) | $ 1.7 | — |
| 1973 | (8.1) | (5.9) | (2.2) | (6.2) | 1.9 | — |
| 1974 | (2.2) | (1.8) | (0.4) | (0.9) | 1.3 | $ 2.4 |
| 1975 | (5.3) | (4.4) | (0.9) | (4.7) | 0.6 | 1.3 |
| 1976 | (5.0) | (2.6) | (2.4) | (5.0) | 0.0 | 0.0 |
| 1977 | (8.6) | (4.9) | (3.7) | (4.0) | 4.6 | 0.2 |
| 1978 | (6.9) | (5.3) | (1.6) | (5.4) | 1.5 | 6.9 |
| 1979 | (21.7) | (18.9) | (2.8) | (18.8) | 2.9 | 34.4 |
| 1980 | (15.3) | (13.5) | (1.8) | (8.3) | 7.0 | 29.2 |
| 1981 | (36.6) | (36.0) | (0.6) | (29.7) | 6.9 | 107.5 |
| 1982 | (20.6) | (24.1) | 3.5 | (5.7) | 14.9 | 24.7 |
| 1983 | (13.1) | (26.8) | 13.7 | 6.0 | 19.1 | (44.1) |
| 1984 | (73.4) | (79.3) | 5.9 | (41.6) | 31.9 | 47.2 |
| 1985 | (112.6) | (124.9) | 12.3 | (5.9) | 106.7 | 4.0 |

*Including bond mutual funds.
SOURCE: Goldman Sachs based on Federal Reserve Board Statistics.

The latest New York Stock Exchange shareownership study portrays the average shareowner in 1985 as being 44 years old with a household income of about $37,000 and median portfolio size of $6,200. While the average profile in 1981 was older (46 years old) and less affluent ($29,200 annual income), the average shareowner household income has consistently remained 65 percent above the total U.S. median.

Interestingly, the typical *new* adult shareowner is female, 34 years old, married, employed in a professional/technical position, has a $2,200 portfolio, and has a household income of about $35,000 per year.

In the aggregate, as shown in Table 17–3(A), individual investors have been liquidating direct ownership of common stocks for many years, instead favoring mutual funds, particularly those of a fixed income nature. As shown in Table 17-3(B), individual investor ownership of equities as a percentage of total financial assets has been less than 25 percent since 1976, a level well below previous years when the popularity of common stock investing was heightened by a long-term trend of rising share prices.

# ■ INSTITUTIONAL INVESTOR OBJECTIVES

Institutional investors are governed by a somewhat different set of constraints from those affecting individual investors. The most important influences on the investment behavior of an institution are:

*Table 17–3(B)    Individual Investor Holdings of Equities, 1968–1985 ($ billions)*

| Year | Total Financial Assets | Equities | |
| | | Amount | Percent of Total |
|---|---|---|---|
| 1968 | $1,911 | $ 858 | 44.9% |
| 1969 | 1,860 | 746 | 40.1 |
| 1970 | 1,926 | 729 | 37.8 |
| 1971 | 2,151 | 833 | 38.7 |
| 1972 | 2,382 | 909 | 38.1 |
| 1973 | 2,297 | 706 | 30.7 |
| 1974 | 2,201 | 498 | 22.6 |
| 1975 | 2,559 | 647 | 25.3 |
| 1976 | 2,900 | 766 | 26.4 |
| 1977 | 3,076 | 723 | 23.5 |
| 1978 | 3,347 | 741 | 22.1 |
| 1979 | 3,827 | 892 | 23.3 |
| 1980 | 4,503 | 1,188 | 26.4 |
| 1981 | 4,802 | 1,135 | 23.6 |
| 1982 | 5,345 | 1,275 | 23.9 |
| 1983 | 6,011 | 1,455 | 24.2 |
| 1984 | 6,587 | 1,491 | 22.6 |
| 1985* | 7,209 | 1,719 | 23.8 |

*As of September 30.
SOURCE: Goldman Sachs based on Federal Reserve Board Statistics.

1. The nature of the institution's obligations to its clients—its reason for being.
2. Legal regulations applicable to its investments.
3. Taxation of its investment income.
4. Intangible considerations, such as the psychology of its clients and of its own personnel, and competitive pressures among the institutions themselves.

These factors influence each institution's investment objectives with regard to current income, capital gains, marketability, liquidity, and safety. The institution then attempts to balance these objectives—which are often in conflict—in the management of its portfolio.

As shown in Table 17–4, private pension funds are by far the largest institutional holder of equities, almost three times the size of the next largest group—state and local government retirement portfolios. Our remaining discussion will focus on pension funds as illustrative of the various factors dictating institutional investment behavior.[3]

Pension fund assets represent the nation's largest aggregation of institutional capital. The market value of private pension fund assets totaled $623.3 billion at the

---

[3]For a discussion of the investment practices and constraints of other institutional investors such as investment companies, insurance companies, deferred profit sharing plans, endowment funds, and private foundations, see previous editions of this text. See also Jay Vawter, "Determination of Portfolio Policies: Institutional Investors," *Managing Investment Portfolios, A Dynamic Process,* ed. Maginn and Tuttle.

TABLE 17–4  *Sector Holdings of Corporate Equities ($ millions)*

| Year | Market Value of Corporate Equities | Household Holdings | Private Pension Funds | State and Local Retirement Funds | Life Insurance Companies | Other Insurance Companies | Open-End Investment Companies | Rest of World | Mutual Savings Bank | Brokers and Dealers |
|---|---|---|---|---|---|---|---|---|---|---|
| 1946 | $ 111.0 | $ 103.3 | $ 0.3 | — | $ 1.2 | $ 1.7 | $ 1.0 | $ 2.6 | $0.1 | $ 0.4 |
| 1950 | 146.0 | 133.6 | 1.1 | — | 2.1 | 2.5 | 2.8 | 2.9 | 0.1 | 0.5 |
| 1955 | 317.0 | 286.3 | 6.1 | $ 0.2 | 3.6 | 5.4 | 6.9 | 6.6 | 1.0 | 0.9 |
| 1960 | 451.0 | 395.5 | 16.5 | 0.6 | 5.0 | 7.5 | 14.8 | 9.3 | 1.3 | 0.5 |
| 1965 | 749.0 | 635.6 | 40.8 | 2.5 | 9.1 | 12.0 | 30.9 | 14.6 | 2.3 | 1.2 |
| 1970 | 906.2 | 728.6 | 67.1 | 10.1 | 15.4 | 13.2 | 39.7 | 27.2 | 2.8 | 2.0 |
| 1975 | 892.5 | 646.9 | 102.1 | 24.3 | 28.1 | 14.2 | 33.7 | 35.3 | 4.4 | 3.4 |
| 1980 | 1635.5 | 1188.2 | 209.5 | 44.3 | 47.4 | 32.3 | 42.2 | 64.6 | 4.2 | 2.9 |
| 1981 | 1568.5 | 1134.3 | 195.6 | 47.8 | 47.7 | 32.4 | 37.2 | 64.6 | 3.2 | 5.6 |
| 1982 | 1810.5 | 1274.8 | 248.4 | 60.2 | 55.7 | 38.5 | 48.9 | 76.7 | 3.3 | 3.8 |
| 1983 | 2151.5 | 1466.2 | 306.2 | 89.6 | 64.9 | 48.1 | 73.5 | 97.2 | 4.3 | 1.4 |
| 1984 | 2183.8 | 1492.5 | 294.1 | 98.1 | 63.8 | 50.0 | 79.9 | 94.5 | 4.3 | 6.5 |
| 1985-3Q | 2504.2 | 1718.8 | 327.8 | 113.0 | 69.6 | 50.6 | 99.1 | 107.9 | 4.8 | 12.5 |

*Sector Percentage Ownership of Corporate Equities*

| Year | Market Value of Corporate Equities | Household Holdings | Private Pension Funds | State and Local Retirement Funds | Life Insurance Companies | Other Insurance Companies | Open-End Investment Companies | Rest of World | Mutual Savings Bank | Brokers and Dealers |
|---|---|---|---|---|---|---|---|---|---|---|
| 1946 | 100% | 93.1% | .2% | .0007% | 1.1% | 1.5% | .9% | 2.4% | .2% | .4% |
| 1950 | 100 | 91.5 | .8 | .02 | 1.4 | 1.8 | 2.0 | 2.0 | .1 | .3 |
| 1955 | 100 | 90.3 | 1.9 | .1 | 1.1 | 1.7 | 2.2 | 2.1 | .3 | .3 |
| 1960 | 100 | 87.7 | 3.7 | .1 | 1.1 | 1.7 | 3.3 | 2.1 | .3 | .1 |
| 1965 | 100 | 84.9 | 5.4 | .3 | 1.2 | 1.6 | 4.1 | 1.9 | .3 | .2 |
| 1970 | 100 | 80.4 | 7.4 | 1.1 | 1.7 | 1.5 | 4.4 | 3.0 | .3 | .2 |
| 1975 | 100 | 72.5 | 11.4 | 2.7 | 3.1 | 1.6 | 3.8 | 4.0 | .5 | .4 |
| 1980 | 100 | 72.6 | 12.8 | 2.7 | 2.9 | 2.0 | 2.6 | 3.9 | .3 | .2 |
| 1981 | 100 | 72.3 | 12.5 | 3.0 | 3.0 | 2.1 | 2.4 | 4.1 | .2 | .4 |
| 1982 | 100 | 70.4 | 13.7 | 3.3 | 3.1 | 2.1 | 2.7 | 4.2 | .2 | .2 |
| 1983 | 100 | 68.1 | 14.2 | 4.2 | 3.0 | 2.2 | 3.4 | 4.5 | .2 | .1 |
| 1984 | 100 | 68.3 | 13.5 | 4.5 | 2.9 | 2.3 | 3.7 | 4.3 | .2 | .3 |
| 1985-3Q | 100 | 68.6 | 13.1 | 4.5 | 2.8 | 2.0 | 4.0 | 4.3 | .2 | .5 |

SOURCE: Shearson Lehman Brothers based on Flow of Funds Accounts, Federal Reserve Board.

**TABLE 17–5  Largest Corporate Pension Funds (in millions of dollars)**

| Fund | Assets |
|------|-------:|
| General Motors | $26,300 |
| AT&T | 24,887 |
| General Electric Co. | 15,812 |
| IBM Corp. | 13,939 |
| Ford Motor Co. | 11,000 |
| E. I. du Pont de Nemours & Co. | 9,665 |
| NYNEX Corp. | 9,447 |
| Ameritech | 8,300 |
| Exxon Corp. | 8,008 |
| U.S. Steel Corp. | 8,000 |
| Bell Atlantic Corp. | 8,000 |
| Bell South Corp. | 6,983 |
| GTE Corp. | 6,740 |
| Pacific Telesis Group | 6,316 |
| Chevron Corp. | 6,004 |

SOURCE: *Pensions and Investment Age,* January 20, 1986.

end of 1984, with approximately 47 percent of the total invested in equities and a slightly larger amount in credit market instruments.[4] Table 17–5 lists the largest corporate pension funds in America.

## Objectives of Corporate Pension Funds

Pension fund assets represent a pool of capital being set aside for the specific purpose of meeting *future* benefit payments. Each plan has its own unique characteristics which in turn requires that investment policies and portfolio strategies reflect the particular needs of the sponsoring organization. In order to determine these effectively, trustees usually review a variety of income and financial statement items as well as the actuaries' report covering employee and retirement trends.

Traditionally, investment managers of a pension fund had more flexibility than virtually any other type of investor, individual or institution. They were relatively unfettered by law. Their relative lack of liquidity needs enabled them to seek higher yields in off-the-beaten path investment media. Tax exemption has permitted them to do this without distinguishing between current income and capital gain. It also allowed them to switch out of overpriced investments and into undervalued situations without regard to tax consequences. If they felt unable to time cyclical turning points, their steady fund inflow enabled them simply to dollar average. It also permitted them to restructure their portfolios by reallocating the investment of new fund inflows without being forced to sell existing holdings if doing so would upset prices.

Many of these investment advantages still prevail. However in late 1974, Congress passed the Employee Retirement Income Security Act of 1974, now popularly re-

---

[4]Michael H. Sherman and Leslie S. Kogod, "Stock Market Flow of Funds, Annual Survey 1985," Shearson Lehman Brothers, p. 27.

ferred to as ERISA. Passage of this comprehensive and complex legislation ushered in a new series of investment constraints for corporate pension fund trustees and perhaps for other institutional investor categories.[5]

The bill created for the first time a uniform federal standard for fiduciary conduct relating specifically to the establishment and maintenance of corporate employee benefit plans. The overall purpose of this lengthy legislation is to assure that pension plans are financed and managed in a manner guaranteeing employees their benefits. Certain provisions have already changed the portfolio behavior of this important institutional group, and recent interpretations of other provisions are likely to produce greater and perhaps more surprising changes.

For example, ERISA includes a number of extensive provisions covering the vesting and funding of corporate pension plans. Prior to the passage of ERISA, there was no legal requirement for employers to amortize their unfunded pension liabilities. At the same time, ERISA essentially converted pension liabilities from their origin as a fringe benefit to a legal claim by beneficiaries against the corporation, enforceable by federal regulation.[6] In the event of a plan's termination, if pension assets are unable to satisfy vested benefits, then the Pension Benefits Guaranty Corporation, created by ERISA to guarantee plan benefits, is empowered to attach a lien up to 30 percent of the sponsoring corporation's net worth to satisfy the funding shortfall.[7] This pension claim assumes the status of a federal tax lien and ranks before the claims of other corporate creditors. However, despite this substantive change in the legal position of pension fund liabilities, the impact on actual investment policy decisions has been negligible as far as we can tell.

Section 404 of ERISA relates to the "Prudent Man Rule" and has been responsible for a great deal of confusion regarding the appropriate composition of portfolio assets. Generally accepted trust law, under the Prudent Man Rule, focuses solely on the risk of loss and on minimizing such risk on *each security* in a portfolio rather than on the portfolio as a whole.[8] Under this concept, risk is viewed apart from the return that a risky investment may contribute to the total portfolio.

Consequently, portfolio managers and trustees initially interpreted ERISA as, for example, prohibiting pension investments in small companies. At the same time, the

---

[5]See, for example, Harvey E. Bines, *The Law of Investment Management, 1983 Cumulative Supplement* (New York: Warren, Gorham & Lamont).

[6]New Financial Accounting Standards Board (FASB) standards require companies whose computed pension plan liabilities exceed plan assets to place a new liability on the balance sheet. However, the purchase of annuities from an insurance company, to cover the shortfall, will allow a sponsor to avoid balance sheet disclosure. For a comprehensive review of current pension fund accounting issues see Lee J. Seidler, "Accounting Issues," *Investment Research,* Bear, Stearns & Company, Inc., January 24, 1986.

[7]The Pension Benefit Guaranty Corporation (PBGC) currently insures the pension benefits of 38 million people. As of October 1985, the PBGC had taken over more than 1,200 pension plans covering 190,000 persons, and had accumulated a deficit of about $1.3 billion, more than two thirds of it in 1985. See *Economic Report of the President 1986* (Washington, D.C.: U.S. Government Printing Office, 1986), p. 206.

[8]The Prudent Man Rule was first articulated in 1830 by the Supreme Court of Massachusetts, *Harvard College v. Amory,* 26 Mass (9 Pick) 446, and contained the following wording: "All that can be required of a trustee to invest is that he shall conduct himself faithfully and exercise a sound discretion. He is to observe how men of prudence, discretion and intelligence manage their own affairs, not in regard to speculation, but in regard to the permanent disposition of their funds, considering the probable income, as well as the probable safety of the capital invested."

level of diversification was increased; that is, the percentage of the total portfolio concentrated in the top 10 or top 20 holdings was reduced.

In order to resolve the confusion over investment prudence and to prevent a total lack of financing for small and developing companies, the Department of Labor issued a clarifying statement on Section 404 of ERISA which accepted the total portfolio approach to pension fund investments, a clear endorsement of modern portfolio theory.[9]

Obviously, the provisions of ERISA affect different pension plans in different ways. Pension fund trustees now recognize that their particular needs find difficulty in being serviced effectively when portfolios are managed by large organizations responsible for hundreds and often thousands of clients all with different objectives. To rectify this problem, trustees have drifted away from granting total discretion to their managers by establishing new constraints and restrictions on investment selections. In some cases, direct control of the portfolio has been returned to the sponsoring organization through the hiring of an internal portfolio manager. Table 17–6 shows the largest 25 pension fund portfolios using internal pension fund management

**TABLE 17–6   Sponsors with Internal Pension Fund Management ($ millions)**

| Fund | Assets |
| --- | --- |
| TIAA-CREF | $40,000 |
| California Public Employees | 29,166 |
| New York State Common Fund | 22,792 |
| N.Y. State Teachers System | 12,644 |
| General Electric Co. | 12,504 |
| New Jersey Division of Investment | 12,494 |
| Texas Teachers | 11,188 |
| Wisconsin Investment Board | 10,800 |
| Michigan State Employees | 10,516 |
| Ohio Public Employees | 10,500 |
| Ohio State Teachers | 10,178 |
| North Carolina Employees | 8,645 |
| U.S. Steel Corp. | 8,000 |
| E. I. du Pont de Nemours | 7,841 |
| AT&T | 6,100 |
| Georgia State Systems | 6,053 |
| IBM Corp. | 5,900 |
| University of California | 5,200 |
| N.Y.C. Retirement Systems | 5,132 |
| Colorado Public Employees | 5,024 |
| Alabama Retirement Systems | 4,744 |
| Florida Dept. of Admin. | 4,643 |
| United Nations Joint Staff | 4,354 |
| Tennessee Consolidated | 4,249 |
| Texas Employees | 3,300 |

SOURCE: *Pensions and Investment Age,* January 20, 1986.

---

[9]Department of Labor Pension and Welfare Benefit Programs Office (29 CFR Part 2550) Rules and Regulations for Fiduciary Responsibility, April 25, 1978.

***TABLE 17–7  How Control of Investment Policies Varies between Company and Managers***

| Investment Policy | Company Specifies Policies | Company Provides Guidelines | Managers Have Full Discretion | No Answer | Uncertain |
|---|---|---|---|---|---|
| Amount invested in real estate | 54% | 7% | 11% | 17% | 11% |
| Amount invested in foreign securities | 50 | 12 | 10 | 18 | 9 |
| Ability to write call options | 49 | 7 | 12 | 20 | 12 |
| Stock/bond ratio | 45 | 17 | 24 | 6 | 8 |
| Amount invested in private placements | 40 | 12 | 22 | 17 | 9 |
| Minimum quality ratings for bonds | 37 | 26 | 26 | 6 | 6 |
| Minimum total rate of return | 26 | 39 | 27 | 3 | 5 |
| Average maturity of bond portfolio | 13 | 25 | 50 | 6 | 6 |
| Rate of negotiated brokerage commissions | 7 | 21 | 59 | 7 | 6 |
| Volatility or beta of equity portfolio | 7 | 23 | 57 | 7 | 6 |
| Minimum income that must be earned | 4 | 39 | 46 | 6 | 6 |

SOURCE: "Report to Participants on Large Corporate Pensions 1985," Greenwich Associates, Greenwich, Connecticut.

to supervise all or part of their investment portfolios. Maximization of total return is now rarely established as the investment objective irrespective of risk tolerance levels.

Table 17–7 shows how the control of investment policy varies between the sponsoring company and the independent portfolio manager.

According to the most recent Greenwich study of large corporate pension plans, companies most often establish specific policies to direct their investment managers on the following issues: (1) amount invested in real estate, (2) amount invested in foreign securities, (3) ability to write call options, (4) stock/bond ratio, and (5) amount invested in private placements.[10]

The study also reveals that most companies provide general guidelines to their managers with regard to: (1) minimum total rate of return, (2) minimum income requirements to be earned annually, and (3) minimum quality rates for bond holdings. Managers are most often given full discretion with regard to:

1. Rate of negotiated brokerage commissions.
2. Volatility or beta of equity portfolio.
3. Average maturity of bond portfolio.

A number of forces coalesced during 1982–86 to suggest some dramatic changes in aggregate pension fund investment behavior. These can be summarized as follows:

Portfolio returns exceeded actuarial assumptions for an extended period of time.

Wage gains, which are a driving force behind pension fund contributions, moderated significantly.

Past service liabilities were segregated from other pension fund liabilities and

[10]See "Report to Participants on Large Corporate Pensions 1985," Greenwich Associates, Greenwich, Connecticut.

**TABLE 17–8   Portfolio Returns and Wage Changes, 1970–1985**

| Year | Return from a Balanced Fund* | Growth in Wages per Employee† | Difference |
|---|---|---|---|
| 1970 | 6.6% | 6.7% | (0.1) |
| 1971 | 13.6 | 7.1 | 6.5 |
| 1972 | 15.5 | 6.4 | 9.1 |
| 1973 | (9.6) | 6.1 | (15.7) |
| 1974 | (10.9) | 8.0 | (18.9) |
| 1975 | 24.2 | 8.3 | 15.9 |
| 1976 | 19.8 | 7.2 | 12.6 |
| 1977 | (3.6) | 7.0 | (10.6) |
| 1978 | 3.1 | 7.7 | (4.6) |
| 1979 | 8.8 | 8.0 | 0.8 |
| 1980 | 16.1 | 9.2 | 6.9 |
| 1981 | (0.1) | 9.1 | (9.2) |
| 1982 | 28.4 | 7.1 | 21.3 |
| 1983 | 12.0 | 5.2 | 6.8 |
| 1984 | 10.3 | 4.4 | 5.9 |
| 1985 | 29.6 | 3.6 | 26.0 |

*Consists of returns from the S&P 500, long-term government bonds, and T-bills. Each asset weighted based on Federal Reserve Board Flow of Funds data.
†Average hourly earnings index from 1970–1976; employment cost index thereafter.
SOURCE: Goldman Sachs.

funded with specialized portfolios with increasing frequency (primarily dedicated bond portfolios, which will be discussed in the next chapter).

A large number of defined benefit programs were terminated and replaced with guaranteed annuities.

Each of these deserves some further, albeit brief, discussion. Table 17–8 shows the return earned from a portfolio constructed to match the actual disposition of pension fund assets over the period 1970–85. Averaging the annual rates (not shown in Table 17–8) results in a return of about 10 percent per annum. Actuarial assumptions, the pension fund's best estimate of the portfolio's future rate of growth needed to meet future liabilities, are currently about 8.5 percent per annum,[11] but were much lower for most of the period under review. It is also interesting that better funded plans tend to use lower assumptions.[12] Also, according to Table 17–8, portfolio returns have generally been in excess of wage growth.

Bond dedication, the designing of fixed income portfolios to match cash flow from coupon payments with liability requirements, generally results in reduced corporate contributions. Dedicated bond portfolios, according to Greenwich Associates, are

---

[11]Vicky Cahan and Stuart Weiss, "The Huge Pension Overflow Could Make Waves in Washington," *Business Week,* August 12, 1985, p. 71.

[12]Patrick J. Regan and Steven D. Bleiberg, "Overfunded Pension Plans," *Financial Analysts Journal,* November/December 1985, p. 11.

presently being used by 17 percent of the companies surveyed, with another 8 percent expecting to utilize such techniques shortly.[13]

Plan terminations emanate from a number of different pressures. Perhaps the most important is that overfunded plans (a situation in which the value of a pension fund exceeds the required level of value to discharge liabilities) represent a sizable new source of funds for the sponsoring corporation. By replacing benefit obligations with guaranteed annuities, the plan sponsor is able to recapture sizable assets for redeployment into other corporate uses. Another contributing factor is that many large corporations have initiated severe employee reduction programs, thereby reducing the amount of future liabilities. The hectic pace of large scale mergers and acquisition activity has also stimulated plan terminations.[14]

Collectively, these forces are partly responsible for the sharp increase in the use of passive portfolio management techniques, which will be discussed in the next chapter.[15]

## Pension Fund Investment Behavior

Recent studies looking into the actual behavior of pension fund investment managers and fund trustees suggest three disturbing conclusions. One, a surprisingly large number of funds still have no formal statement of investment policy. Two, most pension fund portfolios have a similar profile even though the pension plans themselves have substantial differences. Three, major changes in the complexion of portfolio holdings frequently have been ill-timed and counterproductive.[16]

Shifts in the complexion of pension fund portfolio holdings often occur agonizingly slow over long periods of time but sometimes very abruptly. Figure 17–3 shows pension fund holdings of bonds, stocks, and liquid assets as a percentage of total financial assets. Here's how *The Bank Credit Analyst* interprets the data:

> Pension funds increased their holdings of stocks at the expense of bonds during the post-war period until the early 1970s. Pension funds increased their demand for stocks as prices rose, reaching their maximum relative exposure at the top of the secular bull market. To a great extent they helped create the overshooting which occurred during this period as stocks became far overvalued.
>
> During the early 1970s a series of reversals occurred. First their holdings of stocks fell sharply—mostly due to falling asset values in the 1973–74 bear market. Due to a sharp contraction in net equity purchases, equity holdings as a percentage of total

[13]"Report to Participants on Large Corporate Pensions 1985," Greenwich Associates, 1985, p. 31.

[14]According to the Pension Benefit Guaranty Corporation, 236 plans with 284,665 participants terminated their plans in 1984 and recaptured $2.75 billion in excess assets. As of June 30, 1985, there were 216 plan terminations pending with another $2.75 billion in assets to be recaptured. For a comprehensive review of this controversial maneuver, see Arturo Estrella, "Corporate Use of Pension Overfunding," *FRBNY Quarterly Review,* Spring 1984. See also Regan and Bleiberg, "Overfunded Pension Plans," p. 12.

[15]See, for example, Ed Christman, "Managers Win Top Spots with Passive Products," *Pensions & Investment Age,* February 3, 1986.

[16]See, for example, Arthur Sharplin, "Stalking the Elusive 'Real Return' on Investment," *Pension World,* January 1986, p. 41.

**FIGURE 17–3    Private Pension Funds: Portfolio Holdings**

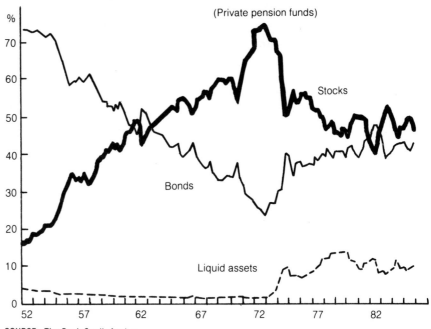

SOURCE: *The Bank Credit Analyst.*

financial assets fell steadily until 1982. It appears that the funds realized their mistake of overemphasizing equities at the top of the market and over the next 10 years maintained a much less aggressive stance towards equities.

The second significant development was a sharp increase in the trend of bond holdings after 1972, albeit from very depressed levels. The third change was in the liquid assets category. Their holdings almost nonexistent prior to 1972, rose dramatically. The rise in inflation, increased economic instability, and deregulation of short-term deposits all combined to increase pension funds' preference for liquid assets.

During the past five years or so, private pension funds have not changed their asset preference a great deal. Despite the rise since 1972, holdings of bonds are still only about one half of those of the late 1940s (when interest rates were much lower in an absolute sense and particularly relative to the equity yields which existed). Holdings of equities are well down from the peak levels of the late 1960s and early 1970s but are still above the levels of the 1940s and 1950s. In addition, liquid assets have stabilized at around 10 percent of all financial assets.

In recent years private pension funds have been extremely volatile. See Table 17–9. They purchased record amounts of equities during 1982/83 and then actually became net sellers during the bear phase in 1983/84. Performance pressures, huge equity retirements and a volatile equity market have all contributed to these rapid swings during the 1980s.[17]

[17]*The Bank Credit Analyst,* February 1986. Abstracted with permission. Donald H. Straszheim and Robert A. Schwartz of Merrill Lynch adds this perspective to the phenomenon: "The proportion of new acquisitions going into stocks versus bonds can and does vary widely over time. Such wide swings tend to reflect the 'herd' instinct of market participants." See Donald H. Straszheim and Robert A. Schwartz, "Financial Market Developments," Merrill Lynch, November 1985, p. 17.

***TABLE 17–9     Private Pension Fund Investment Patterns; Selected Data for Stocks and Bonds***

| Year | Year-End Portfolio Asset Mix | | Annual Cash Flow Allocation | |
|---|---|---|---|---|
| | Stocks | Bonds* | Stocks | Bonds* |
| 1950 | 16% | 75% | 29% | 65% |
| 1955 | 33 | 59 | 32 | 54 |
| 1960 | 43 | 48 | 49 | 37 |
| 1965 | 49 | 35 | 58 | 24 |
| 1970 | 61 | 29 | 66 | 30 |
| 1971 | 68 | 24 | 126 | (16) |
| 1972 | 75 | 22 | 66 | 33 |
| 1973 | 67 | 28 | 40 | 45 |
| 1974 | 51 | 37 | 12 | 48 |
| 1975 | 55 | 37 | 29 | 73 |
| 1976 | 55 | 36 | 41 | 42 |
| 1977 | 49 | 39 | 21 | 44 |
| 1978 | 45 | 40 | 7 | 53 |
| 1979 | 46 | 40 | 23 | 60 |
| 1980 | 51 | 38 | 36 | 62 |
| 1981 | 45 | 43 | 14 | 78 |
| 1982 | 48 | 43 | 37 | 68 |
| 1983 | 50 | 40 | 32 | 45 |
| 1984 | 47 | 42 | (9.7) | 80 |
| 1985 | 52 | 39 | 26 | 64 |

*Corporate and governments combined.
SOURCE: Shearson Lehman, based on flow of funds.

All this is not to suggest that the use of modern portfolio theory could have improved the timing of pension fund investment trends but rather to convey the belief that a better understanding of risk and return by trustees is likely to prevent unwarranted change in long-term planning following short-term performance problems.

In addition to poor timing, pension fund trustees have frequently been criticized for maintaining too conservative a posture with regard to asset allocation policies. More recently, however, pension fund trustees have shown significant investment creativity. Their interest in real estate investments has grown, and they have expanded their investigations into the possible benefits of diversifying portfolios in international markets and adding oil and gas ventures and other nontraditional assets to their portfolios. Table 17–10 shows the results of the survey asking pension fund trustees to estimate their portfolio holdings by category by 1995.

Surprisingly, a number of surveys by Greenwich Associates reveal: "no significant differences in portfolio composition due to any of the following differences: size of company, size of plan, percent of plan participants now working or retired, benefit formula, average age or length of service of plan participants, or actuarial interest rate assumption."[18]

---

[18]See, for example, Report to Participants on Large Corporate Pensions 1985, Greenwich Associates, 1985.

**TABLE 17–10   Estimated Portfolio Mix: Private Pension Funds 1995**

|  | Percent | Dollars (billions) |
|---|---|---|
| Cash and equivalents | 6.0 | 300 |
| Equities | 48.0 | 2400 |
| Fixed income | 30.0 | 1500 |
| Real estate | 4.0 | 200 |
| Commingled real estate equity funds | 4.5 | 225 |
| Mortgages | 2.0 | 100 |
| International investments | 3.5 | 175 |
| Venture capital | 1.5 | 75 |
| Collectibles and precious metals | –0– | –0– |
| Other | .5 | 25 |
|  | 100.0% | $5000 |

SOURCE: Money Market Directories 1986.

## Establishing Basic Investment Policies

Part of the failure of pension funds to achieve better performance can be attributed to the lack of a clear, concise statement of investment policy. The same is true for other investor groups, including individual investors.[19] As was already pointed out in Part 2, portfolio management is an integrated, dynamic process—not a destination. The process starts, to be effective, with the creation of investment policy, a set of decisions defining portfolio goals and objectives along with the methods by which they will hopefully be achieved. As such, investment policy is a broad concept, linking the various critical elements that comprise the scope of investment decision making. Its high purpose, according to Charles Ellis, is to establish useful guidelines for investment managers that are genuinely appropriate to the realities of the investor's objectives and the realities of the investment marketplace. These are the internal and the external realms of investing, and investment policy must be designed to work well in both realms. In addition, good investment policies are "right" for both the long-term and for the many short-term periods that will be experienced in the market.[20] The principal reason for articulating long-term investment policy explicitly, and preferably in writing if a professional manager is being employed to do the investing, is to protect the portfolio from ad hoc revisions of sound long-term policy, and to help the portfolio managers hold to long-term policy when short-term exigencies are most distressing and the policy is most in doubt.[21]

---

[19]A recent survey of financial planners and investment advisers indicates that the second most common mistake made by individual investors with regard to portfolio planning is the failure to establish clearcut investment objectives and investment policy guidelines. The first mistake was the failure to consider tax considerations as part of the portfolio decision-making process. See Michael C. Thomsett, "10 Common Investment Mistakes," *American Way,* April 1, 1986.

[20]Charles D. Ellis, *Investment Policy, How to Win the Loser's Game* (Homewood, Ill.: Dow Jones-Irwin, 1985), p. 57.

[21]Ibid. p. 53.

**FIGURE 17–4  Portfolio Management Flow-Chart**

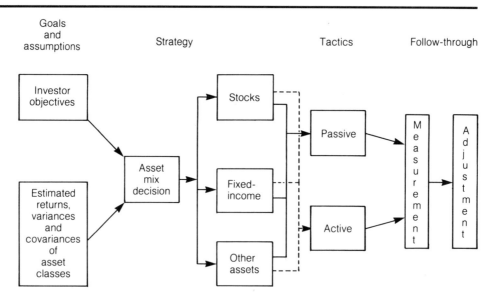

Figure 17–4 has been designed to show how the various elements interconnect. They should be viewed in the context of material previously presented, particularly in Part 2. As Maginn and Tuttle so appropriately point out:

> Portfolio management is a process which, complete with feedback loops for monitoring and adjustment, is continuous and systematic. The process can be as loose or as disciplined, as quantitative or as judgmental, and as simple or as complex as its operators wish it to be.[22]

While portfolio management, as seen through investment policy statements, tends to be a "personalized" affair, meaning different things to different investors, all investment policy statements share certain common concerns. For example, reasonable objectives must be set, giving careful consideration to the needs and constraints of the portfolio's sponsor or owner (as in the case of individuals). As shown in Figure 17–4, these must be blended with rational capital market expectations. Then guidelines must be established governing how the various asset categories to be used are to be mixed in the portfolio. Next, a variety of strategic decisions must be made involving how the portfolio is to actually manage assets within each category. This is discussed in the next chapter. Performance measurement, discussed in Chapter 5, requires matching results with predetermined goals and objectives—not just the market or against other members of a similar investor grouping. Finally, adjustments must be made to reflect and recognize important changes in any of the elements making up the entire process, which then starts once again.

Designers of investment policy statements must also carefully identify responsibil-

---

[22]John L. Maginn and Donald L. Tuttle, "The Portfolio Management Process and Its Dynamics," in *Managing Investment Portfolios, A Dynamic Process,* (New York: Warren, Gorham & Lamont, Inc.: © 1983, 1985), p. 2.

**TABLE 17-11   Fiduciary Responsibilities and Investment Management**

| Decision | Responsibility | Frequency of Review |
|---|---|---|
| Determination of investment objectives. | Board of Trustees or delegative committee. | Very infrequent, unless highly unusual circumstances present themselves. |
| Structural deployment of assets to achieve these goals. | Board of Trustees or delegative committee (May on occasion be left to investment managers). | Same as above. |
| Specific investment management guidelines and restrictions. | Board of Trustees. | Same as above. |
| Establishment of criteria by which to measure investment results. | Board of Trustees (Usually with outside consultation). | Same as above. |
| Selection of investment managers. | Board of Trustees. | At least three years unless unusual circumstances present themselves, but other time periods may be also found appropriate. |
| Disposition of portfolio assets within guideline framework; portfolio decisions. | Investment managers. | Determined by investment philosophy, portfolio strategy, and decision-making procedures of investment manager. |
| Review of current economic and investment posture. | Management appointed committee and investment manager representatives. | Three or four times a year supplemented by in-between written and oral communication, particularly covering significant developments or major changes. |
| Monitoring of transaction activity. | Delegated management representative. | Continuously. |
| Performance review. | Board of Trustees. | Quarterly, with an intensive review on an annual basis. Judgments to be made over a full market cycle, normally three years. |
| Adjustments to investment policy. | Board of Trustees. | In conjunction with investment managers. Frequency of review is at least annually. |

ity for each phase of activity. That is, who is responsible for what. Table 17–11 shows how one large pension fund views the problem. Part of the purpose behind such articulation was to separate policy decisions from operational maneuvers. As Ellis points out, "Portfolio operations should clearly be the responsibility of the investment manager. Policy is the responsibility of the client. Of course, they are not kept in isolation from each other."[23]

Figure 17–5 shows some examples of actual investment policy statements created by different types of investors. We will use the large corporate pension fund as a case study for the remainder of our discussion.[24] This, as all investment policy statements, should be viewed in the context of whether or not it meets the following criteria.[25]

[23]Ellis, *Investment Policy, How to Win the Loser's Game*, p. 60.

[24]Readers should keep in mind that this investment policy statement and the capital market expectations contained therein were used at the time of implementation several years ago. It is against this framework that results will be assessed later.

[25]Ellis, *Investment Policy, How to Win the Loser's Game*, p. 62.

**FIGURE 17–5   Investment Policy Statement: Large Corporate Pension Fund**

**Investment objective**

The primary objective of the Merrill Lynch Pension Fund is to earn a total rate of return from portfolio assets which will permit payment of benefits at current or higher levels and will maintain the funded ratio of the plan (assets as a percentage of plan continuation liability) at its present level of 85 percent and to maintain a contribution rate of no more than 4.9 percent of payroll, based on current plan benefits and existing actuarial requirements.

**Planning horizon**

Based on an analysis of prospective rates of return, a recently completed actuarial study, and other factors, the Merrill Lynch Pension Fund Trustees have decided to organize portfolio planning decisions on a five year time horizon, with results to be measured annually, on a calendar basis, and to be reported quarterly.

**Capital market assumptions**

The following capital market assumptions (implied rates of return) have been used for the determination of broad investment policy.

|  | Average Annual Rate of Return | Standard Deviation of Annual Return |
|---|---|---|
| Stocks | 17.0% | 27.0% |
| Bonds | 11.5 | 9.5 |
| Cash | 8.0 | 2.0 |
| Inflation rate | 8.0 | |

**Asset mix***

It is the general policy of the pension fund to be invested with a bond/stock relationship of 50/50. The pension fund trustees can, however, adjust this ratio within a range of 70/30, in either direction, based upon their view of prospective market conditions and upon consultation with professional investment advice. It is contemplated that asset mix decisions will be made at least once a year, although unusual market advice may necessitate more frequent review.

**Expected return**

It is expected that a portfolio which invested 50 percent in common stocks and 50 percent in bonds would, over the planning period, produce an average annual real rate of return of 3 percent. Attainment of this rate of return would maintain, approximately, the current contribution rate of 4.9 percent by 1984. Concomitantly, the funded ratio by 1984, assuming the indicated rate of return, would drop from its current level of 85.2 to 84.0.

NOTE: While this level of expected real returns appears conservative in view of the 9% real return expected from stocks, the Trustees were advised by their portfolio managers of the likelihood that equity investments would be at the low end of the permissible range during the early years and adjusted expectations accordingly.

*Subsequent to the creation of these investment policy guidelines, pension fund trustees expanded the range of asset categories to include real estate up to 15 percent of the total portfolio. Common stock guidelines were broadened to enable non-U.S. equities to be held.

1. Is the policy carefully designed to meet the real needs and objectives of this specific client?
2. Is the policy written so clearly and explicitly that a competent stranger could manage the portfolio and conform to the client's intentions?
3. Would the client have been able to sustain commitment to the policies during the capital markets that have actually been experienced over the past 50 or 60 years—particularly over the past 10 years?
4. Would the investment manager have been able to maintain fidelity to the policy over the same periods?
5. Would the policy, if implemented, have achieved the client's objectives?

**FIGURE 17–5 (continued)    Investment Policy Statement: Value Oriented Mutual Fund**

The investment objective of the Fund is to seek capital appreciation† and, secondarily, income by investing in securities, primarily equities, that management of the Fund believes are undervalued and therefore represent basic investment value. The Fund seeks special opportunities in securities that are selling at a discount, either from book value or historical price-earnings ratios, or seem capable of recovering from temporary out-of-favor considerations. Particular emphasis is placed on securities which provide an above-average dividend return and sell at a below-average price-earnings ratio. There can be no assurance that the objective of the Fund will be realized.

The investment policy of the Fund is based upon the belief that the pricing mechanism of the securities markets lacks total efficiency and has a tendency to inflate prices of securities in favorable market climates and depress prices of securities in unfavorable climates. Based upon this premise, management believes that favorable changes in market prices are more likely to begin when securities are out-of-favor, earnings are depressed, price-earnings ratios are relatively low, investment expectations are limited, and there is no real general interest in the particular security or industry involved. On the other hand, management believes that negative developments are more likely to occur when investment expectations are generally high, stock prices are advancing or have advanced rapidly, price-earnings ratios have been inflated, and the industry or issue continues to gain new investment acceptance on an accelerated basis. In other words, management believes that market prices of securities with relatively high price-earnings ratios are more susceptible to unexpected adverse developments while securities with relatively low price-earnings ratios are more favorably positioned to benefit from favorable, but generally unanticipated, events. This investment policy departs from traditional philosophy. Management of the Fund believes that the market risk involved in this policy is moderated somewhat by the emphasis on securities with above-average dividend returns.

The current institutionally-dominated market tends to ignore, to some extent, the numerous secondary issues whose market capitalizations are below those of the relatively few larger-size growth companies. It is expected that the Fund's portfolio will generally have significant representation in this secondary segment of the market.

†This statement of investment objectives is fairly typical of those contained in mutual fund prospecti. However, from the vantage point of portfolio theory, there is still some "fuzziness" as to just what is expected in terms relative to the market performance and whether or not return expectations are to be considered in real or nominal terms. Consequently, performance measurement judgments also tend to become clouded.

SOURCE: Merrill Lynch Basic Value Fund.

## Applying Portfolio Theory

Many investors—individual and institutional alike—believe sincerely that outperforming the stock market, both up and down, is a valid performance expectation. That is, the combination of astute stock selection and/or good timing decisions should result in superior (above market) returns regardless of market trend. When the market is rising, investments are expected to produce greater-than-average gains, and when prices are falling, investment decisions are supposed to limit losses to less than the general experience. These are fairly typical desires of most *active* market participants. But are they reasonable?

Let's consider as an example a fairly commonplace set of investment objectives, which could easily apply to an individual as well as an institutional investor. Our illustrative investor would like to (1) preserve capital and (2) achieve growing wealth and income by holding a reasonably high-quality, diversified common stock portfolio. More precisely, the investor hopes to earn a total annual rate of return 25 percent

**FIGURE 17–5 (concluded)    Investment Policy Statement: National Health Organization**

---

**Objectives**

The overall portfolio is expected to produce, over three- to five-year market cycles, a total rate of return net of investment expenses at least 3 percent per year in excess of the rate of inflation. Such results will also be evaluated in comparison with a *yardstick portfolio* invested as follows:

   50% in S&P 500 Stock Index.
   40% in the Shearson Lehman Government/Corporate Bond Index.
   10% in the average record of a sample of open-end equity real estate accounts.

**Guidelines**

1.   No equity investment (common stock and securities convertible into common stock) shall be made which would increase such holdings to more than 60 percent of the total assets under management, based on market value. And no sales should be made to decrease such holdings to less than 40 percent of such assets. In no event, moreover, shall equities amount to more than 60 percent or less than 40 percent of assets for more than six consecutive months.

2.   No investment in fixed-income-type vehicles shall be made which would increase such holdings to more than 50 percent of the total assets under management. And no sales should be made which would decrease such holdings to less than 30 percent of such assets. In no event, moreover, shall fixed income assets amount to more than 50 percent or less than 30 percent of assets for more than six consecutive months.

3.   At least 20 percent of total assets shall be kept invested in fixed-income vehicles with low variability of returns and which allow for the payment of benefit distributions required by the Plan without any penalty or adjustment in asset value.

4.   Real estate assets should be gradually accumulated over a three to five year period to reach a 10 percent of invested asset target ratio. It is not expected that market timing will play a significant role in the establishment of this position.

**Measurement of performance and reporting requirements**

The Committee will review performance on a quarterly basis, and any significant deviations from the target results over a significant time period will lead to a reevaluation of the program.

**Investment policy review**

The Committee will, at least annually, review this statement of Policy Objectives and Guidelines to assure its continued relevance to the Plan's requirements.

---

better than the market (S&P 500) during an up cycle but incur only 85 percent of the market's loss on the down side—in other words, superior performance during both bull and bear markets, as summarized on the next page.

Capital asset pricing theory highlights the inconsistency of such common investor desires. Figure 17–6 illustrates expected returns in terms of various levels of risk, as expressed by the beta coefficient of alternative portfolios. A well-diversified portfolio carrying a beta of 1.0 would represent the market as measured by, say, the S&P 500 Stock Price Index. The graph assumes that the average rate of return on the S&P 500 (appreciation plus dividend income) will be 15 percent per annum, that the average risk-free rate will be 10 percent, and that periodic bear markets will produce negative market returns of 15 percent during those bear market years. Using the market line concept, Figure 17–6 illustrates the expected rate of return of a portfolio with beta other than 1.0.

## Investment Expectations (annual percent change)

|  | S&P 500 | Trust Fund |
|---|---|---|
| Bull markets | + 30% | + 37.5% |
|  | + 20 | + 25.0 |
|  | + 15 | + 18.75 |
|  | + 10 | + 12.5 |
|  | + 5 | + 6.25 |
| Bear markets | − 5 | − 4.25 |
|  | − 10 | − 8.5 |
|  | − 15 | − 12.75 |
|  | − 20 | − 17.0 |
|  | − 30 | − 25.5 |

Let us consider in this context the set of investment objectives described above. Our investor seeks a return of 18.75 percent during the year when the market returns 15 percent. In order to achieve this level of return, Figure 17–6 indicates that the portfolio's beta coefficient will have to be slightly higher than 1.5. (To simplify the discussion, it is assumed for the moment that alpha is zero; i.e., stock selection produces no incremental return, either positive or negative.) Even if one questions the notion that there is a clear linear relationship between beta and rate of return, surely the implication of the market line is that the portfolio required to achieve the upside objective represents a position significantly more risky than the market. Moreover, the portfolio probably would violate the desire for a diversified portfolio of quality investments with preservation of capital, since it is difficult to find a large

**FIGURE 17–6  A Framework for Establishing Long-Term Investment Objectives**

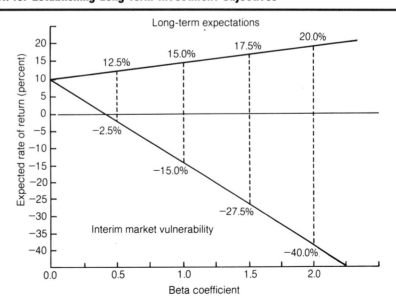

number of quality stocks with high betas, and leveraging a low-beta portfolio would not be considered acceptable by most investors.

This incompatibility of objectives stands out when we consider the portfolio results during a bear market. Recall that the investment manager is being asked to achieve a loss of only 12.75 percent when the market declines 15 percent. Does our market line model, even if we recognize its imperfections, accommodate these expectations? Clearly it does not. We can see in Figure 17–6 that under the assumptions of our model, a portfolio with a beta of 1.5 can be expected to generate a return of $-27.5$ percent when the market declines 15 percent (and the risk-free rate is 10 percent).

In order for the portfolio to achieve a return of $-12.75$ percent when the market return is $-15$ percent, the beta would have to be reduced from 1.5 to about 0.9. This is derived as follows:

$$R_p = R_f + B(R_m - R_f)$$
$$-12.75\% = 10\% + B(-15\% - 10\%)$$
$$-22.75\% = B(-25\%)$$
$$B = \frac{-22.75\%}{-25\%}$$
$$B = 0.9$$

It would appear rather utopian, however, to expect portfolio managers to forecast a bear market long enough in advance and be willing to incur the high transaction costs involved to shift the beta of their portfolios from 1.5 to 0.9. And it would appear equally utopian, in view of the evidence provided in Chapter 5, to expect portfolio managers to be so expert at security selection that a sufficient alpha can be achieved to offset the results of having an inappropriate beta.

The capital asset pricing model suggests that a goal of substantially outperforming the market on the upside involves a large exposure to proportionately greater under-performance on the downside. This leveraged exposure to underperformance is a function of the risk-free rate being included in the market line model, which seems reasonable, since an investor always has the alternative of owning risk-free assets. Recall that the market line is $R_p = R_f + B(R_m - R_f)$. If $R_m$ is expected to be greater than $R_f$, the only way to "beat the market" substantially, absent great security selection skills, is to have a portfolio with a high beta. But undertaking a high beta in the expectation that $R_m$ is greater than $R_f$ exposes one to the risk that if $R_m$ is less than $R_f$, $R_p$ will reflect the difference magnified by the beta of the portfolio.

For example, as Figure 17–6 shows, a portfolio with a 1.5 beta, when the risk-free rate is 10 percent, has the potential of producing a $-27.5$ percent return against a long-term potential of 17.5 percent per annum, a spread of 45 percent. When the portfolio beta increases to 2.0, the range of returns between interim risk ($-40$ percent) and longer term returns (20 percent) expands to 60 percent. In other words, a 0.5 or one-third increase in a portfolio's beta enlarges the spread between interim risk and longer term potential by one third (from 45 to 60 percent). But even if this strict linearity is not accepted as the norm, the market line concept is useful in clarifying investment objectives and indicating what a set of objectives implies in terms of market timing (adjustment of beta) and the ability to secure gains (alphas) from the astute selection of undervalued securities. For institutional investors, this produces a greater degree of understanding on the part of both client and investment manager and can provide the basis for a better relationship than generally exists. Individuals, on the other hand, will be better able to understand the vulnerability of high-risk portfolios since it is clear that some investors do not possess the temperament to endure bear markets in the pursuit of ambitious investment returns.

Let us next explore the process by which modern portfolio theory can be applied to selecting strategies for achieving the desired objectives.

## Selecting Efficient Strategies

Once objectives are clarified, investors must determine how most efficiently to distribute portfolio assets. Few investors, operating in the traditional intuitive manner, achieve portfolios which lie on the efficient frontier described in Chapter 4. More often than not, a portfolio will be at some interior point *P* of Figure 17–7. (The illustration relates to a portfolio manager who is unable to employ leverage to raise the risk level, even though capital asset pricing theory assumes such leverage can be used to increase portfolio risk.)

Through the use of portfolio optimization mathematics, given certain information inputs to be described below, the portfolio manager can determine what actions would be necessary to shift from point *P* to any one of four (or more) points on the efficient frontier.[26]

**FIGURE 17–7   *Alternative Points on the Efficient Frontier***

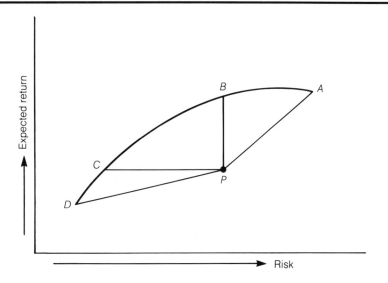

------

[26]It is not necessary for each investment management organization to develop and maintain its own complicated programming and computer capability to make these determinations. There are available to most institutional investors a variety of service firms which will perform quantitative portfolio analysis on a regular basis. Frequently, this can be arranged through a New York Stock Exchange firm which will accept commissions as payment.

> At point *A* he would minimize portfolio risk at the maximum level of
> expected return which his universe of securities is capable of providing.
>
> At point *B* he would maximize the portfolio's expected return at the *existing
> level of risk*.
>
> At point *C* he would minimize portfolio risk at the *existing level of expected
> return*.
>
> At point *D* he would maximize the portfolio's expected return at the
> minimum risk level which his universe of securities is capable of providing.

In determining the investment composition required to arrive at these points on
the efficient frontier, most of the available computer programs allow for the inclusion
of a variety of portfolio constraints. The most important of these involves the pre-
determination of some maximum or minimum level of commitment (in terms of a
percentage of total portfolio value) for any one class of security, any one issue, or
any one industry classification. This type of constraint can be critical because many
investment organizations (e.g., mutual funds) have legally mandated diversification
requirements.

***Asset Mix Decisions.***     The concept of efficient frontiers can be applied to the
problem of deciding how investors should divide their assets among the major categories—stocks, bonds, real estate, etc. Creating the appropriate composition of portfolio assets (that is, a mix that accurately reflects objectives) is perhaps the most
important aspect of effective investment management.

Consider the deliberations facing the trustees of our case study, a large corporate
pension fund sponsored by a leading diversified financial services company. The
trustees have already decided that the primary objective of the fund is to earn a total
rate of return from portfolio assets which will permit payments of benefits at current
or higher levels and will maintain the funded ratio of the plan (assets as a percentage
of plan liability) at its present level of 85 percent and to maintain an annual contribution rate of not more than the present 4.9 percent of payroll, based on current
planned benefits and the existing actuarial requirements of 7.0 percent. An analysis
by a special consulting firm determined that a real rate of return, over the planning
period, of 3.0 percent per annum would be required to achieve the trustees' primary
investment objectives.[27] (Earning the actuarial rate of 7.0 percent would be insuffi-
cient in light of revised inflation forecasts and concern over a number of factors not
included in the original actuarial rate determination.) The market value of the portfolio is approximately $132 million, and the annual cash flow (contributions less
payments to retired employees) amounts to $17 million. The major question then is
"How are portfolio assets to be distributed?"

Such concerns are not limited to institutional investors. For example, contemplate
the portfolio planning problems of a middle-aged heart surgeon earning $250,000 a
year from his medical practice and having a portfolio of approximately $650,000.
The doctor, now 50, desires to continue his practice until age 60. His primary in-

---

[27]As a matter of fact, prior to conducting a study along the lines described in this chapter, the
pension fund was 70 percent invested in stocks and 30 percent in long-term, fixed-income securities.
Further, the trustees prior to their analysis, had no knowledge as to the level of returns actually
required to meet their objectives.

vestment goal is to assure himself adequate retirement funds; current income is of minimal importance. The doctor must decide what rate of return would be required to provide a future asset base sufficient to yield real income equal to his needs after retirement, and he must then determine how assets are to be positioned to maximize the probability of actually achieving this return.

***Capital Market Assumptions.*** One of the major difficulties usually facing investors in deciding how much of a portfolio to allocate to each asset category is their limited experience with the actual interaction between investment returns. Consequently, notions of appropriate asset mix tend to be based upon intuition rather than evidence and experience. Portfolio theory, however, highlights the value of beginning asset mix deliberations with an analysis of expected returns for a number of "efficiently" constructed portfolios, such as those shown in Table 17–13, which is based on the capital market assumptions shown in Table 17–12.[28] Note that our analysis is stated in terms of *real* returns, i.e., net of inflation, which is more helpful than using *nominal* returns for two important reasons: First, pension funds are, or at least should be, in the final analysis interested in real returns since inflation affects both the asset return and liability sides of the equation approximately equally. Second, it avoids distracting arguments over the prospective rate of inflation, which has not proved susceptible to reliable forecasting.[29]

Furthermore, these assumptions are used merely to illustrate the process, and alternative judgments can easily be incorporated into computer programs if the user believes that capital market movements over the planning period will depart from the historic pattern.

The risk inherent in a portfolio mix can be further clarified by consideration of ranges of uncertainty (or confidence intervals) for expected dispersion of returns over various time horizons. As an example, consider the 4 percent expected real return portfolio in the six asset case which has an annual standard deviation of returns of 7.2 percent. For this particular portfolio, two ranges of uncertainty for 1- to 15-year time horizons are depicted in Figure 17–8.

The narrower band of uncertainty is based upon one standard deviation from the expected return and includes 68 percent of the probability distribution. In other words, the interval defined by the first range of uncertainty encompasses 68 percent of the returns produced by the asset mix comprising this particular portfolio. As an example, the one year 68 percent confidence band ranges from +11.2 percent (4 percent expected return plus 7.2 percent annual standard deviation) to −3.2 percent (4 percent expected return minus 7.2 percent annual standard deviation). This return interval from +11.2 percent to −3.2 percent covers 68 percent of the annual returns produced by this portfolio. The wider band of uncertainty is based upon two standard deviations from the expected return and includes 95 percent of the probability distribution. While negative real returns are a distinct possibility in the nearer

---

[28]This section draws heavily on material used by Prudential Asset Management Company, a subsidiary of the Prudential Insurance Company of America, to explain these concepts to corporate pension fund trustees.

[29]Unfortunately, most trustees or investment managers do not conceptualize their responsibilities in terms of purchasing power or real rates of return. See, for example, Arthur Sharplin, "Stalking the Elusive 'Real Return' on Investments," *Pension World*, January 1986.

**TABLE 17–12   Capital Market Assumptions**

| Asset Type | Expected Annual Real Returns | Expected Annual Standard Deviation |
|---|---|---|
| Short-term investments | 0.0 | 3.0 |
| Intermediate bonds | 1.5 | 5.5 |
| Foreign bonds | 2.1 | 8.0 |
| Long-term bonds | 2.5 | 8.3 |
| Real estate | 4.0 | 13.5 |
| Large stocks | 7.5 | 15.5 |
| Foreign stocks | 7.6 | 17.0 |
| Small stocks | 9.0 | 19.0 |

**Interrelationships***

| | Short-Term Investments | Intermediate Bonds | Foreign Bonds | Long-Term Bonds | Real Estate | Large Stocks | Foreign Stocks | Small Stocks |
|---|---|---|---|---|---|---|---|---|
| Short-term investments | 1 | | | | | | | |
| Intermediate bonds | .27 | 1 | | | | | | |
| Foreign bonds | .13 | .49 | 1 | | | | | |
| Long-term bonds | .21 | .95 | .41 | 1 | | | | |
| Real estate | .20 | −.11 | −.09 | −.13 | 1 | | | |
| Large stocks | .16 | .39 | .25 | .40 | .15 | 1 | | |
| Foreign stocks | .17 | .39 | .72 | .35 | .09 | .52 | 1 | |
| Small stocks | .22 | .44 | .24 | .42 | .10 | .89 | .54 | 1 |

*The interrelationships are expressed by the correlation coefficient, which ranges from +1.0, indicating perfect positive correlation, to −1.0, perfect negative correlation. A correlation of zero indicates no relationship.
SOURCE: Prudential Asset Management Company.

term, they are increasingly unlikely in the longer run as shown by the convergence of the uncertainty band toward the 4 percent expected real return.

Looking at Table 17–13, it is clear that risk (as measured by the standard deviation of annual returns) and return are positively correlated. Also, the higher the expected real return, the greater the proportion of common stock in the portfolio. Table 17–14 compares two three-asset class portfolios, one expected to provide a 5 percent average annual real return and one expected to produce a 2 percent average annual real return. The 3 percent increase in expected real returns requires a portfolio mix of significantly more stocks and bonds and substantially less cash. At the same time, risk, the standard deviation of annual return, more than doubles.

Armed with this information, let's see how a few different investors might apply our table of expected returns (Table 17–12) to their own purposes.

Consider first, on the institutional side, the case of a pension fund. Pension funds can usually plan their investment strategy for long and extended periods. However, most trustees remain very sensitive to short-term results, both in the absolute and relative to other managers. Use of these techniques holds the key, according to one observer, to keeping the proper focus between the two horizons in that "asset allocation models can have a therapeutic function in correcting myopic responses to a condition requiring foresight."[30]

---

[30]Gifford Fong, "An Asset Allocation Framework," *Journal of Portfolio Management*, Winter 1980, p. 64.

**TABLE 17–13   Asset Mix at Various Levels of Expected Returns**

### Eight-Asset Class Portfolio
### Asset Mix (Percent)

| Average Real Return | Standard Deviation | Cash | Intermediate Bonds | Long-Term Bonds | Real Estate | Large Stocks | Small Stocks | Foreign Bonds | Foreign Stocks |
|---|---|---|---|---|---|---|---|---|---|
| 1.00 |      | 62 | 18 | 0  | 7  | 3  | 0  | 9  | 0  |
| 2.00 | 4.1  | 40 | 24 | 0  | 13 | 10 | 0  | 12 | 2  |
| 3.00 | 5.5  | 24 | 16 | 10 | 19 | 12 | 3  | 13 | 5  |
| 3.50 |      | 16 | 8  | 17 | 21 | 12 | 4  | 14 | 7  |
| 4.00 | 6.9  | 9  | 1  | 24 | 24 | 13 | 6  | 15 | 8  |
| 4.50 |      | 0  | 0  | 27 | 27 | 14 | 7  | 15 | 10 |
| 5.00 | 8.4  | 0  | 0  | 26 | 28 | 15 | 9  | 6  | 16 |
| 6.00 | 10.1 | 0  | 0  | 15 | 29 | 17 | 15 | 0  | 24 |
| 7.00 | 12.1 | 0  | 0  | 0  | 27 | 17 | 27 | 0  | 30 |

### Six-Asset Class Portfolio
### Asset Mix (Percent)

| Average Real Return | Standard Deviation | Cash | Intermediate Bonds | Long-Term Bonds | Real Estate | Large Stocks | Small Stocks |
|---|---|---|---|---|---|---|---|
| 1.00 |      | 63 | 25 | 0  | 7  | 5  | 0  |
| 2.00 | 4.3  | 39 | 35 | 0  | 14 | 12 | 0  |
| 3.00 | 5.7  | 16 | 41 | 3  | 20 | 15 | 4  |
| 3.50 |      | 9  | 35 | 9  | 24 | 17 | 6  |
| 4.00 | 7.2  | 1  | 31 | 16 | 27 | 18 | 8  |
| 4.50 |      | 0  | 10 | 30 | 30 | 19 | 11 |
| 5.00 | 8.8  | 0  | 0  | 33 | 31 | 20 | 16 |
| 6.00 | 10.7 | 0  | 0  | 16 | 32 | 24 | 28 |
| 7.00 | 12.9 | 0  | 0  | 0  | 32 | 26 | 42 |

### Three-Asset Class Portfolio
### Asset Mix (Percent)

| Average Real Return | Standard Deviation | Cash | Long-Term Bonds | Large Stocks |
|---|---|---|---|---|
| 1.00 |      | 79 | 12 | 9  |
| 2.00 | 4.8  | 61 | 18 | 21 |
| 3.00 | 6.4  | 43 | 25 | 32 |
| 3.50 |      | 35 | 28 | 37 |
| 4.00 | 8.2  | 25 | 32 | 43 |
| 4.50 |      | 17 | 35 | 48 |
| 5.00 | 10.1 | 8  | 38 | 54 |
| 6.00 | 12.1 | 0  | 30 | 70 |
| 7.00 | 14.3 | 0  | 10 | 90 |

SOURCE: Prudential Asset Management Company.

As mentioned earlier, the trustees of our pension plan had determined a 3 percent average annual real return would be sufficient to meet their primary investment objectives. Table 17–13 shows that the optimal portfolio (based on the capital market expectations contained in Table 17–12) using a six-asset mix would be: 16 percent cash equivalent (T bills), 41 percent intermediate-term bonds, 3 percent long-term

**FIGURE 17–8  Two Ranges of Uncertainty for a Six-Asset Portfolio**

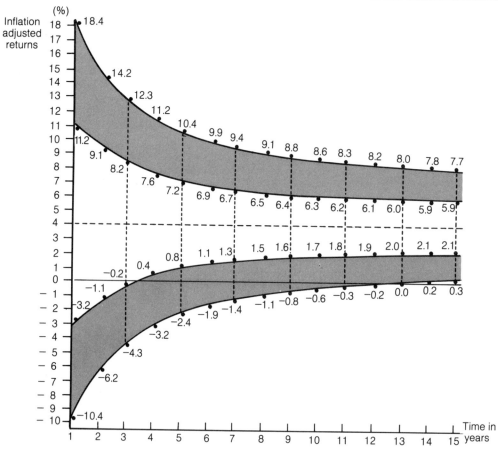

SOURCE: Prudential Asset Management Company.

bonds, 20 percent real estate, 15 percent large capitalization common stocks, and 4 percent small stocks. Note that this distribution of assets would not fall within the original guidelines established by the investment policy statement shown previously in Figure 17–5 because real estate was not included in the asset mix at that time.

Further, adoption of such a portfolio mix carries with it the clear understanding that during a bull market this portfolio's return would most likely be much lower than the general market's and lower than portfolios more heavily invested in common stocks. In other words, while the objective would be achieved, relative performance would be poor. Conversely, during a bear market, relative performance would be much better.

Given this recognition, combined with the need for most trustee groups to give at least some consideration to relative returns over the planning period, a decision was actually made to allow the pension fund's investment manager to position the portfolio in as little as 20 percent common stocks when conditions warrant. At the same

**TABLE 17–14  Portfolio Comparisons**

| | Average Expected Return | Standard Deviation | Portfolio Mix | | |
|---|---|---|---|---|---|
| | | | Cash | Bonds | Stocks |
| | 5.00% | 10.1% | 8% | 38% | 54% |
| | 2.00 | 4.8 | 61 | 18 | 21 |

SOURCE: Table 17–13.

time, the trustees made it very clear to the investment manager that they expected returns to increase commensurately during periods when a more risky position was actually undertaken.

Now, what about our 50-year-old doctor with a $650,000 portfolio planning for retirement 10 years hence? Based on the lines of our discussion thus far, the doctor's decision-making process should focus on the following vital questions:

1. What retirement income will be needed?
2. How much principal will be required to generate this income assuming, for example, a nominal risk-free rate of 7.5 percent and an equivalent rate of inflation (i.e., a zero real return on risk-free investments, as in Table 17–12.
3. At what rate must the current portfolio grow over the next 10 years in order to achieve the required principal?
4. What portfolio mix provides the most likely prospect for achieving this return (under the capital market assumptions discussed earlier)?

If we assume that the doctor decides on the need for a risk-free return equal to one half his present earnings, annual income must come to $125,000. A risk-free rate of 7.5 percent calls for a portfolio value of approximately $1.7 million to produce such income. In other words, the present portfolio of $650,000 must grow at an annual rate of 10 percent over the doctor's remaining working life. If we further assume that annual income tax liabilities on dividends, interest, and realized capital gains will amount to one third of each year's total return, the present portfolio must produce, under these assumptions, an average annual rate of return of 15.0 percent or about 7.0 percent in real terms per annum. Since most individual investors tend to consider stocks, bonds, and bills in their investment planning, the portfolio from Table 17–13, representing the most efficient mix for the doctor's planning purpose would be one comprised of almost all comon stocks. Such an investment profile is considered by most investors to be very risky, as indicated by the standard deviation of annual returns of more than 14 percent.

Another alternative available to the doctor would be to lower his age-60 portfolio goal and plan to meet his retirement income requirements by "cannibalizing" principal to supplement investment income. (Of course, his children and other heirs might not take too kindly to this idea, but let's put such considerations aside.) For example, instead of trying to build up his $650,000 into a $1.7 million portfolio, which requires a 10 percent per annum return net of taxes, he might shoot for a $1.25 million portfolio, which would require only 6.75 percent per annum net.

We have said that the doctor wants to spend $125,000 per year during his retirement. In relation to a principal amount of $1.25 million, $125,000 is 10 percent. With a risk-free rate of only 7.5 percent, clearly interest income will have to be supplemented by withdrawals of principal. There is a formula that can be used to calculate the number of years such principal withdrawals can be continued before it is exhausted.[31] Application of this formula leads to the conclusion that a portfolio having a value of $1.25 million would run out in about 20 years.

Mortality tables in use by insurance companies today indicate that the doctor would be expected to live almost 20 years after retirement at age 60. Therefore, he would probably be on pretty thin ice with a retirement portfolio of $1.25 million.

Still another alternative would be for the doctor to purchase an annuity from an insurance company when he retires. As of this writing, an annuity purchased for $1.7 million woud provide a *guaranteed lifetime income* of approximately $151,000 per year, while an annuity purchased for $1.25 million would provide $89,000 per year for life. Thus, it would appear that the doctor's goal should be to build up a retirement fund in excess of $1.25 million, but it needn't be as great as $1.7 million.

### *Asset Mix in the Real World.*

An important point must be stressed at this juncture. Asset mix deliberations are not merely an academic exercise but play an important role in real-world investing. A recent study shows that well over half of the pension plan sponsors surveyed rank long-term asset allocation decisions as the most important decisions in pension plan management. As shown in Table 17–15, no other aspect of pension plan management matches the long-term asset allocation decision in perceived importance. What is surprising, at least to us, is the relatively large percentage of survey respondents who believe other elements are more important.

Pension fund trustees have good reason to believe in the primary importance of asset allocation. Done well, it pays off in improved performance. For example, a study by SEI (a large, well-known investment performance measurement consulting organization) of 97 large pension funds for the 10-year period ended in 1983 showed that an incredible 87 percent of differential performance was related to asset class selection and only 9 percent was related to manager selection. A Hamilton Johnson (another highly regarded consulting firm) study demonstrated that by correctly alternating between stocks, bonds, and cash, over 10 years, annual returns three times those of the typical balanced fund can be realized.[32]

Leon G. Cooperman and Steven G. Einhorn of Goldman Sachs have looked into

---

[31]The formula for determining how long a pool of capital will support a withdrawal rate in excess of investment returns is:

$$x = \frac{i}{1 - (1 + i)^{-N}}$$

where

$x$ = Percentage of original capital to be withdrawn annually; i.e., the excess of (*a*) the amount you wish to spend as a percent of capital minus (*b*) the interest rate you expect to earn on the declining capital balance.

$i$ = Assumed compound rate of portfolio earnings over the withdrawal period.

$N$ = Number of years before capital is exhausted.

For a more detailed explanation see: Lawrence R. Rosen, *The Dow Jones-Irwin Guide to Interest,* Revised ed. (Homewood, Ill.: Dow Jones-Irwin, 1981), pp. 17–20.

[32]Barton M. Biggs, "Asset Allocation is Crucial," Morgan Stanley Perspectives, April 9, 1985.

**Table 17–15   Pension Plan Sponsor Views on Investment Management Decisions**

| | Rank of Importance | | | | | | | Average Rank |
|---|---|---|---|---|---|---|---|---|
| | **1** | **2** | **3** | **4** | **5** | **6** | **7 or blank** | |
| Long-term asset allocation | 29 | 5 | 5 | 2 | 4 | 3 | 1 | 2.2 |
| Strategic asset allocation | 8 | 17 | 5 | 5 | 5 | 7 | 2 | 3.2 |
| Specialty asset allocation | 0 | 1 | 5 | 3 | 5 | 14 | 21 | 5.8 |
| Alternative investments | 1 | 3 | 10 | 10 | 17 | 4 | 4 | 4.4 |
| Equity management | 7 | 15 | 14 | 10 | 2 | 0 | 1 | 2.8 |
| Bond management | 2 | 5 | 13 | 15 | 10 | 4 | 0 | 3.8 |
| Balanced management | 2 | 1 | 2 | 1 | 5 | 9 | 29 | 6.0 |

SOURCE: *Financial Analysts Journal,* September–October 1985.

**TABLE 17–16   The Potential Benefit of the Asset Allocation Decisions
(for equity-only private pension funds)**

| Year | (1) Stocks | (2) Cash | (3) S&P 500 | (4) T Bill | (5) Adjusted Portfolio | (6) Normal Portfolio | (7) Potential Benefit of Asset Allocation Decision |
|---|---|---|---|---|---|---|---|
| 1973 | 89% | 11% | (14.8)% | 6.9% | (10.1)% | (12.5)% | 2.4% |
| 1974 | 82 | 18 | (26.4) | 8.0 | (14.1) | (20.3) | 6.2 |
| 1975 | 86 | 14 | 37.2 | 5.8 | 37.2 | 32.7 | 4.5 |
| 1976 | 90 | 10 | 23.6 | 5.1 | 23.6 | 21.8 | 1.8 |
| 1977 | 87 | 13 | (7.4) | 5.2 | (4.3) | (5.8) | 1.6 |
| 1978 | 83 | 17 | 6.4 | 7.4 | 6.7 | 6.5 | 0.2 |
| 1979 | 82 | 18 | 18.2 | 9.5 | 18.2 | 16.6 | 1.6 |
| 1980 | 82 | 18 | 32.3 | 11.4 | 32.3 | 28.6 | 3.7 |
| 1981 | 83 | 17 | (5.0) | 14.2 | 1.5 | (1.7) | 3.3 |
| 1982 | 83 | 17 | 21.4 | 11.4 | 21.4 | 19.7 | 1.7 |
| 1983 | 86 | 14 | 22.4 | 8.8 | 22.4 | 20.5 | 1.9 |
| 1984 | 85 | 15 | 6.1 | 10.0 | 7.3 | 6.7 | 0.6 |
| Average | | | 7.8 | 8.6 | 10.7 | 8.2 | 2.5 |

SOURCE: Goldman Sachs Research.

the question of whether asset allocation or active stock selection (varying common stock holdings as issues became both under- and over-priced) is the more important determinant of portfolio performance.

Admitting to some crudeness in their exercise, the Goldman Sachs strategists created Table 17–16 to measure the difference between stock selection and asset allocation over the 1973–84 period. "The portfolio unaffected by asset allocation decisions (the normal portfolio) provided an average annual return of 8.2 percent. The adjusted portfolio (which allows for adjustments to cash and equity exposure) yielded an average return of 10.7 percent. If one could forecast the relative performance of stocks and cash, the net benefit of the asset allocation decision would have averaged 2.5 percentage points annually in the last dozen years. This 2.5-percentage-point incremental return is significant: Equity money managers that outdistanced the S&P 500 by such a spread in the last decade would rank in the top 5 percent."[33]

***Adjusting the Asset Mix.***     Asset mix decisions are importantly influenced by expected rates of return, which in turn shift as market levels fluctuate. Some observers believe that a 1 percent change (plus or minus) in rate of return assumptions can change the optimal asset weighting by 10 percent in each category.[34] Furthermore, portfolio managers and trustees are advised constantly as to how to adjust their holdings in light of expected developments. Most major Wall Street research organizations publish periodic advice as to how portfolio assets should be distributed to achieve an optimum risk-return profile in light of market expectations.[35] Most of these suggestions, such as the one shown in Table 17–17, are predicated on the "strategists'" own short-term view of capital market movements, rather than being the product of matching expectations against historical experience. For example, Goldman Sachs states, "In setting our allocations for financial assets, our time horizon is approximately 12 months. Given the illiquid nature of real estate and the transaction costs involved, our time horizon is 5 to 10 years."[36] Morgan Stanley maintains a similar perspective.[37]

Our own experience indicates that most trustee groups tend to review portfolio allocation intensively at least once a year, usually at the beginning, in conjunction with a performance appraisal of the prior year's results. Such a schedule is particu-

**TABLE 17–17  *Recommended Portfolio Models***

| | Large Pension Fund | | | Large Equity Mutual Fund | | | Smaller Aggressive Mutual Fund | | |
|---|---|---|---|---|---|---|---|---|---|
| | Current Asset Allocation | Normal Range | Cash-Flow Allocation | Current Asset Allocation | Normal Range | Cash-Flow Allocation | Current Asset Allocation | Normal Range | Cash-Flow Allocation |
| Cash | 10% | 0–25% | 10% | 20% | 0–35% | 20% | 20% | 0–50% | 20% |
| Bonds | 30 | 10–35 | 30 | — | — | — | — | — | — |
| Property | 10 | 10–20 | 5 | — | — | — | — | — | — |
| Equities | 50 | 45–65 | 55 | 80 | 65–100 | 80 | 80 | 50–100 | 80 |
| | 100% | | 100% | 100% | | 100% | 100% | | 100% |

SOURCE: Goldman Sachs.

[33]Leon G. Cooperman and Steven G. Einhorn, "Investment Strategy Highlights," *Portfolio Strategy,* March 1985, p. 1h.

[34]See Lawrence S. Speidell, "Handle With Care: A Study of Asset Allocation Models," *Pensions & Investment Age,* October 29, 1984.

[35]Another method of reconstituting asset mix is to use interest rate and stock index futures contracts to change the portfolio exposure to equity and fixed-income markets. By altering the portfolio's risk using stock index and interest rate futures contracts, an investment manager is, effectively, changing asset allocation; nonetheless, capital does not move from one market to the other. Therefore, we can assume that a change in an asset's exposure to the risk of the market is, effectively, a change in asset allocation. See, Ravi Dattatreya and Mark A. Zurack, "Asset Allocation Using Futures Contracts," Goldman Sachs Stock Index Research, February 1985; and Pavan Sahgal, "Mapping Dynamic Asset Management Strategies," *Wall Street Computer Review,* March 1986. See also Edgar E. Peters, "Index Futures and Index Funds: The New Investment Marriage," *Pension World,* April 1986.

[36]Leon G. Cooperman, *Investment Strategy Highlights,* Goldman Sachs, February 1986, p. 1m.

[37]Barton M. Biggs, *Investment Perspective,* Morgan Stanley, February 4, 1986, p. 1.

larly appropriate for pension funds if quarterly or annual contributions in the new year will represent significant infusions of new capital into the portfolios. Generally, interim or short-term asset allocation decisions tend to focus more on the disposition of new cash flow rather than the redeployment of the entire portfolio. However, trustees and other investors are well advised to approach this vital aspect of the investment decision-making process with care and to predicate asset shifts by looking through short-term or transient forces. This is not to say that periodic review of current or pending capital market conditions should not be considered, but rather that the focus should be on the longer-term horizon. Investors, after periods of unusually strong or weak securities markets, sometimes lose sight of the normal, realistic rates of return they should expect to earn from their stocks and bonds.[38] Eugene B. Burroughs puts it this way: "As investors, we tend to look in the rearview mirror a bit too long and thus there is a lag in our perceptions versus the changing realities."[39]

To prevent such myopia from affecting objectivity, asset allocation discussions should concentrate on several fundamental factors which, considered in combination, are likely to lend to effective judgments. Recognizing that no "checklist" can cover each possible or even reasonable set of circumstance, Figure 17–9 has been prepared to serve as an initial agenda for asset mix discussions. Adherence to such an outline will reduce the much irrelevant conversation and personal opinions characteristic, we are sure, of most committee meetings on the subject.

As a matter of fact, trustees of our case study pension fund actually held an asset allocation discussion based on the material shown in Figure 17–9, just about five years after implementing the investment policy statement shown earlier in this chapter. The discussion took place at a time when the portfolio was distributed as follows: 40 percent stocks; 43 percent bonds, including a significant position in zero coupon issues purchased when yields to maturity were significantly higher; 9 percent real estate; and 8 percent cash equivalents. The trustees also reflected that actual rates of return over the first five-year planning period substantially exceeded their original expectations, and inflation, conversely, was much lower than forecasted. See Table 17–18. In view of this favorable performance, and considering the various items detailed in Figure 17–9, the trustees decided to first adjust investment market expectations downward for the next five-year planning period and to essentially maintain the current asset mix of the portfolio.

The basic reasoning behind the decision to maintain the asset distribution of the portfolio was three-fold. First, revised capital market expectations indicated a significant real investment return over the five-year planning horizon. Second, the stock market's advance over an extended period of time placed broad market evaluations at a level approaching bull market peaks, and increased exposure to equities did not seem warranted. Third, the original asset allocation study indicated that the pension fund should follow a more conservative risk policy because of the high correlation between the sponsoring company's profits and pension fund portfolio returns. In

---

[38]H. Bradlee Perry, "What Sort of Returns Should Investors Expect?" *The Babson Staff Letter*, David L. Babson & Co., Inc., January 17, 1986, p. 1.

[39]Eugene B. Burroughs, "Perspective on Investments: How Does Inflation Affect Performance of Asset Classes?" *Pension World*, November 1985, p. 60.

# FIGURE 17-9  Agenda for Asset Allocation Decision Meeting

| Discussion Point | Data Reference | Comments/Judgments to Be Drawn |
|---|---|---|

**Recent returns versus historical experience**

### Returns from Cash, Bonds and Stocks

| | 1952–1965 (Disinflation) | 1965–1980 (Inflation) | 1981 | 1982 | 1983 | 1984 | 1985p | 5-Year Average 1981–1985 |
|---|---|---|---|---|---|---|---|---|
| Cash | 3.2 | 10.9 | 15.1 | 12.0 | 8.8 | 10.0 | 8 | 11 |
| Bonds | 3.8 | 3.9 | 3.6 | 42.8 | 2.0 | 16.1 | 32 | 19 |
| Stocks | 16.0 | 8.2 | −5.0 | 21.4 | 22.4 | 6.1 | 31 | 15 |
| Inflation | 1.4 | 6.9 | 8.9 | 3.9 | 3.8 | 4.0 | 4 | 5 |

Cash: 1 month Commerical Paper; Federal Reserve
Bonds: Aaa Corporate Bonds; Ibbotson & Sinquefeld, Moody's
Stocks: S&P 500
Inflation: CPI Year-to-year, Dec. to Dec.; U.S. Department of Labor
SOURCE: Rosenkrantz, Lyon, & Ross, Inc.

*Comments/Judgments:* Real returns for the 1981–85 period exceeded significantly those of the prior fifteen years. However, common stock returns were still well below those experienced during the 1952–1965 period of "disinflation."

**Market valuations**

| S&P 400 | Average at Market Troughs | Average at Market Peaks | Recent Figure |
|---|---|---|---|
| Dividend yield | 5.1% | 4.0% | 3.06% |
| Price-to-book-value multiple | 1.27 | 1.76 | 1.99 |
| Price-earnings multiple | 10.6 | 16.7 | 16.68 |

SOURCE: Fortune.

*Comments/Judgments:* Broad market valuations are approaching or exceeding the average levels reached at bull market peaks over the past fifty years. However, price-to-book and price-earnings ratio levels may not be as extreme as they appear. Stocks, on average, according to some observers, are selling at only 75 percent of replacement book value, which more accurately reflects the current worth of plant and equipment after years of high inflation. As for price-earnings ratios, continued low inflation rates should result in higher evaluations of current earnings, and stocks have sold at significantly higher levels in the past. but, the warning signals from broad valuation standards are flashing.

| | |
|---|---|
| Business cycle outlook | See Table 17–19 which shows a typical Wall Street economic forecast. |
| | Real GNP in 1986 forecasted to rise 3.3 percent over 1985 average. Reported inflation estimates lowered for second and third quarters of 1986 to reflect energy price declines, but thereafter assumed tax increase offsets much of the impact. For the year 1986, the CPI is lowered to a 3.4 percent rise from our earlier estimate of 4.1 percent. Profits are expected to rise about 9 percent in 1986, after a decline of 2.9 percent in 1985. Despite continued economic growth, interest rates are expected to decline modestly, and inflation is likely to remain subdued. |
| Technical position of the market | Table 17–20 contains a summary of one leading technician's assessment. Items not covered in Chapter 8 have been eliminated. A number of important indicators are at or near bearish parameters. |
| Significant exogenous factors | Important long-term trends instrumental to better capital market performance around the world remain very positive. The rising tide of capitalism and the retreat of state-oriented economic systems continue to provide a backdrop for further improvement in stock and bond prices. Political attitudes remain conservative and some budget reform is likely. Despite some concern over foreign policy developments and the potential for a reemergence of protectionism trends, the basic political and economic outlooks remain positive. |
| Changes in investment objectives | Portfolio returns over the past five years have significantly improved the financial position of the pension fund despite sharply higher future liabilities caused by a rapidly expanding employee base. The ratio of assets to the actuarial present value of plan liabilities is 95.5 percent, and contributions as a percentage of wage costs remain well below the guideline target. Despite the improved position of the pension fund, trustees voted to continue the existing investment policy statement. |

**TABLE 17-18   Investment Market Performance against Expectations**

|  | Expected Annual Rates of Return | Actual Annual Rates of Return | Revised Expectations |
|---|---|---|---|
| Stocks | 17.0% | 19.5% | 12.0% |
| Bonds | 11.5 | 15.8 | 9.0 |
| Cash | 8.0 | 11.0 | 6.0 |
| Inflation | 8.0 | 5.0 | 4.0 |

**TABLE 17-19   Macroeconomic Forecast**

| Forecast Summary | Annual Estimates | | | | | | | |
|---|---|---|---|---|---|---|---|---|
|  | 1984 | % Change | 1985 | % Change | 1986 | % Change | 1987 | % Change |
| % change in real GNP | — | 6.6 | — | 2.3 | — | 3.3 | — | 2.6 |
| % change in GNP deflator | — | 4.2 | — | 3.3 | — | 3.2 | — | 4.2 |
| % change in Consumer Price Index | — | 4.3 | — | 3.5 | — | 3.4 | — | 4.3 |
| Civilian unemployment rate (%) | 7.5 | — | 7.2 | — | 6.5 | — | 6.9 | — |
| Profits after-tax ($ billions) | 144.0 | 10.9 | 139.8 | −2.9 | 152.5 | 9.1 | 153.5 | 0.7 |
| **Main components of GNP (billions of 1982 $)** | | | | | | | | |
| Personal consumption expenditures | 2239.8 | 4.4 | 2313.0 | 3.3 | 2370.6 | 2.5 | 2424.4 | 2.3 |
| Durables | 318.6 | 12.4 | 345.0 | 8.3 | 352.3 | 2.1 | 350.1 | −0.6 |
| Nondurables | 828.0 | 3.4 | 847.0 | 2.3 | 867.0 | 2.4 | 885.9 | 2.2 |
| Services | 1093.3 | 3.0 | 1121.0 | 2.5 | 1151.2 | 2.7 | 1188.3 | 3.2 |
| Nonresidential fixed investment | 430.3 | 19.5 | 471.7 | 9.6 | 493.0 | 4.5 | 487.9 | −1.0 |
| Equipment | 281.6 | 22.2 | 305.8 | 8.6 | 327.0 | 7.0 | 333.9 | 2.1 |
| Structures | 148.7 | 14.7 | 165.9 | 11.6 | 166.0 | 0.0 | 154.0 | −7.2 |
| Residential investment | 168.4 | 13.2 | 171.3 | 1.8 | 176.6 | 3.1 | 171.8 | −2.8 |
| Government spending | 675.9 | 4.3 | 716.1 | 5.9 | 737.5 | 3.0 | 745.8 | 1.1 |
| Federal | 292.6 | 6.2 | 322.2 | 10.1 | 332.3 | 3.1 | 333.0 | 0.2 |
| State and local | 383.3 | 3.0 | 393.9 | 2.8 | 405.3 | 2.9 | 412.8 | 1.9 |
| Final sales to domestic purchasers | 3514.3 | 6.4 | 3672.1 | 4.5 | 3777.7 | 2.9 | 3829.7 | 1.4 |
| Net exports | −85.0 | — | −106.7 | — | −111.5 | — | −69.9 | — |
| Final sales of GNP | 3429.3 | 4.5 | 3565.4 | 4.0 | 3666.3 | 2.8 | 3759.8 | 2.6 |
| Inventory change | 62.7 | — | 5.6 | — | 21.6 | — | 22.5 | — |
| Gross National Product | 3492.0 | 6.6 | 3571.0 | 2.3 | 3687.9 | 3.3 | 3782.3 | 2.6 |
| **Other key indicators** | | | | | | | | |
| Real disposable income (1982 $) | 2468.4 | 5.7 | 2508.9 | 1.6 | 2570.0 | 2629.3 | 2.3 | |
| Savings rate (%) | 6.5 | — | 4.6 | — | 4.1 | — | 4.3 | — |
| Industrial Production Index (1977 = 100) | 121.8 | 11.6 | 124.5 | 2.3 | 129.8 | 4.2 | 132.0 | 1.7 |
| Capacity utilization (%) | 81.2 | 8.7 | 80.6 | −0.7 | 81.5 | 1.1 | 80.3 | −1.5 |
| Housing starts (millions of units) | 1.77 | 3.8 | 1.74 | −1.4 | 1.83 | 4.8 | 1.74 | −4.8 |
| Single family | 1.10 | 3.5 | 1.07 | −2.7 | 1.20 | 11.8 | 1.18 | −2.1 |
| Multi-family | 0.66 | 4.2 | 0.67 | 0.7 | 0.63 | −6.5 | 0.56 | −10.0 |
| Automobile sales (millions of units) | 10.39 | 13.2 | 11.13 | 7.1 | 10.65 | −4.3 | 10.35 | −2.8 |
| Domestic | 7.95 | 17.1 | 8.28 | 4.2 | 7.60 | −8.2 | 7.13 | −6.2 |
| Imports | 2.44 | 2.2 | 2.84 | 16.6 | 3.05 | 7.3 | 3.23 | 5.7 |
| **Interest rate forecast (%)** | | | | | | | | |
| 91-day Treasury bills | 9.5 | — | 7.5 | — | 6.4 | — | 5.8 | — |
| Prime rate | 12.0 | — | 9.9 | — | 8.4 | — | 7.4 | |
| Treasury bonds—10 years or more | 12.0 | — | 10.8 | — | 8.1 | — | 7.8 | |
| Treasury bonds—30 years | 12.4 | — | 10.8 | — | 8.3 | — | 8.0 | |
| Corporate bonds—seasoned AA | 13.3 | — | 11.8 | — | 9.1 | — | 8.6 | |
| Utility—new issue AA | 13.5 | — | 11.8 | — | 9.3 | — | 8.8 | — |
| Utility—seasoned BAA | 14.6 | — | 13.0 | — | 10.1 | — | 9.6 | |
| Municipal bonds—bond buyer | 10.1 | — | 9.1 | — | 6.8 | — | 6.5 | — |

NOTE: These projections represent the views of the Dean Witter Reynolds Economic Research Group alone and are not to be construed as necessarily reflecting the official corporate position of Dean Witter Reynolds Inc. SOURCE: Dean Witter Reynolds, February 21, 1986.

**TABLE 17–20** *Summary of Technical Indicators*

| Indicator | Current Reading | Current Description | Extreme Bearish Level | Extreme Bullish Level |
|---|---|---|---|---|
| **Secular Indicators** | | | | |
| Stock-bond allocations: | | | | |
| Pension funds | 10.5% | Low & rising | 100% | 0% |
| State and local retirement funds | 18.5% | Low & rising | 100% | 0% |
| Insurance companies | 18.8% | Low & rising | 30% | 0% |
| Individuals: | | | | |
|   Total equity investments | Less than zero | Still liquidating | 100% | 0% |
|   Mutual funds only | 18% | Low | 100% | 0% |
| **Cyclical Indicators** | | | | |
| Liquidity: | | | | |
|   Mutual fund cash | 8.9% | Remains high | 5.5% | 9.5% |
|   Bank and pension fund cash | 6.0% | Very low | 9.0% | 17.0% |
| Supply/demand: | | | | |
|   New equity financing (Three-month average) | $3.3 Billion | High & rising | $3 billion | $1 billion |
|   Insider sell/buy ratio (Eight-week average from Vickers) | 4.23 | Very high | 3.00 | 1.25 |
| **Medium-term Indicators** | | | | |
| Advisory services (Investor's Intelligence): | | | | |
|   Bulls | 66.7 | Excessive | 60.0% | 20.0% |
|   Bears | 21.7 | Low & extreme | 20.0% | 60.0% |
| CBOE Put/Call Ratio (10-day MA) | 0.45 | Low, near sell signal | 0.40 | 0.70 |
| Adjusted CBOE Put/Call Ratio (10 day MA) | 0.29 | Low, gave sell signal | 0.26 | 0.50 |
| E. F. Hutton Naked Put/Call Ratio (10-day MA) | 0.42 | Giving sell signal | 0.50 | 2.00 |
| Relative Option Premiums (Five-week MA) of Put/Call Ratio) | 0.43 | Near sell signal level | 0.40 | 1.00 |
| Nonmember Short Sale Ratio | 2.461 | High, but probably distorted by arbitrage | 1.200 | 2.200 |
| Block Uptick/Downtick Ratio (10-day MA) | 1.18 | Flat, gave sell signal | −0.20 versus Two-week high | +0.20 versus Two-week low |
| Margin Account Activity (10-day MA) | | | | |
| E. F. Hutton: NYSE | 1.13 | High, gave sell signal | 1.15 | 0.80 |
| ASE | 1.28 | High | 1.40 | 0.60 |
| OTC | 1.34 | High, gave sell signal | 1.40 | 0.60 |
| Trendlines Over-Under 30-week MA | 82% | Rising slightly | Turning down from over 80% | Turning up from under 20% |
| New Highs/New Lows (Weekly NYSE total) | 857/35 | Still confirming new highs in averages | Nonconfirmation of new highs; expanding new lows | Nonconfirmation of new lows; expanding new highs |

SOURCE: E. F. Hutton.

other words, if expected investment returns did not materialize, there would be a strong likelihood that the sponsoring company's operating results would also be disappointing. Consequently, the trustees decided not to increase the risk position of the portfolio even though expected returns looked positive.

# ■ *SUMMARY*

Thus far in the portfolio management process, we have shown the need for planning the broad strategy. Before moving on, reiteration of the major points discussed is appropriate, since most investors still fail to appreciate the need for comprehensive decision making to determine specific objectives, establish a portfolio designed to meet those objectives, provide for the realignment of holdings as conditions change, and monitor performance achievements against expectations. Instead, most investors, professional and amateur alike, continue to behave as if these activities are unrelated.

First and foremost is the recognition that effective portfolio supervision is a continuous process, responsive to ever-changing capital market conditions. It starts with the determination of rational goals based on rational expectations. These two elements must be incorporated into a set of policy guidelines which defines the investment character of the portfolio and provides benchmarks for performance evaluation. Once investment objectives have been defined in terms of acceptable levels of risk, portfolio theory offers investors a number of useful tools to further clarify the planning process. The most important of these is focusing sufficient attention on the asset configuration of the portfolio. In other words, what types of assets are to be owned and how much of each, within a defined range, are to be held. Traditionally the mix has been confined to stocks, bonds, and cash equivalents, but real estate has gained in popularity; and the other categories have been subdivided into a wider number of groupings.

The next series of steps involve a number of tactical decisions required to implement these investment policy decisions. This is the subject of the next chapter.

# SUGGESTED READINGS

Doors, Richard C. *The New Mutual Fund Advisor*. Chicago: Probus Publishing, 1986.

Ellis, Charles. *Investment Policy: How to Win the Loser's Game*. Homewood, Ill.: Richard D. Irwin, 1985.

Fogler, Russell H., and Darwin M. Baystow. *Improving the Investment Decision Process: Quantitative Assistance for the Practitioner—and for the Firm*. Homewood, Ill.: Dow Jones-Irwin, 1984.

Good, Walter R. "Accountability for Pension Fund Performance." *Financial Analysts Journal*. January-February 1984.

Mennis, Edmund A., and Chester D. Clark. "Understanding Corporate Pension Plans." Charlottesville, Va.: Financial Analysts Research Foundation, 1983.

Milne, Robert D. "Determination of Portfolio Policies: Individual Investors." In *Managing Investment Portfolios, A Dynamic Process,* ed. John L. Maginn and Donald L. Tuttle, 1983. Boston, MA Warren, Gorham & Lamont.

Tuttle, Donald L., ed. "The Revolution in Techniques for Managing Bond Portfolios." Charlottesville, Va.: The Institute of Chartered Financial Analysts, 1983.

Vawter, Jay. "Determination of Portfolio Policies: Institutional Investors." In *Managing Investment Portfolios, A Dynamic Process,* ed. John L. Maginn and Donald L. Tuttle, 1983.